Second Edition

FUNDAMENTALS OF PARLIAMENTARY LAW AND PROCEDURE

The Rules of Procedure for Deliberative Assemblies

Miriam H. Butcher, *Editor*

Associate Editors

Leo G. Athans	Jane M. Klausman
John E. Baird	Joyce C. Parks
Lee Demeter	Eve M. Wilkinson

Previously entitled Parliamentary Law and Procedure Student Workbook

Copyright © 1987, 1992 by American Institute of Parliamentarians

ISBN 0-8403-8135-2

Printed in the United States of America
10 9 8 7 6 5 4 3 2 1

Contents

FOREWORD

This new edition of *Parliamentary Law and Procedure*, successor to the first edition published in 1988 as two separate but complementary manuals that were subtitled *The Instructor's Manual* and *The Student's Workbook*, represents a blending into one volume and an updating, expansion, reorganization and substantial revision of the material contained in the two predecessor manuals.

The objective of the book remains the same: specifically, to serve as (1) a unique textbook for teaching parliamentary law and procedure at the college level; (2) an effective self-instruction manual; and (3) an authoritative reference source on parliamentary law and procedure.

Upon satisfactory completion of this course, the student should be able to:

1. Practice as an effective and credible parliamentarian.
2. Preside with confidence and expertise at any deliberative assembly, and rule in matters involving serious procedural difficulties and differences of opinion in parliamentary situations.
3. Formulate and interpret bylaws, rules and parliamentary procedures for deliberative assemblies of any size and of any nature.
4. Possess academic and practical knowledge of the application of parliamentary law and procedure in all its various forms and complexities.
5. Exercise a sound understanding of the philosophical and conceptual principles underlying the discipline of parliamentary law and procedure.

The need for familiarity with, and indeed mastery of, parliamentary law and procedure has never been greater than it is today. More than half a century ago the prescient Henry M. Robert declared: "Some knowledge of parliamentary law may be justly regarded as a necessary part of the education of every man and woman, every boy and girl." Mr. Robert also stated: "Ignorance of the rules and customs of deliberative assemblies is a heavy handicap to anyone who expects to influence the policy of a society." If these assertions made sense in the America of the 1920's, they have added significance in the America of the 1990's.

Consider for a moment these mind-boggling numbers:

- There are more than 1.375 million* nonprofit organizations in the United States.

- There are thousands upon thousands of governmental bodies at the local, county, state and national levels.

- A research study, "How to Make Meetings Work," funded by the Carnegie Corporation and the Rockefeller Foundation, and conducted by Ventura Associates in New York City, reveals that more than 11 million meetings are held in the United States <u>every day</u>, that middle management spends approximately 35 percent of its working day in meetings, that in top management the figure could be 50 percent or more. This means that more than half one's organizational life could be spent attending or conducting meetings!

- The typical adult American at any one time belongs to an average of six organized groups, to say nothing about informal organizations.

Granted that some of the aforementioned groups may respect the rules of parliamentary procedure, more in the breach than in the observance. Still, even they tend to abide by its basic principles of equality, justice and fair play, decorum and civility, the right of all individuals to be heard and, ultimately, the right of the majority to rule the organization.

Thus, it would be no exaggeration to say that much of the "business" of America today, in whatever field of human activity, in whatever type of group, be it incorporated or unincorporated, for-profit or not-for-profit, tax exempt or not tax exempt, is conducted in varying degrees of conformity with the fundamental principles and/or rules of parliamentary procedure.

Meetings are all around us today; they have become as American as apple pie. And parliamentary procedure has developed into the engine of our democratic processes and the balance wheel of our society. To the degree that members of an organization properly use parliamentary procedure, their meetings are likely to be conducted expeditiously, productively and harmoniously.

Nonprofit Almanac, 1992, p.23.

Publication of this new edition by the American Institute of Parliamentarians (AIP) was made possible—as was the first edition— by a grant from the William Randolph Hearst Foundations. The national program with the schools is directed and administered through the AIP Parliamentary Education Project for Colleges and Universities, and sponsored by the Hearst Foundations.

The Hearst Foundations support the proposition that parliamentary law and procedure studies at the college level in our nation's schools would be of significant benefit to students entering the mainstream of our social, business, civic and professional activities upon graduation. These initial grants by the Hearst Foundations were the start of an on-going national program for providing parliamentary education programs— not only for the four-year schools of higher learning, but also for community colleges and select secondary schools.

In this regard, the AIP-Hearst National Parliamentary Education Project lists more than 35 nationally recognized professional parliamentarians, teachers and educators who, on a wholly volunteer basis, serve as consultants to schools requiring assistance in establishing parliamentary law and procedure classes, or conducting seminars or workshops. The services of the consultants are free to the schools; they receive no compensation for their services.

We are indebted to editor Miriam Butcher and the associate editors: Dr. John E. Baird, Dr. Lee Demeter, Jane M. Klausman, Joyce Parks and Eve M. Wilkinson, who reorganized, revised, expanded and updated the lesson material in this new edition.

Finally, profound appreciation and well-earned recognition is extended to all those volunteers who are doing a magnificent pioneer job in serving the parliamentary needs of the schools; to the American Institute of Parliamentarians for its continuing support in the development of this second edition; and to the contributing authors, all of whom are nationally recognized certified professional parliamentarians. It is they who provided the written material for the book's 32 lessons and the five appendixes.

Leo G. Athans
Project Director

THE PROJECT

This parliamentary education work is authorized by the American Institute of Parliamentarians (AIP) and known as the AIP National Parliamentary Education Project for Colleges and Universities. The Project was originated and developed by Leo G. Athans and Floyd M. Riddick (Parliamentarian Emeritus of the United States Senate) and is sponsored by the William Randolph Hearst Foundations.

All talent and time to produce this book, and all management, administrative, and promotional activities are fully donated and performed by volunteers. All authors and contributors donated their works. No person involved in the Project receives compensation or obtains any financial benefit.

PROJECT ORGANIZATION

Board of Trustees:
Dr. Leo G. Athans, Chairman
Miriam Butcher, CPP*
Dr. Floyd M. Riddick, Ph.D., CPP

Project Director:
Leo G. Athans, Th.D., CPP

National Coordinator
for Schools:
John E. Baird, Ph.D., CPP

Consultants to
the Project:
Cleon C. Babcock, CPP, President of AIP
Dr. Lee Demeter, CPP
Prof. Herman W. Farwell, CPP
Jane M. Klausman, CPP

(Continued on the following page.)

*CPP - Certified Professional Parliamentarian

Project Area Coordinators for Schools

Prof. Raphael Antonio
Alfaro-Garcia, CPP
Eleanor G. Nenstiel
Lucille Alt, CPP

Margaret A. Banks, CPP

Robert Burr Cade, Ph.D.

Harold E. Corbin

Prof. Imogene Emery, CPP

Elbert F. Floyd, J.D.

Paula J. Hook

Wanda E. Hotchiss, CPP

Dr. Charles H. Johnson, CPP

Prof. Larry E. Larmer

James Lochrie, CPP

Richard E. Lucas, CPP

James T McCabe, CP

Prof. Joyce C. Park, CPP

Alan D. Pauw

Edda R. Pittman

Alice N. Pohl, CPP

Veda J. Price

Dr. James Gaut Ragsdale, CP

Maurice L. Redd, CPP

Dorothy M. Ruccick, CPP

Sherry C. Strange

P.R. "Tony: Tonelli"

Leona M. White, CPP

Please Note: Schools wishing assistance or information may direct their requests to – Project Director, American Institute of Parliamentarians, 33760 Westchester Dr., 1000 Palms, CA 92276. Telephone (760) 343-1924, Fax (760) 343-3914.

LIST OF CONTRIBUTORS

Leo G. Athans .... Th.D., CPP, Instructor
College of the Desert
Palm Desert, California;
National University
Palm Springs, California

John E. Baird .... Ph.D., CPP, Educator
California State University
Hayward, California

M. Eugene Bierbaum .... Ph.D., CPP, PRP, Educator
State University of New York
at Cortland, New York

Miriam Butcher .... CPP, PRP, Educator
Chair, Education Committee
American Institute of
Parliamentarians, Ft. Wayne,
Indiana

Robert Burr Cade .... Ph.D., Educator
University of Southern
Mississippi
Hattiesburg, Mississippi

Lee Demeter .... Ed.D., CPP, PRP, Educator
Adjunct Professor
Long Island University, N. Y.
Hofstra University, New York

Jon L. Ericson .... Ph.D., Drake University,
Educator
Des Moines, Iowa

Hermon Farwell .... CPP, Educator
Professor Emeritus
University of Southern
Colorado
Pueblo, Colorado

Jane M. Klausman .... CPP, PRP
Professional Paliamentarian,
Liverpool, New York

Joyce C. Parks .... M.A., CPP, Educator
Bob Jones University
Greenville, South Carolina

Gregg Phifer .... Ph.D., CPP, Educator
Florida State University
Tallahassee, Florida

Emil Pfister .... Ph.D., CPP, Educator
Central Michigan University
Ambassador College
Pasadena, California

Alice N. Pohl .... CPP, PRP, Instructor
Professional Parliamentarian
Tigard, Oregon

Floyd M. Riddick .... Ph.D., CPP, Parliamentarian
Emeritus, U. S. Senate,
Washington,
District of Columbia

Donald L. Wolfarth .... Ph.D., CPP, Educator
University of Wisconsin
Eau Clair, Wisconsin

ACKNOWLEDGMENTS

Many individuals have supported and encouraged the authors and editors during the development of this book. Specifically, a deep sense of gratitude is felt and expressed to the William Randolph Hearst Foundation for its on-going financial support.

Grateful appreciation is given to the authors, educators, and professional parliamentarians who took the time to read and reread the several drafts of the manuscript, correct and revise parliamentary questions and answers, and in so many ways gave freely of their time and talents.

The editor sincerely acknowledges the valuable assistance of the associate editors: Leo G. Athens, John E. Baird, Lee Demeter, and Jane Klauisman. During the past two years, they provided much of the research, the writing and the testing, and the rewriting of the many drafts of the manuscript. Joyce Parks and Eve Wilkinson made significant contributions to the various parts of the manuscript.

Finally, special recognition is extended to Leo G. Athans who put the manuscript together, coordinated the work of the authors and editors, developed the format with the publisher and produced this book in its present form.

Miriam H. Butcher

TO THOSE WHO TEACH

> Whereas, Proper use of parliamentary law helps
> keep principles of democracy alive; and
> Whereas, Use of parliamentary procedures is a
> valuable tool for making decisions; and
> Whereas, Its purpose must be understood, that its use
> is to help, not to hinder;
> *Resolved,* That it is necessary and rewarding
> to study the subject of parliamentary law.

For teaching to be effective, consider the following suggestions:

- *Be Prepared.* Study the lesson in advance. Rehearse it. Be in control of it. Assurance comes with the authority of knowing what has been assigned for study.

- *Ambiance.* Classes should be held in a comfortable place. Heat, lighting, ventilation and seating are important, including desks or tables for writing notes. All teaching tools, such as audiovisual aids and sheets for distribution, should be ready and in good working order.

- *Aptitude.* Teachers should be sincerely concerned with the students' progress and the subject being taught. The teacher role is to help students gain self-confidence from gainful learning experiences. Patience, tact, goodwill are required. Use of pertinent humor speeds the assimilation of information. The student should never be embarrassed for errors made. Come early, stay late.

- *Class Time.* Set a definite day and time for all classes. Start on time. Allow adequate class time to read, discuss, participate. Provide a short break during class hours.

- *Lecture.* Explain each lesson's objective. Present lesson material carefully, clearly so all may hear, with enthusiasm. For the reading assignments to become meaningful, check that the students fully understood the reading. Allow time for pertinent questions. Illustrate with related anecdotes when available. Anecdotes involve the listeners and liven up the lesson.

- **Methods**. Teaching methods should be varied. Keep lessons lively by encouraging student participation. Encourage questions to reinforce points under discussion, but avoid unnecessary argument. Use teaching tools as available. Hold mock meetings. Play parliamentary games. Have team contests. Distribute problems for students to solve and then hold critiques. Assign students to write a specific bylaw, resolution, committee report followed by discussion. Practice handling committee recommendations or any of the parliamentary functions.

"A good teacher is one whose spirit enters the soul of the pupil."

John Milton - Poet *(Paradise Lost)*

TO THOSE WHO LEARN

To gain the most from your class meetings, consider the following suggestions:

- **Be Prepared**. Study the lesson in advance. Do the assigned reading. Then read the discussion in this book. If it is not possible for you to do all of the reading assigned, at least do the reading assignment designated "Robert."

- **Test Yourself**. Testing material is included with each lesson. Write the answers on a separate piece of paper. Then check your answers with those given in the back of this book. Analyze any errors that you made.

- **Preview Your Class**. Anticipate what the instructor will be covering in lecture. Note particularly any questions you have coming from your reading or your self-testing. If the lecture doesn't answer these questions, raise them with the instructor during class or after class.

- **Attend Classes**. Arrive on time, prepared to listen and to take notes. Participate in class discussion. Ask questions. Take part in any class exercises assigned by the instructor. Be a good listener.

- **Be a Leader**. Don't be afraid of making a mistake; be decisive. When you are called upon to rule, decide and announce your ruling clearly. If you are wrong, the group can correct you or your instructor can correct you. Follow the old principles for effective public speaking: "Stand up to be seen, speak up to be heard, and shut up to be appreciated."

- **Be Helpful to Others**. Contribute to the discussion. When others are leading, be a cooperative follower. Act toward your fellow students as you expect them to act toward you.

- **Re-Test Yourself**. Take the tests given with each lesson. Check your answers. If there are still things you don't understand, make a note to ask your instructor at the next class meeting.

KNOW THE AUTHORITIES

This book is based on the writings of a number of popular parliamentary authorities. These names should become familiar to you:

- **Demeter**. George Demeter was a Boston attorney, a former member of the Massachusetts legislature, and a nationally known parliamentarian. His book, ***Demeter's Manual of Parliamentary Law and Procedure,*** is published by Little, Brown and Company. The citations given here are taken from the Blue Book edition, published in 1969.

- **Deschler**. Lewis Deschler served as Parliamentarian of the U.S. House of Representatives from 1928 until 1974 and continued as consultant to the House on parliamentary matters. He is the author of ***Deschler's Rules of Order***.

- **Ericson**. Jon L. Ericson is a professor of Speech at Drake University, Des Moines, Iowa. He has lectured on parliamentary procedure and served as parliamentarian for organizations throughout the country. He recently authored a book, ***Notes and Comments on Robert's Rules***.

- **Farwell**. Hermon W. Farwell, a retired educator, wrote ***The Majority Rules: A Manual of Procedure for Most Groups*** in an attempt to simplify the rules of parliamentary procedure for ordinary groups that rarely face the complexities discussed in other manuals.

- **Hills**. George S. Hills was senior partner in the New York City law firm of Rogers Hoge & Hills. He has over 40 years of experience in handling corporate meetings and is the author of ***Managing Corporate Meetings: A Legal and Procedural Guide***.

- *Jefferson*. Thomas Jefferson, third President of the United States, had been the presiding officer of the U.S. Senate while serving as Vice President (1797-1801). Seeing the need for a manual to guide Senate deliberations, he published his *Manual of Parliamentary Practice* in 1801, which was subsequently adopted as an authority by the Senate, various state legislatures, and other groups.

- *Mason*. Paul Mason was the parliamentarian for the California State Legislature and the author of a *Manual of Legislative Procedure*, adopted as an authority by a number of state legislatures.

- *O'Brien*. Joseph O'Brien was Professor of Speech at Pennsylvania State University and the author of a number of articles on parliamentary procedure published in professional journals.

- *Petyt*. G. Petyt was an English author whose book, *Lex Parliamentaria*, written in 1689, was a pocket manual of procedure which assembled materials from the Journals of the House of Commons for the use of members of Parliament.

- *Riddick*. Floyd M. Riddick is Parliamentarian Emeritus of the U.S. Senate and author of the most authoritative guides to procedure and usage in the Senate. His book, *Riddick's Rules of Procedure,* was coauthored by **Miriam H. Butcher,** a former president of the American Institute of Parliamentarians. In form, this book is like an encyclopedia, with the important terms in parliamentary procedure presented and discussed in alphabetical order.

- *Robert*. General Henry M. Robert was a distinguished river and harbor engineer with the U.S. Army. He was active in civic and educational affairs in many parts of the country, and he sought to adapt the rules of the U.S. House of Representatives for the use of ordinary groups nationwide, thus bringing unity to American parliamentary practice. He personally wrote the first five editions of his manual, which has become the most popular parliamentary authority with American organizations. The citations given here are taken from the Scott, Foresman *Robert's Rules of Order Newly Revised, 1990 Edition*.

- ***Sturgis.*** Alice Sturgis taught parliamentary procedure at the University of California and Stanford University. She was an advisor to the American delegation to the conference establishing the United Nations, and she worked with hundreds of national and international organizations. **Sturgis** was particularly interested in the legal aspects of parliamentary procedure. Her ***Standard Code of Parliamentary Procedure*** has been adopted by many organizations as their parliamentary authority. She was the author of the first two editions of this book. A third edition, done under the auspices of the American Institute of Parliamentarians, was published in 1988 by the McGraw-Hill Book Company. It is this third edition which is cited here.

PARLIAMENTARY AUTHORITIES REFERENCE

Robert's Rules of Order Newly Revised 1990 Edition
Scott, Foresman & Co., Glenview IL

Sturgis Standard Code of Parliamentary Procedure 1988
3rd Edition
McGraw-Hill, New York NY

Demeter's Manual of Parliamentary Law and Procedure 1969
Little, Brown and Company, Boston MA

Riddick's Rules of Procedure, Riddick-Butcher, 1985
Charles Scribner's Sons, New York NY

The Majority Rules, H.W. Farwell, 1980
High Publishers, Pueblo CO

Mason's Manual of Legislative Procedure, Paul Mason
1989 Revised Edition
National Conference of State Legislatures, Denver CO
West Publishing Co., St. Paul MN

Deschler's Rules of Order 1974
Prentice Hall Inc., Englewood Cliffs NJ

Managing Corporate Meetings, George S. Hills, 1977
Ronald Press Co., New York NY

Notes and Comments on Robert's Rules, Jon L. Ericson
1991 Revised Edition
Southern Illinois University Press, Carbondale and Edwardsville IL

Parliamentary Law, Henry M. Robert, 1975 Edition
Irvington Publishers Inc., New York NY

Parliamentary Law and Practice for Non-profit Organizations
H. Oleck & C. Green, 1991 2nd Edition
ALI-ABA American Law Institute—American Bar Association,
Philadelphia PA

LESSON 1
PRINCIPLES AND RULES
OF PARLIAMENTARY LAW

"There are five great principles underlying the rules of parliamentary law, namely:

ORDER. That is, there must be orderly procedure.
EQUALITY. That is, all members are equal before the rule or law.
JUSTICE. That is, 'justice for all.'
RIGHT OF THE MINORITY to be heard on questions.
RIGHT OF THE MAJORITY to rule the organization."

Demeter, *Manual of Parliamentary Law and Procedure*

LESSON OBJECTIVE

To understand that principles are more important than rules.

READING ASSIGNMENT

Robert pp. xxv-xliv   **Demeter** pp. 4-8
Sturgis pp. 1-10   **Riddick** - Introduction

LESSON MATERIAL

Most of the rules of parliamentary procedure flow naturally from and constitute a logical application of basic principles. They are the reasonable application of the five principles as stated by **Demeter**, rules by which we govern ourselves in voluntary organizations.

These rules are not statutory but have become so established and tested by time that many have become customs known as common law.

These rules provide protection for freedom of choice and equal rights for all members, whether present or absent.

Robert wrote: "Where there is no law, but every man does what is right in his own eyes, there is the least of real liberty."

BASIC PRINCIPLES

Order

Only one piece of business may be handled at one time, meaning only one substantive motion may be pending at one time. Members should not be permitted to digress or introduce different subjects.

One piece of business must be disposed of in some way before another subject may be considered. The simplest, most direct action is always preferred.

All business shall be conducted fairly and impartially, with order. The presiding officer must protect members from unfair treatment or abuse, recognize members impartially, give each member the opportunity to speak, while preserving proper conduct and decorum during debate.

Procedures must be orderly. Motions must be resolved according to reasonable methods, with those that are immediately pending being resolved first.

Equality

All members have equal rights, responsibilities, obligations and privileges according to their status as members as defined in the bylaws.

This means that each member has equal opportunities to propose motions, to participate in debate, to vote, to serve on committees or as an officer, to share in organization activities, according to the member's talents, skills and desires.

Justice

All members have the right to be informed, to ask questions, to have complex motions explained or clarified by the Chair. No one should be asked to vote if that person is ignorant of the facts or the possible results.

Procedural rules must be understood. Meetings must be conducted with fairness and in good faith.

Minority Rights

The minority must be protected. Dissenting members also have equal rights to be heard, to express opposing opinions, to be allowed the opportunity to persuade with the hope of becoming the majority. The majority should be willing to listen to members' reasons for opposition. For this reason, debate should not be closed too soon or too easily.

Will of Majority Prevails

The power and authority of the organization is vested in its members. No members, board or officers have the right to dictate or control decisions unless the members grant such rights.

Members may take any action not in conflict with national, state or parent organization laws.

Decisions are made according to the will of the majority.

Members are expected to accept the will of the majority. They have no right to sabotage majority decisions but may try to persuade the majority to change its decision later.

PROCEDURAL RULES AS TOOLS

Properly understood and applied, rules become the indispensable tools of democratic procedure. These tools facilitate and improve situations instead of having to submit to the frustration and delay that occur when rules are lacking. A group in close agreement and accord would need less strict adherence to rules of conduct than a group with differences of opinion where stricter rules should be applied. More formality should be observed in ratio to the sharpness of discord or discussion. Rules of procedure must apply in all cases, however, if fairness, order and efficiency are to prevail.

Procedural Rules Provide For:

1. Assurance of fair play. Each member has a turn to speak and to vote.
2. Free and frank discussion, pro and con, through a meaningful debate.
3. Ample time for discussion, cut off only by a two-thirds vote.

4. Orderly procedure, eliminating confusion or frustration.
5. Open discussion before all members present.
6. Protection of the sensibilities of members because all remarks must be addressed to the Chair and kept impersonal.
7. Uniformity of application: the same rules are used for every meeting.
8. Business regulated by an agenda, not subject to the caprice of the Chair or manipulation by a few members.
9. Expeditiousness. Discussion is kept germane. Time-wasting irrelevancies are prohibited.

Application Of Rules

Knowing rules is not enough. Interpretation of rules requires common sense, tact, fair play -- rather than the application of the letter of the law. As long as the principles are not violated, flexibility of interpretation may be permitted. When in doubt, the Chair may ask the parliamentarian to give an opinion as to the meaning of the rules upon which the presiding officer acts, subject to appeal, or else the problem may be submitted to the membership. Courts rule on legality, not fairness alone.

┌─PRACTICE EXERCISE─────────────────────┐

1. What does "parliamentary law" or "parliamentary procedure" mean to the average citizen?
2. As you listen to groups conducting business, do you hear terms you find confusing or difficult to understand? What are some of these expressions?
3. Would groups act more efficiently if they could forget about parliamentary rules entirely? Why or why not?

┌─REVIEW QUESTIONS ──────────────────────┐

1. Q. Must I be required to use the exact terms used in accepted books by parliamentary authorities?

   A. No. Proper use of parliamentary language should be encouraged and practiced, but rigid use of terms is not required. The Chair would accept a statement or motion if the meaning were clear.

2. Q. Does the use of parliamentary rules complicate the discussion?

   A. No. Proper use of parliamentary rules speeds up business and provides ways to keep discussion germane, brief and to the point, preventing everyone from talking at once or as long or as often as one chooses.

3. Q. If some members know parliamentary rules and others do not, does that not give an unfair advantage?

A. Unfair? No, because rules provide for fair play and protect the rights of members from both sides to be heard and for all to choose by majority vote.

Advantage? Yes. Knowledge is power, power to use rules with skill in order to improve a situation.

RELATION OF CIVIL LAW TO PARLIAMENTARY LAW

Parliamentary Law is based on usage and custom, tried and tested until accepted as common law.

Civil Law, in relation to parliamentary law, includes those statutes that have been applied in court decisions where parliamentary law has been in question. When a presiding officer makes a ruling, it is subject to appeal by the members.

Thomas Jefferson believed that parliamentary law is upheld by common law, and its rules are binding upon the assembly. These rules have the effect of law, because the courts have ruled that organization members who do not obey the rules they have adopted, or act contrary to these rules, are liable to action in court.

COURTS HAVE ACCEPTED AS VALID, IN DESCENDING ORDER

- Federal and state applicable statutory law.

- The Charter of Articles of Incorporation if incorporated.

- Procedures as set forth in bylaws and any special rules adopted for use by an organization.

- Parliamentary laws as codified in manuals that have been adopted.

- Parliamentary law as explained in a manual as cited by the court.

- Common parliamentary law as derived from rules, customs and usages.

- Testimony of qualified parliamentarians as expert witnesses.

- Common law or case law as established by court decisions.

┌─Review Quiz #1 ──────────────────────────────┐

LESSON 1: PRINCIPLES AND RULES OF PARLIAMENTARY LAW

1. Write your definition of the purpose of parliamentary law.

_____

_____

_____

2. What are some of the principles of parliamentary law?

_____

_____

_____

3. What is the difference between parliamentary and statutory laws?

_____

_____

_____

4. What parliamentary rules does an organization adopt?

_____

_____

_____

5. Why did **Jefferson** write his *Manual?*

_____

_____

_____

_____

6. Are parliamentary rules an end in themselves?

_____

_____

_____

_____

7. List the procedures that evolved as **Petyt** presented them.

_____

_____

_____

_____

8. If a society adopts a parliamentary authority, what does it mean?

_____

_____

_____

_____

9. Where is the primary authority in an organization?

_____

_____

_____

_____

10. Why do rules change over the course of time?

_____

_____

_____

_____

11. Name some advantages of using parliamentary procedures.

_____

_____

_____

_____

Review Quiz #2

LESSON 1: PRINCIPLES AND RULES OF PARLIAMENTARY LAW

Write in which **principles** are violated in the following examples.

1. The Chair declared the motion adopted as "nearly unanimous."

   _____

   _____

   _____

2. The Chair declared the motion adopted after taking the vote, which appeared to be the same for both sides.

   _____

   _____

   _____

3. The Chair, after hearing several speakers in favor of the motion and none in opposition, declared the motion adopted.

   _____

   _____

   _____

4. A motion to give an honorarium to a speaker was amended to increase the salary of the secretary.

   _____

   _____

   _____

5. A member moved that the society purchase club pins for each member and to close debate on the motion.

   _____

   _____

   _____

6. A member abstained from debating or voting on a motion to raise dues and then complained bitterly when the motion was adopted.

_____

_____

_____

7. A member voted "No" on a motion that each member be assigned a committee membership. The motion was adopted. The member said that since he voted against the motion, he was not bound by the decision.

_____

_____

_____

8. A member rose to speak against a motion. Another member called out, "Sit down. We want this motion passed. You are wasting our time."

_____

_____

_____

9. After a lengthy proposition had undergone several changes, the Chair put the motion to a vote without repeating the motion as altered.

_____

_____

_____

10. Some members complained that they had not been told of a special meeting called to consider the purchase of certain property.

_____

_____

_____

LESSON 2
DELIBERATIVE ASSEMBLIES
MEETINGS

"The rule derived from common law is based on the concept that the private procurement of a written assent signed by a majority of members will not supply the want of a meeting. Such an expedient deprives those interested of the benefit of mutual discussion and subjects them to the hazards of fraudulent misrepresentation and undue influence."

George S. Hills, *Managing Corporate Meetings*

LESSON OBJECTIVE

To understand various types of meetings and the nature of effective participation.

READING ASSIGNMENT

Robert pp. 1-24, 82-96
Sturgis pp. 97-103

Demeter pp. 13-21, 203
Riddick pp. 21-22, 81-82, 108-109

LESSON MATERIAL

A **meeting**, other than for social purposes, is a gathering of persons who meet officially under rules of conduct, all members having been notified, and each member having equal rights to make motions, to debate and vote, and to transact business face to face. Except at the meeting itself, no group decisions can be made. A meeting may recess briefly, after which business continues from the point of interruption. No meeting is valid without the presence of a presiding officer and a secretary.

Assemblies are meetings of groups of members, or of more than a few persons, who come together for a definite purpose—to transact business. Such a body meets to deliberate (debate, discuss pro and con, sift evidence, learn facts, ask questions, persuade and convince) and to reach decisions on proposed items of business arrived at by a vote, nearly always that of a majority of those present and voting.

Sometimes the assembly does not make a decision to adopt or reject but disposes of the proposition by using some other form of parliamentary action.

Whatever the outcome, the action taken is recorded in the minutes as the sense of the assembly. All discussion is conducted under procedural rules established by the parent body or other adopted parliamentary authorities, which the members must obey.

Each meeting has its **order of business**. Members should attend promptly and remain until the meeting is adjourned. They should be ready to participate in the discussion, keeping within the rules of decorum. A productive meeting requires good management, careful planning and a competent Chair. Both officers and members should know the rules of their organization and the parliamentary rules of procedure so that business may be resolved with order and efficiency. Decisions made by the collective body should be promptly and properly implemented.

THERE ARE MANY KINDS OF MEETINGS

Regular meetings are those convened periodically as set by the society's documents of authority. The business transacted at the meetings must be within the adopted objects or jurisdiction of the society. Regular meetings should be specified and defined in the bylaws; therefore, no further notification to the members is usually required.

Adjourned meeting, or continued meeting, provides for the continuance of the same meeting when business that cannot wait until the next meeting fails to be completed at the time of adjournment. After the call to order of the continued meeting and the reading of the minutes of the previous meeting, business begins from the point of interruption at the regular meeting. Any business that would properly be presented before the regular meeting may be considered at a continued meeting. Special notice of an adjourned meeting is not required, since the meeting is a continuance of the previous meeting. The motion to set the time and place of an adjourned meeting, according to the parliamentary authority chosen, may be a privileged motion or a fully debatable main motion.

Special meetings are unscheduled meetings held at times specified in the call to meeting. Provisions for calling special meetings should be provided in the bylaws of an organization. Only the business stated in the call may be considered unless otherwise provided. The usual order of business is not in effect in a special meeting. Minutes are not read. The Chair reads the call to the special meeting, and the purpose stated in the call is then under consideration.

Annual meeting is the window dressing or the showpiece of the organization's achievements and should be prepared with care. Bylaws provide for annual meetings, at which time members hear reports of the retiring administration, the officers, the board, the standing committees and the president. They also listen to the report of the audit of the financial records and any other business that relates to the work that was undertaken and accomplished. Because the organization looks to the future, recommendations to the future administration are frequently submitted. Elections and the installation of new officers are generally included in the program; therefore, notice to the members of time and place of the meeting is required. The minutes of annual meetings are read for approval at the next regular meeting unless an alternative method of approval is used.

Mass meetings are those called by an unorganized group for whatever purpose was announced by the sponsor in the call to the meeting. Often the call is for the purpose of organizing. Persons may be notified in the press, by mail, by invitation or by some other means, and the sponsors have the right to restrict attendance to certain categories of persons as stated in the call. For example, a call for a meeting, as published in a newspaper, might say, "Those families interested in forming a children's theater club for children ages six through 12 will meet in the high school auditorium on Friday, October 10, 19_, at 7 p.m." Although anyone may attend, after such a public notice it is reasonable to expect that only those who are parents or guardians or those interested in promoting the purpose would respond to the call. Those opposed to the meeting or not in sympathy with the purpose may be excluded by the sponsors of the meeting as nonmembers who intend to obstruct the purpose. All who attend are considered members comprising a quorum with the right to debate and vote.

Legislative meetings by legislatures and some other lawmaking bodies are also deliberative meetings. No member can participate unless elected to membership. Such groups have the power to investigate, enact, amend or repeal statutes as delegated to them by their constituents.

Conventions are deliberative assemblies whose members are composed of delegates elected to represent constituent units. Conventions, other than those called to form an association or merger, must be provided for in the bylaws of the parent organization. Each convention makes its own rules, adopted for the duration of that convention. Any business not arrived at by adjournment ceases to exist. Conventions may consist of one or a series of meetings. Although many members and guests attend a convention, only elected delegates, officers and certain specified members may vote. The business of a convention consists of reports on issues of general concern to all representative units and frequently includes nominations and/or the election of officers. Conventions usually include programs for the education of the members as well as for their pleasure.

Executive session, sometimes called "closed session," is a special kind of meeting in which confidentiality must be observed. Nonmembers must be excluded from attendance. Such a session is necessary at executive level and in legislative bodies, but it has little place in civic or ordinary societies, except under extreme circumstances, and has often been abused. Many state legislatures have enacted "sunshine laws" to protect a citizen's "right to know." Such considerations as personnel, negotiation, property deals and discipline of members normally would be considered in closed session. To go into closed session, a member would rise to a *question of privilege* to present an emergency motion. This motion, when granted by the Chair, is treated like any other main motion and requires a majority vote or *general consent.*

THE FOLLOWING GENERAL REQUIREMENTS ARE APPLICABLE TO ALL MEETINGS

1. All members should be properly notified of the meeting in adequate time to attend. Place and time should be included in the notification.
2. Meetings should start on time, not before, as soon as a quorum is present.
3. The meeting place should be accessible and comfortable, and all equipment to be used should be ready and in working order.
4. Every meeting should have a competent Chair well able to apply procedural rules, a qualified parliamentarian willing to assist before and during the meetings and a secretary to record action taken.
5. The agenda for the proceedings should be carefully planned in advance.

6. Procedural rules should be used in ratio to the size and complexity of the group.
7. Sufficient time should be provided for debates, questions and answers, for all members. No one member should be permitted to dominate the discussion.
8. Limits to debate, when desired, should be established in advance.
9. If material is to be distributed, sufficient copies should be available. No copies of a speech should be distributed in advance.

THE CHAIR HAS THE FOLLOWING RESPONSIBILITIES

1. To come ahead of time and start at, but not before, the appointed time. Start as soon as a quorum is present.
2. To adhere to a well-prepared agenda as adopted.
3. To use procedural rules properly.
4. To preserve order, explain and clarify.
5. To call on members impartially.
6. To take and announce the vote correctly.
7. To stay composed and keep the meeting moving.
8. To use the gavel sparingly to open and close the meeting and to maintain order.
9. To make sure that adjournment does not end action on adopted motions, and to see that those motions are implemented.

THE MEMBERS HAVE THE FOLLOWING RESPONSIBILITIES

1. To arrive on time and remain until adjournment.
2. To attend prepared to participate.
3. To contribute ideas with properly phrased motions and intelligent debate.
4. To observe proper decorum in debate.
5. To obey the legitimate orders of the Chair.
6. To vote, and to accept the decision of the majority.

*BOTH OFFICERS
AND MEMBERS
SHOULD NOTE
THE FOLLOWING
POINTS*

1. If a meeting has been called and a quorum is present but the official presiding officer is absent, the vice president or, if the vice president is also absent, the secretary or another ranking officer may call the meeting to order. If no officer is present, a member may function in this capacity. The members may then make nominations and hold a voice-vote election for a Chair pro tem. A suitable waiting time for the arrival of the presiding officer should be provided. When the president arrives, the acting president withdraws.

2. Business that is postponed to a later day becomes a general order for that day and is introduced under the category of unfinished business before new business is considered.

3. Business once voted on may not be brought up again at the same meeting except by a motion to **Reconsider** or by *unanimous consent.*

4. **Robert's Rules of Order 1990 Edition** requires that business being postponed to a specific time may not be postponed beyond the next regular meeting. At that meeting, it may be postponed once again, however. Other authorities suggest that main motions may not be postponed to a meeting that has not been scheduled nor to any time that would be too late for the postponed motion to be effective if it were adopted.

PRACTICE EXERCISE

1. The lesson lists nine general requirements applicable to all meetings. Who has the primary responsibility for meeting each of these requirements? Who would be expected to assist in meeting each of these requirements?

2. Under what conditions and for what purpose should a society have an "executive session"?

3. Why should "sunshine laws" govern meetings of government bodies? Are there disadvantages with such laws?

REVIEW QUESTIONS

1. Q. What is the difference between a "meeting" and a "session"?

   A. A meeting is a single gathering of the group's members to conduct business. The members continue to act without separating, except, perhaps, for a brief recess.
   A session is an extended meeting or series of meetings devoted to one agenda, with each succeeding meeting continuing the business at the point where the previous meeting left off.

2. Q. How are special meetings and adjourned meetings classified in terms of "meetings" or "sessions"?

   A. A special meeting is classified as a separate session, conducting the business for which it was called.
   An adjourned meeting continues the previous regular meeting and is thus part of the same session.

3. Q. How is a recess different from an adjournment?

   A. A recess is a brief intermission in a meeting.
   An adjournment ends the meeting. If no provision has been made for a continuation of the meeting's agenda at some future time, the adjournment would also end the session.

┌─**Review Quiz** ─────────────────────────────┐

LESSON 2: DELIBERATIVE ASSEMBLIES
MEETINGS

1. List some of the general requirements for a deliberative meeting.

_____

_____

2. What does a call to a mass meeting need to include?

_____

_____

3. What are the requirements for a special meeting?

_____

_____

4. What business is conducted at an adjourned or continued meeting?

_____

_____

5. When may a meeting be called to order?

_____

_____

6. Write the notice required and the business that can be conducted in each type of meeting.

_____

MEETING	Notice	Business
Regular		
Adjourned		
Special		
Annual		
Mass		

LESSON 3
ORGANIZING A SOCIETY

"The idea for a membership organization usually begins in the mind of one individual, who recognizes that he has a need that is shared by others and that the need they share can be met through group action."

Lewis Deschler, *Rules of Order*

LESSON OBJECTIVE

To learn how formal organizations come into being.

READING ASSIGNMENT

Robert pp. 537-555   **Demeter** pp. 314-318
Sturgis pp. 206-209, 217-220   **Riddick** pp. 106-108, 132-135

LESSON MATERIAL

Organizations are formed for a variety of reasons—some for temporary objectives, dissolving as soon as the objective is accomplished, and others for permanence into perpetuity or until dissolved. Some organizations become incorporated, some do not. Some organize for profit, some do not. Most voluntary groups become nonprofit organizations, which means that they may not use any profit they make for any purpose other than for the object as stated in their bylaws. Consequently, some not-for-profit organizations apply for and receive tax-exempt status from the Internal Revenue Service.

When groups get together to share a common view, it is important that all in attendance actually share the same view. A clear and explicit statement of purpose should be stated in the call to the first mass meeting. Plans for the execution of purpose should be carefully prepared so that they meet all legal and parliamentary requirements. Sponsors should obtain a good chairman to promote and develop these plans.

Organizing a society takes at least two meetings. The first meeting is to determine to have an organization, and the second meeting is to adopt bylaws, obtain members and possibly appoint some committee members after officers have been elected.

When any group decides to organize into a club or society, the initial procedure is similar to calling a mass meeting. Only those desired for membership who would be interested in the purpose of organizing would be invited to attend. Such invitations are usually made through personal contact, through the media or by mail.

At the first meeting, usually called to order by a sponsor, temporary officers—the chair and a secretary—are elected by voice vote. The sponsors of the meeting then explain the reasons for becoming an organized group. A resolution, usually prepared in advance, is submitted for adoption:

         Resolved, That this group now form a society for the purpose of _____ .

Or a motion is made:

         "I move that we form a society to be called _____, at this time."

Discussion and amendments may follow, and a majority vote adopts. Adoption of the motion does not create a new society, but it establishes a formal consent to do so. Two additional steps are necessary to create the society.

Bylaws, which may have been prepared in advance by the sponsors or composed by a committee appointed to do so, may be presented when ready, possibly at a second meeting, known as an adjourned meeting, which is a continuance of the first meeting. At that designated meeting the bylaws are discussed, amended and adopted by a majority vote.

After adoption of bylaws, the group recesses for those desiring membership to enroll as members, pay dues as required in the new bylaws and thus become charter members. The organization is now established.

Permanent officers are then nominated and elected according to the bylaw regulations. Organizations planning to negotiate legal contracts will desire to incorporate, and the services of a local attorney may be required.

AGENDA FOR FIRST MEETING

1. Call to order—usually by the sponsor.
2. Election of a Chair pro tem, usually conducted by the sponsor.
3. Election of a secretary, conducted by Chair pro tem.
4. Reading of the call to the meeting.
5. Sponsor or others present reasons for forming a society.
6. Adoption of a resolution, usually prepared in advance, to form a society.
7. Appointment or election of a bylaws committee.
8. Adjournment, with the time, place and date specified for the next meeting.

AGENDA FOR SECOND MEETING

1. Call to order by Chair pro tem.
2. Reading and approval of minutes of the first meeting.
3. Consideration and adoption of bylaws.
4. Recess to enroll members and collect dues.
5. Election of officers according to bylaws.
6. Appointment of committees according to bylaws.
7. Adjournment.

PRACTICE EXERCISE

Divide the class into two groups.

Assign each group a fictitious situation, a problem with at least two opposing alternatives. For example, group #1 might be asked to determine the use for a piece of property donated to the city, with some wanting to construct a racetrack, some wanting to use the land for a park and others wanting to build a shopping mall. Someone in the group should be appointed to sponsor each alternative.

Group #2 should be given a problem with different alternatives. For example, their assignment might be a swamp, which could either be drained for a real estate development or dredged to make a lake and playground. Again, each alternative should have a sponsor.

Assign each group to write a call to a mass meeting, assuming a particular time and place, for public discussion of its problem. At this point the group should determine, by vote, which alternative the members prefer. The sponsor of that alternative becomes the sponsor of the mass meeting.

Group #1 should then conduct its meeting, calling the meeting to order, electing a Chair and a secretary, preparing and adopting its resolution. Discussion time should be limited. Afterward, the members of group #2 should critique the procedure.

Then have group #2 conduct its own meeting, with group #1 doing the critique.

Review Quiz #1

LESSON 3: ORGANIZING A SOCIETY

Mark "T" for True or "F" for False for each statement and explain why statements labeled "F" are incorrect.

____ 1. In contrast to a mass meeting, in a meeting to form a permanent society the persons should be invited to attend by personal contact rather than by public announcement.

____ 2. The person who calls the mass meeting to order conducts the election of both temporary officers, namely the Chair and the secretary.

____ 3. The adoption of a resolution to form a society brings the organization into being.

____ 4. In the first organization meeting for a society, dues may be established to provide finances for funding early expenditures, such as printing bylaws.

____ 5. In advance of the meeting, a bylaws committee should be identified by the sponsor in order to expedite forming a society.

____ 6. A motion should be adopted to fix the date, hour and place for the next meeting, or at the call of the Chair.

____ 7. All permanent societies should be incorporated.

____ 8. Those who enroll and pay initiation fees, if any, and dues at the second meeting are called "charter members."

LESSON 4
ORDER OF BUSINESS
AGENDA

"The business of a meeting is the real reason for the organization's existence. Business is conducted systematically in a predicted sequence as provided for in the order of business of the adopted agenda, so that convenience and consistency are provided."

Riddick Butcher, *Riddick's Rules of Procedure*

LESSON OBJECTIVE

To learn the standard order of business for a formal meeting.

READING ASSIGNMENT

Robert pp. 24-26, 345-359   **Demeter** pp. 14-21, 223-238, 297-298
Sturgis pp. 107-113   **Riddick** pp. 7-11, 130-132

LESSON MATERIAL

Order is the fundamental quality of an organized society. Members of any organization should expect a predictable sequence in handling its business. By definition, **order of business** is the established sequence of topics to be considered at any meeting of the organization. The **agenda** consists of the topics within the order of business, but for general use the terms are often considered synonymous.

Parliamentary procedure is a clear, orderly, understandable, systematic plan for the successful conduct of business. This general principle is demonstrated in the common provision that an order of business be adopted and placed in the standing rules or special orders. This order does not belong in the bylaws, because bylaws cannot be amended or suspended without a special provision to that effect. The order of business frequently needs adjustment or change, something easily accomplished by moving to **Suspend the Rule**, a motion which requires a two-thirds vote. This permits a change in the adopted order, placing an item of business elsewhere on the list.

The items contained in an order of business can vary depending on the purposes of the organization. A "standard" order of business would contain these six headings:

1. Reading and approval of minutes of the previous meeting
2. Reports from officers, boards and standing committees
3. Reports from special committees in the order created
4. Special orders of business, if any
5. Unfinished business and general orders
6. New business

Agenda is the blueprint of the meeting providing the specific sequence in which business will be introduced. Organizations that meet frequently put an adopted agenda in their standing rules. For irregular meetings, the proposed agenda which is adopted is debatable and amendable before business begins. *General consent* or majority vote adopts. Less important items should be scheduled at the end of the agenda to insure sufficient time for consideration of important items. The Chair announces each item of business in turn by stating, "The next business in order is . . . "

Consent agenda is used when a list of routine business items that require action, but not necessarily discussion, may be approved all at the same time, either by a majority vote or *general consent*, with no objection. This all-at-one-time approval is called adoption "en bloc," in totality, in entirety as an undivided whole. Such items as approval for ordering club stationery, accepting resignations, and the like are usually noncontroversial. Any member wishing to do so may ask to have an item removed from the list and placed on the regular agenda. The purpose of consent agenda is to provide more time for priority items in a heavy schedule by disposing of minor items with a single vote.

The term **program** can be used to designate the entire schedule for a series of meetings within an annual convention. For local regularly convened groups, a program may be an item of entertainment that is usually placed just before the group's adjournment. In addition, although **call to order** is technically not regarded as an order of business, it is actually the business of establishing the presence of a quorum and opening a meeting, and **adjournment** is the business of closing a meeting.

The following "expanded" agenda contains 10 headings:

1. Call to order
2. Reading and approval of the minutes of the previous meeting
3. Reports from officers of the organization
4. Reports from boards and standing committees
5. Reports from special committees
6. Unfinished business
7. New business
8. Announcements
9. Program
10. Adjournment

Note: The standard and the expanded orders of business are applied to regular meetings. The order of business for a **special meeting** is significantly different. As the term implies, special meetings are called between regular meetings to deal with very limited business. Only items of business specifically listed in the call of the special meeting may properly be handled. A typical order of business for the special meeting would contain these three steps:

1. Call to order
2. Business stated in the call to meeting
3. Adjournment

The minutes of a special meeting are read at the next regular meeting.

The order of business of a **regular meeting** might be as follows:

Call to order: When the hour for the regular meeting arrives, the presiding officer calls the meeting to order promptly by striking the gavel and announcing, "The regular meeting of the Association for the Study of Contemporary Problems will please come to order."

Approval of the minutes follows, with necessary corrections, after which, either by *general consent* or majority vote, approval is given as "read," "corrected" or "distributed."

Reports from officers vary, depending upon the type of organization. The most common report is that of the treasurer, which should feature receipts and disbursements of funds and a statement of current balance. Properly, the treasurer's report is filed, not approved. The president, secretary or other officers may report under this business heading.

Under the heading of **reports from boards and standing committees** are heard reports, if any, from the board of directors or from an executive committee composed of the elected officers of the organization. Standing committees are permanent organizational committees provided for in the bylaws. Reports of boards or committees are filed unless given in recommendation form. Specific proposals or recommendations may be considered immediately, or the consideration may be postponed until new business.

Under the heading of **reports from special committees**, the organization entertains reports from what can be called the temporary, special or ad hoc committees. The Chair calls for reports only from committees prepared to report and in the order in which the committees were created.

Unfinished business and **general orders of business** relate to items of business from a previous meeting that were pending upon adjournment and to items scheduled for the previous meeting but not yet reached. Also included are items specifically postponed to the present meeting or matters specifically made a general order of business for the next regular meeting.

New business is largely self-explanatory and refers to the specific items of business planned for the current meeting or to new items that arise spontaneously from the needs and interests of the members in attendance.

Announcements provide opportunity for the Chair or other members to make comments for the interest or welfare of the membership.

Program, as applied to regular meetings of ordinary societies, may include cultural, educational or civic activities for the delight or edification of the members. An advantage of placing the program before adjournment is to allow the membership the possibility of voting to commend or endorse some activity described in the program and for the Chair to retain control of the meeting.

Adjournment is the formal termination of a meeting. As it is usually handled, the Chair inquires whether there is further new business to come before the assembly. If none is offered, the Chair may, with no objection, adjourn the meeting. Some parliamentary authorities, however, require a formal motion for adjournment. When a member moves to adjourn and the motion is adopted, the Chair announces the meeting adjourned and strikes the gavel.

Should an organization wish to include **opening ceremonies** (for example, an invocation, the national anthem, a pledge of allegiance to the flag, calling of the membership roll or other ritual), such activities come after the call to order and before the reading of the minutes. These activities may occur without the presence of a quorum.

Some organizations use an item on the agenda called **good of the order**, where a member may offer informal observations regarding the work of the organization or speak to the infractions of rules or reputation of the society or its members. Such an item of business comes after the new business. Action is usually not taken on these discussions at this time but may be introduced as new business at the next meeting.

Orderliness and predictability are important characteristics of meetings, but there are times when some flexibility can better serve the members. An important committee report or some urgent new item of business can be advanced in the agenda in priority of handling. For example, a member may rise asking "unanimous consent to present a specified item at this time," requiring prompt approval. The Chair would ask whether there is any objection to this early consideration. Should there be none, this proposal is promptly considered. A committee wishing either to advance or to delay the time of its report asks permission for this exception to the standard order of business. Either by *unanimous consent* or by a two-thirds vote of the assembly, permission may be granted. The motion to **Suspend the Rules** is frequently employed to make an order of business more flexible and thereby meet the special needs of the organization.

General orders are any subjects placed on the agenda. General orders come up for consideration when that place on the agenda is reached. If business is pending, the general order is taken up as soon as pending business is disposed of, unless a motion is adopted either to lay the pending business on the table or to postpone it until after the general order is resolved.

Special orders of business are not common among ordinary societies and refer to an action of a previous meeting that postponed and elevated a particular item of business to the special priority status of being considered even before the unfinished business. A two-thirds vote is required to create a special order. If a special order appears on the agenda, the subjects of such motions are assigned a special place and hour for their consideration, which can interrupt pending business.

┌─**PRACTICE EXERCISE**────────────────────────┐
└──┘

Have the class use the expanded order of business and create specific agenda items for the meeting of a campus or local organization.

Include specific proposals under unfinished business and new business.

Plan a realistic program.

Review Quiz #1

LESSON 4: ORDER OF BUSINESS
AGENDA

1. What is the order of business for a special meeting?

_____

_____

_____

_____

2. Where in the order of business should the singing of the national anthem be placed?

_____

_____

_____

_____

3. What general principles of parliamentary procedure sustain the wisdom of an order of business?

_____

_____

_____

_____

4. Define "agenda."

_____

_____

_____

5. Give two different meanings of "program" as applied to meetings.

_____

_____

_____

6. How can members seek to adjust priorities of the adopted order of business?

_____

_____

_____

_____

7. Why does unfinished business come before new business?

_____

_____

_____

_____

8. What is meant by "consent agenda" or "consent calendar"?

_____

_____

_____

_____

9. What are special orders?

_____

_____

_____

_____

10. What business comes under good of the order?

_____

_____

_____

_____

┌─Review Quiz #2 ─────────────────────────────┐

LESSON 4: ORDER OF BUSINESS
AGENDA

Match the agenda items below as they would be placed in the order of business.

Identify the item in the order of business where each agenda item fits.

Place the number for that order of business in the blank at the right.

ORDER OF BUSINESS	AGENDA ITEMS	
1. Call to order	Elections	_____
2. Reading and approval of minutes	Report of ways and means committee	_____
3. Reports of the officers	Panel discussion	_____
4. Reports from standing committees	Postponed motions	_____
5. Reports from special committees	Establishment of quorum	_____
6. Special orders	Report on state finances	_____
7. Unfinished business	Report of ad hoc committee	_____
8. New business	Time to cease business	_____
9. Adjournment	Check the record	_____
10. Program	Introduce new proposition	_____

LESSON 5
BRINGING BUSINESS BEFORE THE ASSEMBLY - MAIN MOTION

(Lessons 5 and 6 may be presented as one lesson.)

"A main motion aims to contribute to those policies for which the organization stands."

Joseph O'Brien, *Parliamentary Law for the Layman*

LESSON OBJECTIVE

To learn how to bring business before an assembly and how it is processed to some decision.

READING ASSIGNMENT

Robert pp. 97-122, 31-81   **Demeter** pp. 50-58
Sturgis pp. 30-41, 15   **Riddick** pp. 116-117, 104-105

LESSON MATERIAL

A **main motion** is a statement of proposed action or desired opinion presented for consideration and decision. It is the most important motion, yet it has precedence over nothing and can be introduced only when no other business is pending. Its specific requirements should be understood before it can be properly put to good use.

There are three types of main motions:

1. An **original** substantive main motion introduces a new subject. For example, "I move that we donate $500 to the Boys Club of America." The subject may also be introduced by a resolution.

2. An **incidental** main motion, sometimes called a **specific** main motion or a **restoratory** motion, reintroduces a subject that has already been acted upon. There is no difference in treatment of this motion except that, according to **Robert**, in some instances it requires a two-thirds vote to adopt without previous notice. For example, "I move to

amend Standing Rule #4 to add that smokers be required to sit in the rear of the assembly hall."

3. Certain **privileged, subsidiary and incidental** motions that are introduced *when no other business is pending* are treated as **original** main motions and, being in the nature of main motions, their order of precedence is the same as a main motion and they yield to higher ranking motions—just as all main motions do. Some examples follow: **Schedule an Adjourned Meeting, Adjourn** (under certain circumstances), **Recess, Limit or Extend Debate, Postpone to a Definite Time, Refer to Committee, Amend Something Previously Adopted, Approve Committee Reports and Minutes, Approve Amendments to Bylaws, Choose the Method of Voting, Suspend the Rules, Divide a Question** and the like. Any motion introduced when no business is pending is a main motion and is treated as such in terms of its order of precedence and the rules that govern it.

The following rules govern the original main motion:

1. Cannot interrupt a speaker.
2. Requires a second.
3. Is debatable, for it presents a substantive proposal.
4. Can be amended.
5. Requires a majority vote.
6. Takes precedence over no other motions.
7. Applies to no other motion.
8. Can have applied to it all subsidiary motions, object to consideration and withdraw.

Considering the rules that govern a main motion and the characteristics of a well-constructed motion, the Chair should rule **out of order** motions that do any of the following:

1. Conflict with any laws, or with the bylaws of the organization.
2. Repeat the same question on the same day.
3. Conflict with an already adopted motion.
4. Operate outside the scope, jurisdiction or objects of the organization.
5. Conflict with motions held in committee or otherwise waiting action.
6. Duplicate motions that have been laid on the table.
7. Reflect unacceptable, discourteous language.
8. Appear incomplete, dilatory, incorrect, frivolous.

Before any proposal, the maker should determine that the motion is legal, is in harmony with the purpose of the organization, and can be implemented. The maker may explain briefly, if necessary, the reason for stating the motion, especially if the subject is obscure or complicated. The maker should also be aware of these points:

1. The Chair may require that a motion be submitted in writing.
2. The maker of a motion has first right to speak to it.
3. A member may vote against his own motion, but some parliamentary authorities disallow the member to speak against it.
4. A member may modify his own motion before it is stated by the Chair and offer an amendment after it is stated by the Chair.
5. A member may withdraw his own motion up to the time it is stated by the Chair and after that may withdraw it by permission of the assembly.
6. Modifications accepted by the maker of the motion may be made *before* the motion is stated by the Chair.

THE PROCESSING OF A MAIN MOTION INCLUDES THE <u>FOLLOWING STEPS</u>

Recognition

A member rises, addresses the Chair by the proper title and waits to be recognized. The Chair usually recognizes the member who rose first and addressed the Chair, if that member is entitled to speak at that time. The Chair has full authority to make the selection.

Proposal

After recognition the member states, "I move that . . ." or "I move to . . ." No other form is correct. If the maker has difficulty in formulating the motion, the Chair may offer assistance, stating the motion as agreed to by the maker.

Second

Without waiting for recognition, any member may call out, "I second the motion" or "Second," which signifies that at least two people think the motion worth consideration. (Some authorities no longer require a second because the motion can be objected to if not desired.)

The Chair is not obligated to ask for a second. When there is none, the Chair may say, "There is no second; the motion is not before you" or "Since there is no second, the next business in order is . . ."

Statement

After a second, the Chair states the motion. "It has been moved and seconded that . . . . Is there any discussion?"

Debate

The Chair calls upon members who ask for recognition to debate pro or con, offer amendments or propose other motions that are applicable.

When discussion stops, the Chair will pause, then ask, "Are you ready to vote?", pause again, then put the motion to a vote. If a motion has been made to close debate on the motion, the Chair will take a vote on this subsidiary motion at once. The motion to close debate must be seconded and requires a two-thirds vote. If adopted, the Chair immediately puts the main motion to a vote. If the motion to close debate is lost, debate on the main motion continues.

Vote

First, the Chairman restates the motion. "It has been moved and seconded that . . . ." Both opinions must be voted upon. The Chair says, "All those in favor of the motion to . . . say, "Aye." All those opposed to the motion to . . . say, "No." A majority vote wins, with certain exceptions as provided in the organization's documentary authority, which may require a two-thirds vote. "Majority" is based on the number of those present and voting. Abstentions are not counted.

If a vote was counted, the Chair always announces the result of the count first, then proceeds to announce which side won.

Result

The Chair always announces the result of the vote. No vote is considered final until this has been done. The announcement verifies the result for inclusion in the minutes. The Chair says, "The Ayes have it and the motion to . . . is adopted" or "The Noes have it and the motion to . . . is lost."

If the vote was counted, the Chair always announces the count first by saying, "There being ____ votes in the affirmative (or for the motion) and ____ in the negative (or against the motion to . . .), the Ayes have it and the motion is adopted" or "The Noes have it and the motion is lost (or rejected)."

Except when the vote is taken by ballot, any member has the right to change his vote up until the time the Chair announces the result; after the announcement, the member may change only with the permission of the assembly.

The announcement of the result always should include four parts:

1. The count of the votes and the outcome of the vote. "The Ayes have it."
2. The effect on the motion. "The motion is adopted."
3. A statement as to the effect of the action. "The treasurer will prepare the check for . . . ."
4. An announcement of the next item of business for the assembly.

Implementation

If appropriate, the Chair will then direct the proper member or committee to carry out the directive in the motion.

In the category of *assumed* or *implied motions* are some main motions of little consequence, or motions in which the affirmative decision appears to be obvious with no debate required. The Chair assumes that the motion has been stated and takes the vote by *general consent,* with no objection. If there is an objection, a vote is taken. Such motions are approval of minutes, adjourn when no business is pending, closing polls or nominations and permitting editorial changes in a motion.

┌─**Review Quiz #1** ──────────────────────────┐

LESSON 5:   BRINGING BUSINESS BEFORE THE
ASSEMBLY - MAIN MOTION

1. What steps are used to handle a main motion?

_____

_____

2. What is the difference between an original and an incidental main
motion?

_____

_____

3. What are the characteristics of a main motion?

_____

_____

4. How may main motions be improved to increase popular support?

_____

_____

5. Why must a main motion be accurate and well worded?

_____

_____

6. What kind of motions may be ruled not in order?

_____

_____

7. Once a motion is adopted, what becomes of it?

_____

_____

_____

⌐Review Quiz #2 ⌐

LESSON 5: BRINGING BUSINESS BEFORE THE ASSEMBLY - MAIN MOTION

IMPROPER MOTIONS
Explain why the following motions are incorrect, or are they?

1. I move that we do not march in the Memorial Day parade.

_____

_____

_____

2. I move that free beer be supplied at all meetings.

_____

_____

_____

3. I move that we vote now by a show of hands instead of wasting time on ballot voting as stated in our bylaws.

_____

_____

_____

4. I move that we disagree with the order from our parent group to raise our dues.

_____

_____

_____

5. I object to this motion that was referred to committee.

_____

_____

_____

_____

6. I move that we disregard the standing rule that all members be required to wear badges.

_____

_____

_____

_____

7. I move that we refuse to accept the Chair's decision made this morning that the motion was out of order.

_____

_____

_____

_____

8. I move that we go on record not to support the bond issue.

_____

_____

_____

_____

9. I move that we do something about the filthy condition of the school grounds.

_____

_____

_____

_____

10. I move that we instruct our secretary to write a letter of appreciation to our instructor for his patience with our many questions during class.

_____

_____

_____

_____

┌─ **Review Quiz #3** ─────────────────────────────────┐

LESSON 5:   BRINGING BUSINESS BEFORE THE ASSEMBLY - MAIN MOTION

ORDER OF PROCEDURE

Number the items below to indicate the correct order in which they should appear in the process of making and disposing of a motion.

____ 1. A member, remaining seated, says, "I second the motion."

____ 2. Mr. S., rising, says, "Mr. Chairman."

____ 3. "Is there any discussion?" asks the Chair.

____ 4. "Is there anyone to speak further on the motion?" asks the Chair.

____ 5. "Mr. S.," says the Chair.

____ 6. "Are you ready to vote now?" asks the Chair.

____ 7. Member who made the motion speaks in favor of it.

____ 8. "Those opposed to the motion to . . . say, 'No,'" says the Chair.

____ 9. The Chair says, "It has been moved and seconded to . . . ."

____ 10. A member secures the floor and speaks in opposition.

____ 11. "Those in favor of the motion to . . . , say, 'Aye,'" says the Chair.

____ 12. Mr. S. says, "I move that . . . ."

____ 13. "The Ayes seem to have it, and the motion to . . . is adopted," says the Chair.

┌─ **Review Quiz #4** ────────────────────────────┐

LESSON 5:   BRINGING BUSINESS BEFORE THE
                ASSEMBLY - MAIN MOTION

SUBSTANTIVE MAIN MOTIONS
INSTRUCTIONS: Describe how you, as presiding officer, would process
these motions.

1. **(GARDEN CLUB)** "Mrs. Adkins, the treasurer, tells me that this
   organization is practically broke. I move that we give some serious
   thought to raising the dues."

   _____

   _____

   _____

2. **(ROTARY)** "I move that this organization pay $75.00 toward each
   delegate's expenses at the national convention."

   _____

   _____

   _____

3. **(AMERICAN LEGION POST)** "I move that we follow the suggestions
   of Al Brown for Memorial Day."

   _____

   _____

   _____

4. **(FRIENDS OF THE ART MUSEUM)** "I move that we turn in a fire
   alarm to test the efficiency of our city fire department and that we
   time the interval between the turning in of the alarm and the arrival
   of the first fire engine."

   _____

   _____

   _____

5. **(COMMUNITY CLUB)** "I move that a committee be appointed for studying ways and means of enlisting new members for this organization."

_____

_____

_____

6. **(CITY COUNCIL)** "I move that all dog owners be required to have muzzles on their dogs whenever they appear on the city streets."

_____

_____

_____

7. **(POLITICAL PARTY)** "I move that we set up a roadblock beside the Hastings Road and Route 5 intersection to pass out fliers for our candidate."

_____

_____

_____

8. **(DEBATING CLUB)** "I move that we disregard the constitutional provision against voting at the same meeting on new members, and that we vote on the name of Tom Bennet at once."

_____

_____

_____

9. **(CHURCH)** "I move that the portable air conditioners throughout the church be replaced with a central air-conditioning unit."

_____

_____

_____

10. **(LIONS CLUB)** "I move the guest speaker be denied the floor for further comment because of Rule 10 on political advocacy."

_____

_____

_____

LESSON 6
BRINGING BUSINESS BEFORE THE
ASSEMBLY - RESOLUTIONS

"A main motion—particularly an original main motion—is frequently offered as a resolution."

Henry M. Robert, *Robert's Rules of Order Newly Revised*

LESSON OBJECTIVE

To learn proper form and presentation of resolutions, which are forms of main motions.

READING ASSIGNMENT

Robert pp. 32, 102-107   **Demeter** pp. 50, 58-62
Sturgis pp. 183-187   **Riddick** pp. 69, 174-176,

LESSON MATERIAL

The right to petition is part of the Bill of Rights, and resolutions are the tools for petitioning. Resolutions are written main motions to request action or express opinion, to seek support on action taken by others, to seek legislation or to establish a policy. Because they are frequently controversial and are used for important decisions that are publicized, resolutions require accuracy. Resolutions from a group already in agreement command respect, have clout. They often become official policy.

A resolution may be presented from a committee or by an individual member. The committee chairman states, "By direction of the committee (optional), I move the adoption of the following resolution. . . ." The chairman then reads the resolution.

If there are many resolutions, they may be numbered and considered all at the same time (en bloc) or one at a time, as desired.

Resolutions are identical in function to main motions but are written in a form established by custom. Usually they consist of one or more clauses. There may or may not be a **preamble**, or explanatory clause, beginning with **Whereas**. If a preamble is included, it should state the reason for the resolution briefly. Oral reading of preambles may be omitted, especially if copies have been distributed.

The **Resolve** may also have one or more clauses. It is the resolving clause, sometimes called the enacting clause, that states the desired action. The effecting clause denotes who should carry out the order or be informed, and how this should be done.

Format:

Whereas, comma, is often followed by identification of the makers of the motion beginning with a capital letter or We . . . followed by a semicolon. Then a new paragraph begins with **Resolved**, comma, next word beginning with a capital letter. Each clause ends with a semicolon.

Example:

Whereas, There is no public playground for children in this village; therefore, be it

Resolved, That ample playgrounds should be provided promptly for children; and (be it further—optional)

Resolved, That a committee of five be appointed by the Chair to present this resolution to the village authorities and urge immediate attention to this matter.

Resolving clauses are always amended first, then the preamble, followed by voting on the entire resolution as amended.

A long resolution with several resolves may have each resolve considered one at a time (seriatim).

When the resolution is being amended, it is not necessary to move for editorial changes or number changes. The secretary should be responsible for such changes.

ACTION ON RESOLUTIONS

Resolutions may be adopted, amended, rejected or recommitted if presented by a committee.

A well-drafted resolution is:

1. Clear, accurate and concise, with no surplus language.
2. Legal in all regards.
3. Written with citations and quotations faithful to the original.
4. Enforceable if adopted.
5. Specific about the situation to be addressed.

The preamble should be as brief as possible. It has no legal significance. The resolution can be introduced with "I move" or "On behalf of the committee, I move that . . ." or *"Resolved,* That . . . " A resolution may even be a single statement, such as:

Ordered: That this fire department purchase paramedic supplies for its paramedics at a cost not to exceed $100.00.

or

Resolved: That this PTA make the establishment of a neighborhood preschool its main project for the year.

PRACTICE RESOLUTIONS

Write a resolution to establish a lending library.

Other subjects to be used for practice resolutions:

a.   Laws regarding DWI.

b.   Better supervision of parking facilities.

c.   Returning prayer to schools.

d.   Better gun control.

┌─Review Quiz ─────────────────────────────┐

LESSON 6:   BRINGING BUSINESS BEFORE THE
ASSEMBLY - RESOLUTIONS

1. How is a resolution presented?

_____

_____

2. How does the Chair state the resolution?

_____

_____

3. Why should a preamble be brief?

_____

_____

4. Why is the preamble amended last?

_____

_____

5. What vote adopts a resolution?

_____

_____

6. What are some common forms for writing resolutions?

_____

_____

7. What unusual advantage is gained by presenting a motion as a resolution?

_____

_____

_____

LESSON 7
THE AMENDING PROCESS

"Second only in importance to the main motion, in all parliamentary law, is the motion to amend. Main motions carry the main business of the organization. Motions to amend, in their primary and secondary forms, so perfect the main motion that it embodies the true will of the assembly."

Joseph O'Brien, *Parliamentary Law for the Layman*

LESSON OBJECTIVE

To learn the proper uses of amendment as a method to perfect a proposition.

READING ASSIGNMENT

Robert pp. 127-164, 299-304   **Demeter** pp. 68-82
Sturgis pp. 19, 42-50   **Riddick** pp. 12-20

LESSON MATERIAL

The importance of the proper use of amendments cannot be overstated. Amendments are intended to perfect a proposition, particularly a main motion. They revise the wording of a main motion to make it clearer, more complete and more in harmony with the desires of the majority of the assembly. Since they apply to the main motion, amendments are classed as subsidiary motions, taking precedence over the main motion to which they apply but yielding to other subsidiary motions such as a motion to refer the question to a committee or to postpone the question to some future time. Amendments may also be applied to other motions containing variable factors. For example, a motion to refer the question to a committee could itself be amended in regard to the committee membership or its instructions. A motion to postpone the main question could be amended in regard to the future time to which the question is postponed.

Unfortunately, the amending process sometimes results in confusion when members don't understand the procedure. To amend a motion is to revise its wording. People mistakenly believe that passing an amendment also passes the motion. Such is not the case. The revised motion would still be open to further discussion and amendment before a final vote is taken to pass or to reject the reworded motion itself. In addition, amendments are sometimes offered without adequate forethought or clarity of intent. While main motions and resolutions may be carefully worded and even studied by a committee, proposed amendments may arise spontaneously from the floor, making changes in the main motion that only make it more difficult to understand. Nevertheless, nothing is perfect, and a thoughtful amendment may often make an unpopular motion acceptable to the majority of the group.

RULES GOVERNING THE AMENDING PROCESS

1. Any member may propose an amendment, or it may come from a committee. Presumably, a committee amendment would offer better impact, since the thought and language would have had consideration.

2. The Chair should rule out of order any amendment that is not germane (related) to the motion to which it is applied. An obviously dilatory amendment should also be ruled out of order.

3. The secretary must record each amendment as it is seconded and stated by the Chair. The subsequent disposition of each amendment should also be recorded.

4. Adopting an amendment does not adopt the original main motion, which must be put to a separate vote, whether amended or not.

5. Adoption of the proposed amendment is decided by the assembly, by majority vote.

6. Each member is free to vote on the amendment and on the main motion as he may decide.

7. Noncontroversial *acceptable* amendments may be adopted by *general consent,* if no member objects.

8. Any number of amendments may be offered to a main motion, but each one of these primary amendments must be voted upon and decided before the next one is in order.

9. No amendment is in order that simply proposes a negative to the original motion.

10. The Chair may require an amendment to be put in writing.

Amendments may be made by:

1. Adding words at the end of a sentence or phrase.
2. Inserting words within the context.
3. Striking out words.
4. Striking out and inserting contiguous words; replacing one expression with another.
5. Substituting one major section of the motion with a replacement section. Such a substitution may even replace the entire motion with another motion, provided that the substitute motion is germane to the original motion.

The amendment to a main motion may itself be amended. Thus amendments have two degrees, primary (applying to the main motion) and secondary (applying to the primary amendment). However, the secondary amendment may not be amended, which is to say that a tertiary amendment is never in order.

As a general rule, amendments are accepted one at a time, and a second amendment to the main motion may not be offered so long as a first amendment is being considered. However, a member speaking in opposition to the first amendment might state his readiness to propose a better amendment, once the first one is defeated. In so doing, he could even briefly outline his proposal. These comments would be regarded as discussion, and his proposal could not claim the official attention of the group until the first amendment is rejected and his amendment is properly made and seconded.

Amendments:
1. Cannot interrupt a speaker. The one offering an amendment must properly gain the floor.
2. Must be seconded.
3. Are debatable, if the motion to which they apply is debatable.
4. Are amendable. However, a secondary amendment is not amendable.
5. Require a majority vote even if the motion to which they apply requires a two-thirds vote.
6. Can be reconsidered.

SUBSTITUTE MOTIONS

A substitute motion is an amendment which replaces the entire text of the main motion with an alternative. It is a primary amendment and must be germane to the main motion. As a primary amendment, it may have secondary amendments applied to it. **Robert** outlines the following for handling substitute motions:

1. The substitute is held in suspension while the assembly continues to discuss the original main motion. Other amendments to the main motion may be offered, discussed and voted on at this time.
2. The main motion is then held in suspension while the assembly turns its attention to the proposed substitute. This amendment may now be discussed and amended, as the assembly wishes.
3. The substitute is put to a vote. That is, the assembly is asked to decide, by majority vote, whether the substitute should replace the main motion as the motion before the group.
4. The remaining motion, either the substitute or the main motion, is then open to further discussion, and a final vote is taken on adopting this motion.

Sturgis and some other parliamentary authorities believe that the substitute proposal should be perfected and voted on first. If it is defeated, the original motion is then open to amendment.

FRIENDLY AMENDMENT

A friendly amendment may be defined as a change in wording that the author of the original motion would have made had he thought of it. When such a change is proposed and no one objects, the amendment is adopted by *general consent*.

HOSTILE AMENDMENT

While a proposed amendment must be germane to the main motion, it need not be in accord with the intent of that original motion. In fact, the result of the amendment may be radically different from what the mover of the original motion had in mind. For example, suppose a resolution is pending to "commend" a police officer who discovered a bomb in the wheel well of a bus carrying Olympic contestants. Someone in the group happens to be aware that the officer planted that bomb himself and offers the following amendment: to strike "commend" and insert "censure." Such a proposal would be germane and would be in order. Presumably, the facts of the case would come out in the discussion of the amendment.

Notice, however, that a motion to insert "not" in the original motion—that the group "not commend" the officer—would not be in order. Such an amendment would only reverse the vote on the original motion—to commend or not to commend. One could gain the same result by voting "no" on the motion. But to "censure" is a very different thing than merely "not commending." Thus a motion to strike and insert "censure" would be a proper amendment, while a motion simply to insert "not" would be out of order.

FILLING BLANKS

Sometimes a main motion will contain items such as names, places, times, numbers or amounts that become the subject of controversy. Someone offers a primary amendment to change the amount to a smaller figure. Clearly, the amount is highly controversial, and the process of offering and voting amendments, one at a time, could unnecessarily prolong the meeting.

In such circumstances, the most efficient procedure would be to create a blank in the motion and then fill it with whatever sum the majority desires. The procedure is as follows:

1. The blank is created. The Chair may make the suggestion to create the blank. If no one objects, the figure in the main motion is then a blank. At other times, a member may propose the creation of a blank in the main motion. Such a proposal is an incidental motion which would be in order, requires a second, is not debatable and passes by majority vote—although usually it also passes by *general consent*, with no one objecting. A third possibility for creating a blank also exists. In this case, the member offering the main motion knows that the amount will be controversial, so he offers the main motion with a blank for the amount already included.
2. Suggestions are received for filling the blank. The process is essentially the same as offering nominations as each member may suggest a sum for filling the blank. These suggestions are also debatable as they are being offered. The Chair makes a note of all these possibilities, preferably on a blackboard or chart where they can be viewed by the assembly. This process can be shortened by an incidental motion to "close suggestions." Such a motion would require a second, could not be discussed and would require a two-thirds vote.
3. The Chair decides on the order for voting on the suggestions. The general principle is to vote in order from the least popular toward the most popular suggestion. However, if the blank is to be filled with names, the vote follows the order in which

these names were suggested. In the case of dates, the group may vote from the most distant date back to the nearest date, or from the nearest to the most distant. With amounts, the order is from largest to smallest or smallest to largest, depending on the nature of the case—starting with the sum that would be least popular under the circumstances.

4. The Chair takes the vote on each proposal, following this order. The members are asked to vote "Aye" or "No" on each proposal for filling the blank. "Shall the sum of $50 be inserted in the blank? Those in favor, indicate by saying 'Aye.' Those opposed, say 'No.' The 'Noes' have it, and the sum of $50 is rejected. We will now vote on the sum of $45 for inserting in the blank." The Chair proceeds in this manner until an amount finally receives a majority vote. That sum is then inserted in the main motion, and that motion is then open to further discussion and amendment. Of course, no further amendments would now be allowed pertaining to the recently filled blank. What about the other suggestions, the ones that the Chair did not reach in conducting the vote? These are simply dropped.

Sturgis recommends a slightly different procedure for filling blanks. She would agree with steps 1 and 2 for creating the blank and accumulating suggestions for filling it. However, she would vote on all suggestions in the order in which they were made, whether names, amounts, dates, or whatever. The Chair should take a counted vote on all the proposals. That proposal which receives the largest affirmative vote would then be used to fill the blank.

STRATEGIC USE OF AMENDMENTS

A substitute amendment may be proposed to defeat a main motion by offering an acceptable compromise.

If a motion is in danger of losing the vote, an amendment to it may often make the motion more acceptable.

If amendments become so confused that even the Chair has difficulty in presenting them correctly, a member may propose what is called the "Gordian Knot," a motion to suspend the rules by dropping all confusing propositions and starting over with a clean slate, the original main motion as the proposer first stated it. Such a motion to suspend the rules would require a second and a two-thirds vote, but under the circumstances described, it would probably receive unanimous support and could be done by *general consent*.

Sometimes complex motions and their amendments may be resolved by a motion to refer them to a committee or to recess for a caucus.

Improper amendments are those that:

1. Are not germane to the motion they are to amend.
2. Are equivalent to a rejection of the main motion.
3. Repeat a previously adopted motion.
4. Would change the form of a primary amendment. Primary amendments take one of the five forms listed previously. A secondary amendment which would change this basic form of the primary amendment is not in order.
5. Would strike "Resolve" or other enacting words.
6. Are dilatory or absurd.
7. Would make the main motion incoherent or absurd.

PRACTICE EXERCISE

Select a Chair, members X, Y, Z, S and T.

PROCESS THIS MAIN MOTION WITH TWO AMENDMENTS TO A FINAL VOTE *(Assume that all motions have been seconded).*

Member X, rising:	Mr. President.
Chair:	Member X (recognizing the member).
Member X:	I move we *purchase a **typewriter** for use in our office.*
Chair:	It has been moved and seconded that we purchase a ***typewriter*** for use in our office. Is there any discussion?
Member Y, rising:	Mr. President.
Chair:	Member Y.
Member Y:	I move to amend the motion *by inserting the word **electric** before the word **typewriter**.*

Chair:	An amendment (primary) has been made and seconded to insert *electric* before the word *typewriter*. Is there any discussion?
Member Z, rising:	Mr. President.
Chair:	Member Z.
Member Z:	I move to amend the amendment by *inserting the word IBM before the word electric*.
Chair:	An amendment (secondary) has been made and seconded to insert *IBM* before the word *electric*. Is there any discussion?
	If both amendments are adopted, the motion would read *to purchase a IBM electric typewriter*. Is there any discussion on inserting the word *IBM*?
Member T, rising and calling out:	
	Parliamentary Inquiry. Mr. President, is that amendment to the amendment germane?
Chair:	The Chair rules the amendment germane as it relates to the kind of *electric typewriter* now being considered. Discussion is now on inserting the word *IBM* before the word *electric*.
	Since there is no further debate, the Chair puts the question to vote. (This may be preceded by the question "Are you ready to vote?")
	All those in favor of inserting *IBM* before *electric,* say "Aye." All those opposed, say "No." The Noes have it, and the amendment to insert *IBM* before *electric* is lost. Debate is now on inserting the word *electric* before the word *typewriter*.

Chair: (cont'd)	There seems to be no further discussion. Are you ready to vote? All those in favor of inserting the word *electric* before *typewriter,* say "Aye." Those opposed, say "No." The Ayes have it, and *electric* will be inserted before the word *typewriter.* Debate is now on the main motion as amended, which reads *to purchase an electric typewriter for use in our office.*
Member S, rising:	Mr. President.
Chair:	Member S.
Member S:	I move to amend the amended motion *by adding after the word office the words at a cost not to exceed $600.*
Chair:	It has been moved and seconded *to add after the word office at a cost not to exceed $600.* Is there any discussion? Since there is no debate, are you ready to vote on the amendment *to add at a cost not to exceed $600?*
Chair puts the vote:	All those in favor of adding *at a cost not to exceed $600,* say "Aye." Those opposed, say "No." The motion of $600 is adopted.
Chair:	With no further debate, the vote is now on the motion as amended. It has been moved and seconded that *we purchase an electric typewriter for use in our office at a cost not to exceed $600,* say, "Aye." All those opposed, say, "No." The Ayes have it and motion is adopted.

Implementation

The Chair directs the secretary to investigate, get prices and report to the president.

Note: It is not necessary for the Chair to state the amendments as primary or secondary. This was used for practice.

---Review Quiz #1 ------------------------------

LESSON 7: THE AMENDING PROCESS

1. Why does the amendment process, which seems so deceptively simple, hold so many pitfalls for an organization?

_____

_____

_____

_____

_____

_____

2. What may an amendment legitimately do to a motion?

_____

_____

_____

_____

_____

3. What is not permitted under parliamentary law as to use of amendments?

_____

_____

_____

_____

_____

_____

4. Identify the substitute motion. How should it be handled?

_____

_____

_____

_____

_____

5. Identify the "friendly" amendment. How is this handled?

_____

_____

_____

_____

_____

6. Distinguish between primary and secondary amendments. What is a tertiary (third degree) amendment?

_____

_____

_____

_____

_____

7. For what strategy purposes is the amendment process often used?

_____

_____

_____

_____

_____

┌─ **Review Quiz #2** ─────────────────────────────┐

LESSON 7: THE AMENDING PROCESS

Mark "T" for True or "F" for False for each statement and explain why statements labeled "F" are incorrect.

_____ 1. A substitute is to strike out and insert an entirely new motion on the same subject.

_____ 2. Debate may go into the merits of the main motion and of the substitute motion.

_____ 3. The Chair puts the vote first on the main motion.

_____ 4. If the substitute is adopted, the changed main motion is no longer pending.

_____ 5. An amendment requires a majority vote even if the main motion requires a two-thirds vote.

_____ 6. Only two amendments may ever be applied to a main motion.

_____ 7. Amendments may be adopted by *general consent.*

_____ 8. An amendment that is hostile is not germane to the main motion.

_____ 9. Proposals to fill blanks are not debatable.

_____ 10. Both primary and secondary amendments must be germane to the main motion.

_____ 11. A substitute is treated as a motion to strike out and insert.

_____ 12. Amendments may be used for strategic purposes.

_____ 13. Adopting the amendment adopts the main motion as well.

_____ 14. Amendments alter, perfect or improve the main motion.

_____ 15. Amendments apply to any motion that may be varied in form.

_____ 16. The number of pending amendments is limited.

LESSON 8
PRECEDENCE OF MOTIONS
TABLE OF MOTIONS

"Rules determine the manner and priority of consideration of a question and provide an orderly, methodical plan so that all business may receive proper consideration."

Paul Mason, *Manual of Legislative Procedure*

LESSON OBJECTIVE

To learn the principles of precedence (pre-SEED-ens) of motions.

READING ASSIGNMENT

Robert pp. 61-81, tinted pp. 1-48   **Demeter** pp. 46-50
Sturgis pp. 15-24   **Riddick** pp. 117-120

LESSON MATERIAL

Precedence is the priority, the order in which motions may be proposed, discussed and decided upon. It requires that subsidiary and privileged motions have an order of rank (not importance). They may be introduced from the lowest to the highest rank but are disposed of **in reverse order**, from the highest to the lowest rank. The last motion proposed will be the first motion voted on. The most recently proposed motion is termed "the immediately pending motion." The chair should consistently remind the assembly which motion is immediately pending.

Any motion under consideration may have a motion of higher rank (precedence) proposed, but it would be out of order to have one of lower precedence proposed.

Subsidiary, privileged and incidental motions are called **secondary motions** and may be proposed when the main motion is pending. The consideration of a main motion can involve a number of secondary motions. It is possible to have more than one secondary motion pending at the same time in their order of precedence. This consideration of motions in order of rank is done without violating the rule that only one main motion at a time can be considered by the assembly.

SECONDARY MOTIONS ARE CLASSIFIED AS FOLLOWS

1. **Privileged motions** do not relate to the business at hand, but to the welfare and comfort of the assembly itself or its members. The privileged motions need to be disposed of before any other pending motion or business. They have the highest order of precedence and must be resolved before any other business.

2. **Subsidiary motions** relate directly to the business under consideration. They are designed to expedite or dispose of the pending motion other than to adopt or reject it. Such motions have an order of precedence.

3. **Incidental motions** have no order of precedence. They arise out of business, but they are irrelevant to the business itself. They relate to the procedure required for disposing of the main motion. They must be decided immediately before business can resume.

Some motions change their classification according to the need and situation. Some are debatable; some are not. Motions that are variable in form are amendable; others, of course, are not.

Robert and **Demeter** list all subsidiary motions except to **Lay on the Table** and the privileged motion to **Adjourn** as reconsiderable. Some incidental motions are also listed as reconsiderable.

Sturgis lists only the main motion as reconsiderable, since all motions other than the main motion can be renewed on the same day.

Riddick states that *call for orders of the day* and *point of order* are nearly synonymous in use; therefore, since both relate to procedure, *call for orders of the day* has been eliminated. Because *point of information* and *parliamentary inquiry* both seek information on procedure or a parliamentary situation, the motion *parliamentary inquiry*, the more descriptive, is sufficient for both.

THE STANDARD CHARACTERISTICS OF MOTIONS

1. Precedence.
2. Applicability.
3. Order as to interruptability.
4. Second—required?
5. Debatable—is it?
6. Amendable—is it?
7. Vote required.
8. Can it be reconsidered?

After a main motion has been stated by the Chair, it is before the assembly for consideration to be adopted or rejected or disposed of in some other way.

The main motion, when stated by the Chair, is said to be the "pending" motion. At this time, matters or questions pertaining to the main motion must be taken care of. An orderly method of handling such items is by order of precedence. This order of precedence is fully supported by logic and reason.

TABLE OF MOTIONS

S - Needs a second	V - Vote required
D - Debatable	M - Majority vote
A - Amendable	2/3 - Vote required
I - Can interrupt	R - Reconsiderable
* - Chair decides	R1 - Affirmative vote only
	R2 - Negative vote only

Sturgis permits reconsideration on main motions only, others are renewable. **Robert** qualifies reconsideration on negative votes and on affirmative votes where action on the motion has not begun or on that part not yet implemented.

Privileged Motions	S	D	A	V	R	I
(Highest To Lowest In Precedence)						
Fix a Time for an Adjourned Meeting	S		A	M	R	
Adjourn	S			M		
Recess	S		A	M		
Question of Privilege	*			M		
Orders of the Day (Call for)	*			2/3 to deny		

Subsidiary Motions	S	D	A	V	R	I
(Highest To Lowest In Precedence)						
Lay on the Table	S			M		
Previous Question, Close Debate	S			2/3	R	
Limit or Extend Debate	S		A	2/3	R	
Postpone Definitely, Time Certain	S	D	A	M	R	
Refer to Committee	S	D	A	M	Rbefore action	
Amend	S	D	A	M	R	
Postpone Indefinitely	S	D		M	R1	

Incidental Motions	S	D	A	V	R	I
(No Order Of Rank)						
Appeal	S	D		M	R	I
Suspend the Rules	S			2/3		
Object to Consideration				2/3	R2	I
Division of Assembly	*					
Withdraw a Motion (if stated)	S			M	R2	
Parliamentary Inquiry	*					I
Point of Information	*					I
Consider Seriatim	S		A	M		

Incidental Main or Restoratory Motion	S	D	A	V	R	I
Amend Something Already Adopted	S	D	A	M with notice or 2/3 without notice		
Rescind	S	D	A	M with notice or 2/3 without notice		
Reconsider	S	D		M		
Ratify	S	D	A	M	R	
Discharge a Committee	S	D	A	M with notice or 2/3 without notice		
Take from the Table or Resume Consideration	S			M		
Main Motion	S	D	A	M	R	

It is important to memorize the order of precedence. Use the two mnemonics.

For Subsidiary Motions (memorize the letters: LP, LP, RAP).

L - Lay on the Table
P - Previous Question (Close Debate)
L - Limit or Extend Debate
P - Postpone to a Set Time
R - Refer to Committee
A - Amend
P - Postpone Indefinitely
The three highest subsidiary motions are not debatable.
(Robert) The two highest and the lowest are not amendable.
Note: These motions are proposed in order from the bottom up.
They are disposed of from the top down.

For Privileged Motions (memorize the letters: F, A, R, P, O).

F - Fix the Time to Which to Adjourn
(Move for an Adjourned Meeting)
A - Adjourn
R - Recess
P - Question of Privilege
O - Orders of the Day (Call for)

Note: These motions are proposed from the bottom up. They are disposed of from the top down.

Fix a time to which to adjourn (or for an adjourned meeting) provides for a future time to continue the same meeting.

Fix a time at which to adjourn provides for the hour of adjournment for the same meeting and must be presented as a main motion.

Question of privilege and *call for the orders of the day* (or call for the regular order) are procedural in nature. They are seldom put to a vote but are resolved by the Chair.

─Review Quiz #1 ─────────────────────────────

LESSON 8:   PRECEDENCE OF MOTIONS
TABLE OF MOTIONS

1.   What are the purposes of subsidiary motions?

_____

_____

_____

2.   How do they occur?

_____

_____

_____

3.   What is their power?

_____

_____

_____

4.   How are subsidiary motions disposed of?

_____

_____

_____

5.   What are the purposes of incidental motions?

_____

_____

_____

6.   How are incidental motions disposed of?

_____

_____

_____

7. What is meant by privileged motions?

_____

_____

_____

8. How are privileged motions disposed of?

_____

_____

_____

9. Which motions does **Robert** call incidental main motions?

_____

_____

_____

10. What is meant by precedence of motions?

_____

_____

_____

11. What is a secondary motion?

_____

_____

_____

12. What are the secondary motions?

_____

_____

_____

┌─ **Review Quiz #2** ──────────────────────────────┐

LESSON 8: PRECEDENCE OF MOTIONS
TABLE OF MOTIONS

You are attending a meeting and are interested in what is going on. In each of the situations listed on the following page, decide which of the motions shown below is the best motion to use. Identify the proper motion to use in the blank to the left of each problem.

LIST OF MOTIONS

A. Appeal from the Decision of the Chair

B. Object to Consideration

C. Suspend the Rules

D. Postpone Indefinitely

E. Division of the Question

F. Amend by Striking Out

G. Call for Orders of the Day

H. Fix a Time for the Next Meeting

I. Reconsider

J. Question of Privilege

K. Point of Order

L. Recess

M. Parliamentary Inquiry

N. Point of Information

O. Lay on the Table

PROBLEM SITUATIONS

_____ 1. Immediately after the reading of the minutes you wish the assembly to consider your motion to raise dues.

_____ 2. The motion on the floor is to raise dues from six to 12 dollars a year payable monthly instead of yearly, as in the past. You want the dues raised, but you want them payable yearly.

_____ 3. Another member insults you while having the floor.

_____ 4. You think the motion too silly for discussion.

_____ 5. The Chair calls for new business immediately after the reports of the committee chairmen.

_____ 6. The Chair made a decision. You think his judgment is wrong.

_____ 7. The motion you favor is under discussion. It is obvious that it will be defeated. You do not want this to happen.

_____ 8. You are a member of a group supporting a Valentine dance. Someone outside your group moves to amend for an Easter dance. You wish to consult your fellow supporters of the original motion to decide what action to take.

_____ 9. There is a motion to rescind a main motion. You wish to know the vote required to adopt the motion to rescind.

_____ 10. There is a motion to adjourn pending. What is the only motion in order at this time?

_____ 11. Your motion was adopted, but now you think an addition to it should be made.

_____ 12. You agree with the proposition except for one sentence in it.

LESSON 9
SUBSIDIARY MOTIONS

"The subsidiary motions are the most frequently used motions in parliamentary procedure. In the course of the proceedings, motions are debated, amended, postponed, referred to committees, tabled, etc. Hence, unless you know the rules pertaining to each motion you cannot make proper use of them and, therefore, you cannot apply or promote efficiency in the transaction of the assembly's business."

Demeter's Manual of Parliamentary Law and Procedure

LESSON OBJECTIVE

To understand the precedence and use of subsidiary motions.

READING ASSIGNMENT

Robert pp. 123-216   Demeter pp. 62-102
Sturgis pp. 16, 42-65   Riddick pp. 12-20,116-120

LESSON MATERIAL

Subsidiary motions modify or dispose of main motions and relate directly to the business under consideration. These motions are listed in descending order of precedence:

1. Lay on the Table (or Postpone Temporarily)
2. Previous Question (or Close Debate)
3. Limit or Extend the Limits of Debate
4. Postpone Definitely (or Postpone to a Set or Certain Time)
5. Refer to Committee (or Commit)
6. Amend
7. Postpone Indefinitely

Subsidiary motions provide other means for disposing of the main motions besides acceptance or rejection. The idea of one member, expressed in a motion, may need to be changed in wording. It may need further study by a smaller group. The assembly may wish to set the idea aside temporarily, permanently or for a stated period of time.

Even the discussion and debate about the idea should be controlled by the assembly. The subsidiary motions provide for any or all of these actions.

Since subsidiary motions are used by assembly in processing a main motion, they must all have the power or precedence to displace the main motion temporarily. Some of them even take precedence over other motions as well. An **amendment**, for example, may be offered to any motion that has variable features. However, subsidiary motions also have an order of precedence within their own classification. **Lay on the Table** is the highest ranking and thus the most powerful of these motions, and **Postpone Indefinitely** is the lowest ranking. In between, the order of precedence is the order in which we have listed them. The order is most easily remembered by the initials LP, LP, RAP, moving from highest to lowest precedence. These motions are proposed from lowest to highest, each proposal taking precedence over the previous one. The Chair then leads the assembly in disposing of them in the opposite order, moving from highest (the last proposed) to lowest. Our detailed discussion of these motions will move from highest to lowest.

LAY ON THE TABLE OR POSTPONE TEMPORARILY

This motion is used to set aside the pending motions temporarily. When a main motion, along with any lower ranking subsidiary motions adhering to it, has been laid on the table, it remains set aside until brought back before the assembly by a motion to **Take from the Table** (or to **Resume Consideration**). If **Take from the Table** is passed by a majority vote, the assembly resumes consideration of the main motion just as it was before it was set aside. Some authorities insist that the original motion, once tabled, must be taken from the table during the same meeting or convention. **Robert**, however, would permit the motion to **Take from the Table** in the next session of groups meeting quarterly or more often. If the tabled matter is not taken from the table within these limits, it ceases to exist. **Sturgis** takes the position that tabled matters are best forgotten in subsequent sessions, and suggests that the main motion might simply be renewed at the next session.

The purpose of this motion is to enable the assembly to drop for the time being whatever they may be considering in order to turn to something else, usually to handle some emergency that has arisen. Perhaps the discussion of the main motion has gone on much longer than was anticipated. The members are eager to hear the speaker of the evening, but the speaker must catch an early flight. Under these conditions, a majority of the members, without further discussion, could lay the main motion on the table, hear the speaker and then take up the main motion again after the speaker departs.

The motion to **Lay on the Table** is frequently confused with other subsidiary motions. For example, a member may say, "I move that we lay this matter on the table until our next meeting." Here, the motion is being confused with the subsidiary motion to **Postpone Definitely.** The Chair should treat this motion according to the intent of the member: "It has been moved and seconded that we postpone this matter until our next meeting. Is there any discussion?"

Or the motion to **Lay on the Table** may be confused with the motion to **Postpone Indefinitely.** A member who disapproves of the main motion but who doesn't want to go on record as voting against it may gain the floor and say, "I move that we table it." In this case, the intent is to kill the main motion—to postpone it with the hope that it will never be taken up again. The Chair would have the right to inquire as to the purpose of this member. If an emergency is at hand which requires putting aside the main motion temporarily, the motion can be accepted as a legitimate move to lay the main question on the table. Otherwise, the Chair may choose one of three alternatives:

1. Accept the motion as another form of **Postpone Indefinitely.** In this case, the Chair would rephrase the motion and call for discussion. Note, however, that this subsidiary motion has very low precedence, and it might not be in order at the time.

2. Accept the motion as a move to put the main question aside temporarily, without discussion, but require a two-thirds vote to pass the motion, since debate would not be permitted. The Chair should also remind the assembly that a motion to take the matter from the table might later be used to bring the main motion before the group again.

3. Declare the motion to table out of order as an improper use of the motion.

The member making this motion may express it in many ways. He may move to "lay the main motion on the table," to "set aside the main question temporarily" or to "table the motion." However, this last expression, to "table the motion," is most frequently heard when the member really intends to postpone the main question indefinitely.

Properly used as the highest ranking of the subsidiary motions, the motion to **Lay on the Table** temporarily sets aside pending matters in order to take care of some emergency. Certain rules govern its use. This motion:

1. Cannot interrupt a speaker. The member may express the motion in several different **ways,** but she must be recognized by the Chair in order to offer the motion.
2. Requires a second.
3. Is not debatable.
4. Is not amendable.
5. Takes a majority vote.
6. Takes precedence over all other subsidiary motions.
7. Can apply to main motions only. If passed, it not only postpones the main motion temporarily, but any other pending subsidiary motions are also put aside with the main motion to which they are attached.
8. Can have no motion applied to it. It may not be reconsidered, since it may be renewed after a period of time and since the motion to **Take from the Table** may reverse its action.

PREVIOUS QUESTION OR CLOSE DEBATE

This motion, the **Previous Question,** is intended to stop all discussion and prevent further amendments to the pending question. It is used when there seems to be no need to continue discussion, since the members have heard all the facts and arguments they need to determine their vote.

While the intent of this motion is easy to understand, its name often creates problems for an inexperienced Chair and for many of the members. Someone rises and says, "I move the previous question." One is tempted to try to remember what motion the group considered previously. This motion being offered is not a reference to anything done earlier. Rather, the member is expressing a desire to end the discussion and proceed to an immediate vote. Thus the wise Chair should immediately, once the motion is seconded, rephrase it for the benefit of the members: "It has been moved and seconded that we proceed to an immediate vote. All in favor, please rise."

Another confusing action in connection with ending debate relates to the practice of some members of interrupting the discussion with shouts of "Question! Question!" Such a practice is unruly, in that it interrupts the proceedings, has no parliamentary significance and is certainly not a proper procedure to end the discussion. If the member actually interrupts a speaker, the Chair should call such a member to order and permit the speaker to continue. Otherwise, the Chair may suggest that the member should offer a motion to end the debate. Anyone wishing to end discussion properly should gain the floor in the regular manner, be recognized by the Chair and then say, "I move the previous question" or "I move that we stop the discussion and vote immediately."

Because this motion deprives members of their basic right to speak, it requires a two-thirds vote. It is not debatable or amendable, as these actions would defeat the purpose of the motion. It not only puts a stop to discussion, it also prevents the offering of any further amendments. Therefore, it can be used when any amendable motion is pending, even if that motion is not debatable. For example, the motion to **Fix the Time of the Next Meeting** is a motion of high privilege and is not debatable. Even so, a member could move the **Previous Question** when **Fix the Time** is pending in order to prevent amendments from being offered.

Normally, this motion to end discussion would apply only to the motion being discussed. However, it can also be offered to close discussion on a whole series of motions, provided that it is stated to begin with the motion currently under consideration. That is, a member might say, "I move the previous question on all matters pending." If this motion is seconded and passed by the necessary two-thirds, the Chair proceeds to take an immediate vote on the motion being discussed and then on any other subsidiary motions that might be pending, then finally on the main motion. Until the effects of this motion to end discussion have been completed and the motion exhausted by taking all of the required votes, no other subsidiary motion would be in order except the motion to **Lay the Matter on the Table,** the only subsidiary motion of higher precedence.

While the motion to **End Discussion** can be applied to the immediately pending question or to all pending questions, it does not apply to the preamble of a resolution unless the preamble is under consideration. This motion cannot be moved in a committee meeting, but it may be moved when the assembly is considering a matter informally.

The following rules govern the motion to **Close Debate** or **Order the Previous Question:**

1. Cannot interrupt a speaker.
2. Requires a second.
3. Is not debatable.
4. Cannot be amended.
5. Requires a two-thirds vote, for it prevents or cuts off debate.
6. Takes precedence over all subsidiary motions except to **Lay on the Table (Postpone Temporarily).**
7. Applies to debatable or amendable motions only.
8. Can have no motion applied to it.
9. An affirmative vote can be reconsidered up until the time the group puts it into effect by voting on the motion that was being discussed.

LIMIT OR EXTEND DEBATE

This motion is used to modify the time allowed for debate. It may be used to reduce or increase the number of speeches or the amount of time for each speech. It may also set a time to end debate on the immediately pending question or a series of pending questions, or to extend the discussion time beyond the usual time allowed. It may be made only when a debatable motion is pending. A motion to **Limit Debate** interferes with the basic right of free speech and so requires a two-thirds vote. A motion to **Extend the Limits of Debate** is a motion to suspend the normal rules or procedures of the group, so it also requires a two-thirds vote.

The making of this motion follows the usual rules of precedence. It yields to **Previous Question** and to **Lay on the Table,** but it takes precedence over the other subsidiary motions. Once it is passed, however, it may affect the subsidiary motions that rank below it. If the adopted limitation specifies the time at which a vote must be taken or if it limits the total time to be spent in debate, it thereby makes motions to **Refer to Committee** or to **Postpone Definitely** out of order unless they were already pending. No member could offer them in the face of the new time limitations. On the other hand, if the motion to **Limit Debate** merely reduces the number or length of speeches, motions to **Refer to Committee** or to **Postpone Definitely** would still be in order. If made after the limitations have been imposed, however, these other subsidiary motions would be subject to the new limitations.

The subsidiary motions to **Limit or Extend the Limits of Debate** apply to the pending debatable question or to a series of debatable questions, beginning with the pending motion. Subsidiary motions made after the limitations have been adopted would also be affected. But once the votes have been taken on all of these affected motions, the limitations would no longer apply. If the group should adjourn before all these votes are completed, the debate limitations would not be in effect for the next session. A group also has the power to place limitations on debate for all or a portion of an entire meeting or session, but such an act would be an incidental main motion, without the precedence of this subsidiary motion, and it would thus be a debatable motion. Nevertheless, as a change in the rules controlling free discussion, it would still require a two-thirds vote.

The following rules govern the subsidiary motion to **Limit or Extend the Limits of Debate:**

1. Cannot interrupt a speaker.
2. Requires a second.
3. Is not debatable. (**Sturgis** allows restricted debate.)
4. Can have amendments applied to it, but these are restricted to variations in the hour, the time limits, number of speeches, length of speeches. Proposed amendments would not be debatable themselves but could be passed by majority vote.
5. Requires a two-thirds vote, for it limits freedom of debate or sets aside previously adopted limitations on debate.
6. Takes precedence over **Postpone Definitely, Refer to Committee, Amend** and **Postpone Indefinitely.**
7. Applies to debatable motions only.
8. Can be reconsidered.

POSTPONE DEFINITELY OR POSTPONE TO A SET OR CERTAIN TIME

This motion is used to delay action on a pending motion or series of motions until some later time. The motion must specify the time at which the main question will again be taken up. It thus differs from the motion to **Lay on the Table,** which never specifies a time limit, and the motion to **Postpone Indefinitely,** which serves to kill the main motion. The making of this motion to **Postpone Definitely** takes precedence over motions to **Postpone Indefinitely,** to **Amend** and to **Refer the Question to a Committee.** It yields to motions pertaining to limitations on debate and to the motion to **Lay on the Table.**

Since the motion to **Postpone Definitely** always specifies the time to which the matter is postponed, it may be amended in regard to that time. It is also debatable in regard to the advisability of the postponement and in regard to the time details. If the group meets quarterly or more often, it may postpone a question to any time later in the same session (this meeting or series of meetings) or to the next session. If the group meets less often than quarterly, it may only postpone matters to later in the same session. In no case is the group permitted to postpone a matter beyond its next regular session, for in so doing it would deprive those attending the next session of their right to consider the original motion. However, when the postponed motion comes before the group, the members would then have the right to postpone it once again.

If the motion to **Postpone Definitely** is made when other subsidiary motions are pending (to **Postpone Indefinitely, Amend** or **Refer to Committee),** the postponement applies to all of these pending motions. When the time arrives for the postponed matters to be taken up again, the assembly would resume consideration of these subsidiary motions, just as though the postponement had never taken place.

If a matter is postponed until the next session, it would normally come before the group as an item of unfinished business in that session. If it is postponed to later in the same session, it would come before the group when that time arrives. The matter could only be taken up ahead of time by a motion to **Suspend the Rules,** requiring a two-thirds vote. When the appointed time arrives, however, the postponed matter may be further delayed because the group is considering something else. This postponed matter is called a "general order" for the time specified, and it cannot displace or interrupt a pending question. To avoid such delays and to insure that the postponed motion will receive the attention of the group at the time named, a member may move to postpone the matter and make it a "special order" for a given time. However, this form of the motion to **Postpone Definitely** would require a two-thirds vote.

The motion to **Postpone Definitely** should not be permitted when it makes nonsense of the main motion before the group. For example, one could not postpone a matter to a day when no meeting is scheduled. The group would first need to create a meeting for itself on the day in question; then the main motion could be postponed to that meeting. In similar fashion one could not postpone a motion beyond a time required by the motion itself. For example, if the main motion relates to an event happening tonight, it would make no sense to postpone that motion until tomorrow.

The motion to **Postpone Definitely** (or **to a Set or Certain Time**):

1. Cannot interrupt a speaker.
2. Requires a second.
3. Restricts debate to discussion of reasons for postponement or the time specified.
4. May be amended, but amendments are restricted to the time specified or to making the postponed motion a special order for the time specified. Amendments require a majority vote.
5. Requires a majority vote unless it makes the postponed matter a special order.
6. Takes precedence over **Refer to Committee, Amend** or **Postpone Indefinitely.**
7. Applies to main motions only.
8. Can have applied to it motions to **Amend** and motions to **Limit** or to **Close Debate.**
9. Can be reconsidered.

*REFER A MATTER
TO A COMMITTEE
(TO COMMIT)*

Sometimes a main motion may need more investigation, thought and discussion than the assembly as a whole can contribute. Therefore, the assembly has the power to commit the motion to a smaller group to discuss the whole thing in more detail, search out pertinent information, perhaps calling on experts for their advice, and reach a thoughtful decision which can be brought back to the assembly as a whole. This smaller group, a **committee**, may recommend passing the main motion, rejecting it or making various changes in it. The assembly hears the committee recommendation, then makes the final decision on the original motion. The report of the committee should save time for the total organization and should provide for more intelligent decisions.

Committees are of two types. Standing committees are specified in the bylaws and carry out the duties assigned to them. A main motion pertaining to such duties would ordinarily be assigned to the committee concerned for investigation and recommendation. However, for other motions, the group may prefer to create a special or "ad hoc" committee to exist only for the purpose of considering this one matter. Once this committee has reported, it goes out of existence.

The motion to **Refer a Matter to a Committee** should contain the details about the committee intended. Should this go to a standing committee? If so, the committee should be specified, along with any instructions and the date when a report is to be given. An ad hoc committee would require even more detail. How are the members of this committee to be appointed or elected? How many members should there be? The motion could even specify the names of the committee members. What is the assignment of this committee? When is it to report to the assembly? Committees are sometimes given the power to act in the name of the assembly, and any such powers should be specified in the motion to **Refer.** If the original motion to **Refer to a Committee** is incomplete in any of these respects, it should be completed by the amendment process before it is voted or, once it has been passed, it should be supplemented by additional motions. Nothing but privileged matters should receive the attention of the group until the details pertaining to the committee have been decided.

If the Chair is given the power to appoint the committee, she also has the duty of appointing one committee member as chairman. This member should be named first when the committee is appointed. If the assembly as a whole elects the committee, the assembly has the power to appoint the chairman. If no one is appointed to this responsibility, the committee member named first should call the committee together, and they should elect their own chairman.

The motion to **Refer a Matter to a Committee** takes precedence over the subsidiary motions to **Postpone Indefinitely** and to **Amend.** If the motion to **Postpone Indefinitely** is pending when the motion to **Refer** is passed, **Postpone Indefinitely** is considered to be rejected and is dropped entirely. A pending amendment, however, is considered by the committee along with the main motion to which it is attached. The committee is expected to report on such an amendment, along with its report on the main motion. The motion to **Refer** may be discussed in terms of its advisability and in regard to any of the details of the committee appointment and may be amended in regard to these details.

Both special and ad hoc committees may serve many functions besides detailed consideration of main motions. An assembly always has the right to give an assignment to a standing committee or to create an ad hoc committee to serve some purpose. However, a motion to accomplish these ends, made with no other motion pending, would be an ordinary main motion and would be treated as such.

Committees are subject to the will of the assembly that creates them. Thus the motion to **Refer a Matter to a Committee** may be reconsidered if the committee has not begun to function. Afterward, the assembly may vote to **Discharge the Committee,** thus taking the matter out of the committee's control. A matter that has been reported to the assembly may also be recommitted to the same committee, if the assembly so votes.

The following rules govern the motion to **Refer** or to **Commit:**

1. Cannot interrupt a speaker.
2. Requires a second.
3. May be discussed, but debate is limited to the advisability of the motion to **Refer** and to the selection, membership, duties and instructions of the committee.
4. Can be amended.
5. Requires a majority vote.
6. Takes precedence over **Amend** and **Postpone Indefinitely.**
7. Applies to the main motion and any pending amendment only.
8. Can have applied to it **Amend** and motions related to the conduct of discussion.
9. Can be reconsidered if the committee has not begun to act.

AMEND

(The student should review Lesson 7 for details about this procedure.)

The purpose of the *amendment* is to revise the wording of the motion under consideration. The group may vote to insert words, add words, delete words, replace words or even replace the entire motion with a substitute. A majority vote is sufficient to effect the change. However, amendments only change the wording, and a second vote is necessary to adopt or to reject the main motion itself.

An amendment may be applied to any variable motion. A motion to **Postpone a Matter Until a Specified Time** may be varied in regard to the time stated. Thus the motion is amendable. Laying a matter on the table is not variable; the only choice is to defer or not to defer the matter in question. Thus the motion to **Lay on the Table** is not amendable.

Proposed amendments must be germane to the motion they would amend; that is, they must deal with the same subject matter. However, amendments need not be in harmony with the main motion and may, indeed, be hostile to it. As long as amendments are germane, they may change the intent of the main motion in any way that the assembly wishes. The only limitation is that the amendment may not simply negate the main motion, perhaps inserting a "not" so that a "yes" vote would become a "no" and a "no" vote a "yes."

Amendments are debatable as long as the motion to which they apply is debatable. Debate must be limited to the proposed amendment and should not go into the merits of the main question. A proposed amendment to a main motion is also amendable, and changes may be offered in the wording of the amendment, inserting words, adding words, deleting words, replacing words in the primary amendment. Thus, a **primary amendment** and a **secondary amendment** may be pending at the same time, the primary amendment proposing to reword the main motion and the secondary amendment proposing to reword the primary amendment. However, the procedure may go no further, and a tertiary amendment is not permitted. Amendments are proposed, discussed and voted one at a time, but otherwise there is no limit to the number of changes an assembly may make in a main motion or resolution before finally passing or rejecting it.

The following rules govern the motion to **Amend:**

1. Cannot interrupt a speaker.
2. Requires a second.
3. Is debatable, unless it applies to an undebatable motion.
4. Can be amended, but a **secondary amendment** cannot be amended.
5. Requires a majority vote, even though the motion to which it applies requires a higher vote.
6. Takes precedence over main motions and **Postpone Indefinitely.**
7. Applies to motions that are open to variations in wording such as the **main motion,** the **primary amendment, Refer to Committee, Postpone Definitely, Limit Debate.**
8. Can have applied to it **Close Debate** and **Limit Debate.**
9. Can be reconsidered.

POSTPONE INDEFINITELY

Sometimes members wish to reject a main motion without the necessity of going on record with an actual "no" vote. Perhaps the motion deals with some sensitive issue. The members feel that they cannot support the proposal, but a report in the media that they rejected the motion might reflect adversely on the organization. The best procedure under the circumstances might be to **Postpone the Main Motion Indefinitely,** to kill it without an actual negative vote.

The motion to **Postpone Indefinitely** also has a strategic use. It enables opponents of the main motion to test the support behind that proposal. If **Postpone Indefinitely** passes, the main motion is rejected and dropped. On the other hand, if **Postpone Indefinitely** fails to gain a majority, opponents of the main motion know they are in the minority and must find some other tactics to defeat the main question. In addition, members who have exhausted their right to debate on the main question may renew that right once **Postpone Indefinitely** is offered. It is a separate motion which not only may be debated but which opens all aspects of the main motion to debate once again.

Unfortunately, the term "postpone indefinitely" is not widely understood, and members sometimes move to "table the motion," when their intent is to postpone it indefinitely. This wording is particularly confusing, since it resembles the subsidiary motion of the highest precedence, the motion to **Lay** a matter **on the Table.** The Chair should not be misled by the terms used here. To **Lay on the Table** is intended for emergency situations, to put a main motion aside temporarily to deal with the emergency. **Postpone Indefinitely** is intended to kill the main motion. Judging by the situation and by the intent of the member, the Chair should recognize which motion is being offered and should make it clear to all. To **Lay on the Table** is the highest of the subsidiary motions in precedence and is not debatable. To **Postpone Indefinitely** is the lowest of the subsidiary motions in precedence, is debatable and opens the main question to further debate. The Chair should have these differences clearly in mind as she determines the true intent of the motion to "table" and handles it accordingly.

The following rules govern the motion to **Postpone Indefinitely:**

1. Cannot interrupt a speaker.
2. Requires a second.
3. Is debatable and opens the main motion to debate.
4. Cannot be amended
5. Requires a majority vote.
6. Takes precedence over the main motion only.
7. Applies to main motions only.
8. Can have applied to it motions pertaining to debate.
9. Can be reconsidered if voted in the affirmative.

┌─**PRACTICE EXERCISE**──────────────────────────┐
└──┘

PRECEDENCE OF SUBSIDIARY MOTIONS

The Chair may write each subsidiary motion on the chalkboard or distribute a card to each of seven members. Each card is numbered and has a subsidiary motion written on it.

The seven members start in line, side by side. As each motion is made, the holder of the card steps forward. As each motion is disposed of, the holder of the card steps back in line. All motions are seconded. The Chair recognizes each member.

Chair: It has been moved and seconded that we write to Congress to urge that they provide better protection against acid rain. Is there any discussion?

Member 1:   I move to *postpone* this motion *indefinitely*.

Chair: (Explain the motion. Ask for debate.)

Member 2:   I move to *amend* the motion by adding, "and that this problem be resolved during this congressional session."

Chair: (Explain the use of the amendment. Ask for discussion.)

Member 3:   I move to *refer* the motion *to a committee* of three to be appointed by the Chair, who shall prepare this resolution in proper form.

Chair: (Explain the motion. Ask for debate.)

Member 4:   I move to *postpone* consideration of the main motion until the next regular meeting, so we can bring an expert on this subject to speak to us at the next meeting.

Chair: (Explain the motion. Ask for debate. Note: Debate is only on the merit of postponement.)

Member 5:   I move to *limit debate* on the motion to *postpone* to two minutes.

Chair: (Explain the motion. Call for a vote. Defeat motion.)

Member 6:   I move the *previous question* (to close debate, to vote immediately) on all pending questions.

Chair: (Explain the motion. Call for a vote.)

    Before the vote can be taken, member 7 rises.

Member 7:   I move to *lay* the main motion *on the table*.

Chair: (Explain the motion. Take the vote. Defeat motion. Explain taking the vote in reverse order. Put the vote on motion by member 6. Adopt the motion.)

    (Defeat all motions except amendment and the main motion.)

┌─ Review Quiz #1 ──────────────────

LESSON 9: SUBSIDIARY MOTIONS

What motion would you use to achieve the following?

1. You want to present an idea for consideration.

_____

_____

_____

2. You want to improve the pending motion.

_____

_____

_____

3. You want to limit the discussion time.

_____

_____

_____

4. You want to stop the talking and take a vote immediately.

_____

_____

_____

5. You think the proposition deserves more study.

_____

_____

_____

6. You want to take up a more pressing matter at this time.

_____

_____

_____

Review Quiz #2

LESSON 9: SUBSIDIARY MOTIONS

Mark "T" for True or "F" for False for each statement and explain why statements labeled "F" are incorrect.

_____ 1. Every main motion **must** be seconded.

_____ 2. The member seconding the motion is always in favor of it.

_____ 3. No amendment is in order that changes affirmative to negative by inserting the word **not** in the motion.

_____ 4. The motion to **Postpone Indefinitely** is equivalent, if carried, to a negative vote on the main motion.

_____ 5. The motion to **Refer to Committee** may be postponed indefinitely.

_____ 6. The amendment to the amendment may also be amended.

_____ 7. **Lay on the Table** and **Postpone to a Set Time** have exactly the same characteristics.

_____ 8. **Refer to Committee** is always a subsidiary motion.

┌─**Review Quiz #3** ────────────────────────────────┐

LESSON 9: SUBSIDIARY MOTIONS

How should the Chair handle the following situations?

1. The motion to **Lay on the Table** is being used to kill the main motion, without debate and only by a majority vote.

　　_____

　　_____

2. Members keep calling "Question" without being recognized by the Chair.

　　_____

　　_____

3. A member moves to *refer* a matter *to a committee*, but does not specify which committee, how it will be formed, what members it will have, etc.

　　_____

　　_____

4. A member offers an *amendment* which completely distorts the intent of the motion to be amended.

　　_____

　　_____

5. An *amendment* has been voted which completely changes the purpose of the original motion. Now the maker of the original motion rises to speak against it.

　　_____

　　_____

6. A member wants to *postpone* the main motion until the meeting **after** the next regular meeting of the group.

　　_____

　　_____

┌ Review Quiz #4 ─────────────────────────┐

LESSON 9: SUBSIDIARY MOTIONS

1. The highest subsidiary motion in the order of precedence is

   _____

2. **Postpone Indefinitely** has precedence only over the

   _____

3. Subsidiary motions are designed to dispose of the

   _____

4. If a main motion and an *amendment* have been proposed, we vote
   first on the

   _____

5. If a motion to **Postpone Definitely** is pending, a motion to **Refer
   to Committee** is

   _____

6. Three subsidiary motions that are not amendable are

   _____, _____

   and _____

7. Subsidiary motions that require a two-thirds vote are
   _____ and

   _____

8. The subsidiary motion violating the two-thirds rule is

   _____

9. The Chair disposes of subsidiary motions in _____
   order.

   _____

10. After adoption of an amendment, the vote is on the main motion

    _____

11. A motion to **Lay on the Table** _____ be
    qualified.

12. A motion to **Limit Debate** exists for the duration of

    _____

13. The Chair accepts subsidiary motions in _____
    _____ order.

14. Restricted amendments apply to _____ and
    _____

15. Three subsidiary motions that are not debatable are
    _____, _____ and
    _____

LESSON 10
PRIVILEGED MOTIONS

"It is a general rule, dating from the time of **Thomas Jefferson**, that the question first moved shall be first put. But this rule gives way to . . . privileged motions and privileged questions, which are of different grades and precedence among themselves."

Lewis Deschler, *Rules of Order*

LESSON OBJECTIVE

To learn the purpose of privileged motions and their procedural rules. To differentiate between privileged motions and questions of privilege.

READING ASSIGNMENT

Robert pp. 217-246   **Demeter** pp. 102-120
Sturgis pp. 16, 66-76   **Riddick** pp. 4-6, 132, 150-151, 159-161, 164-165

LESSON MATERIAL

Privileged motions are so important that they are given privileges not accorded other motions. Because of their precedence, they must be decided before any pending motion. Privileged motions relate to the assembly and its members rather than to the business being considered. The five common privileged motions are listed in descending order of precedence. They are:

1. **Fix the Time to Which to Adjourn**
2. **Adjourn**
3. **Recess**
4. **Question of Privilege**
5. **Call for Orders of the Day**

Motions under these *questions of privilege* may be offered at any time. If the matter is urgent, they may even interrupt a speaker.

The Chair will rule on the urgency. *Questions of privilege* and *orders of the day* are usually resolved by the Chair.

FIX THE TIME TO WHICH TO ADJOURN (SET A TIME FOR AN ADJOURNED MEETING)

When business cannot be completed during the meeting, a motion may be presented designating the time and place to which to continue the present meeting, provided that the time designated comes before the next regularly scheduled meeting. Some authorities allow this motion to be proposed while business is pending. Other parliamentary authorities allow "qualified adjournment" of any form only when no other business is pending. The motion is then handled as a main motion.

The motion to **Fix the Time to Which to Adjourn** should not be confused with the motion **To Set a Time *at* Which to Adjourn**, which sets a time for adjournment for the meeting in progress and is not a privileged motion.

The following rules govern **Fix the Time *to* Which to Adjourn** when it is interpreted as the highest privileged motion in order of precedence:

1. Cannot interrupt a speaker.
2. Requires a second.
3. Is not debatable.
4. Is amendable only as to date, hour or place.
5. Requires a majority vote.
6. Cannot be applied to any other motion.

The motion sets a time for continuation of the same meeting in order to complete unfinished business. In the continued meeting, business continues, after reading and approval of the minutes, from the point at which the previous meeting adjourned. This provides for consideration of that business which was pending at the time of adjournment or that which was scheduled but unreached.

If this motion is made when no business is pending, it is treated as a main motion.

This motion is used to terminate a meeting or session. If the motion is qualified in any way—such as to state the time—or if its effect would dissolve the assembly, it loses its privileged status and becomes a main motion. Such a motion is out of order while another motion is pending. After the vote to **Adjourn** has been adopted, the meeting is not officially adjourned until the Chair declares it adjourned as the final action. If there is no further business, the Chair may, with no objection, declare the meeting *adjourned*.

The privileged (unqualified) motion to **Adjourn** can be proposed at any time during the meeting whether or not business is pending, providing a future time has been established for the assembly to reconvene.

A final adjournment dissolves the assembly when there is no provision to meet again. This type of adjournment is termed "adjournment *sine die*" (without day). A motion to **Adjourn** under these circumstances would be an ordinary main motion.

If the motion to **Adjourn** seems untimely, the Chair may inform the members of urgent business requiring attention before taking the vote to adjourn. Unfortunately, if a substantial number of members wish to adjourn but lose on the vote to do so, there is danger of losing a quorum.

The following rules govern the motion to **Adjourn**:

1. Cannot interrupt a speaker.
2. Requires a second.
3. Cannot be debated.
4. Cannot be amended.
5. Requires a majority vote.
6. Can have no motion applied to it.

RECESS

This motion normally is used when a brief break in the meeting is desired. The object is to provide a temporary interval during which the meeting is interrupted. After **Recess**, the meeting may be resumed at the point of interruption. Strategists frequently use this motion as a means to caucus for more votes or support.

No *recess* may extend beyond the time set for the next regular meeting. If *recess* has been provided on the agenda or program, the Chair declares the assembly in *recess* at the time established.

The following rules govern the motion to **Recess**:

1. Cannot interrupt a speaker.
2. Requires a second.
3. Cannot be debated, except **Sturgis** allows restricted debate.
4. Restricts amendments to time or length of *recess*.
5. Requires a majority vote.
6. May be withdrawn by approval of the assembly.

QUESTION OF PRIVILEGE OR RAISE A QUESTION OF PRIVILEGE

This motion relates to the organization or any of its members regarding safety, health, integrity or protection. **Demeter's** mnemonic is **S-H-I-P.**

While this motion is listed as a privileged motion, it is actually a request. There are three types of *questions of privilege*:

1. Those that concern the assembly, from heating, ventilation, seating, disturbance, audibility, conduct of officers or members, to any reflection on the organization itself.

2. Those that relate to individual members, such as inaccurate records concerning a member, or charges or remarks made against a member's character (called *question of personal privilege*).

3. Those that introduce an emergency motion such as moving to a larger room to accommodate the larger attendance, or to adjourn in advance of the coming hurricane, or to go into an executive session (closed meeting). Since these motions must take privileged status, they usually are termed *motions of privilege.*

The motion **Question of Privilege** is introduced with the same phrase as the other forms of *question of privilege*: "I rise to a *question of privilege* in order to present a motion." The Chair will ask the member to state the motion desired and rule whether the matter is urgent. If urgent, the Chair will state the motion which will be handled by the assembly as a main motion. If it is not urgent, the Chair will state that the matter will be taken care of at the conclusion of the pending business. If the Chair rules that the matter does not come under the privileged status or denies the *motion of privilege*, any member may appeal.

The following rules govern the **Question of Privilege**:

1. Can interrupt a speaker if it requires immediate attention and decision.
2. Is not debatable.
3. Is not amendable.
4. Requires no vote as it is ruled on by the Chair.
5. Can be reconsidered when submitted as a main motion (**Robert**).

CALL FOR ORDERS OF THE DAY

This motion is a demand to return to the regularly scheduled order of business if the Chair has ignored or parted from it.

Orders of the day relates to the scheduled agenda for the meeting.

A simplified procedure used by some authorities is to omit this motion and use the usual method of calling an error to the Chair's attention by a *point of order*.

┌─ **Review Quiz #1** ──────────────────────────────┐

LESSON 10: PRIVILEGED MOTIONS

1. Write the privileged motions from highest to lowest in order of precedence.

   _____

   _____

   _____

   _____

2. Why are privileged motions not debatable?

   _____

   _____

   _____

   _____

3. What is the difference between **Recess** and **Adjourn**?

   _____

   _____

   _____

   _____

4. What is the correct form to raise a *question of privilege*?

   _____

   _____

   _____

   _____

5. What is the peculiarity of the motion to **Adjourn**?

   _____

   _____

   _____

   _____

6. When may members move to **Adjourn?**

_____

_____

_____

_____

7. What becomes of unfinished business after a meeting adjourns?

_____

_____

_____

_____

8. When does the Chair have the right to *adjourn* a meeting?

_____

_____

_____

_____

9. What does the motion to **Fix the Time to Which to Adjourn** (set a time for an adjourned meeting) accomplish?

_____

_____

_____

_____

10. When can a *question of privilege* become a main motion?

_____

_____

_____

_____

┌─**Review Quiz #2** ────────────────────────────┐

LESSON 10: PRIVILEGED MOTIONS

These questions review Lessons 7-10. In each case indicate the motion or motions that might be used to remedy the situation.

MOTIONS

1. The time for debate on the motion should be determined.
   The motion is _____

2. The Chair neglected to call for discussion on the pending motion.
   The motion is _____

3. The first item of the resolution needs modification.
   The motion is _____

4. The motion to establish a library needs more facts to support it.
   The motion is _____

5. Some members wish to kill the main motion without voting on it.
   The motion is _____

6. The guest speaker has a plane schedule to meet.
   The motion is _____

7. Debaters are repeating each other's remarks.
   The motion is _____

8. The hour is late, but business is not completed.
   The motion is _____

9. There is no further business.
   The motion is _____

10. The meeting is threatening to interfere with lunch.
    The motion is _____

11. The air conditioner has over-chilled the room.
    The motion is _____

12. Urgent business must be concluded before the next regular meeting.
    The motion is _____

13. There is no quorum.
>   The motion is _____

14. The Chair omitted to ask for approval of the minutes.
>   The motion is _____

15. The debate has gone on and on.
>   The motion is _____

16. A severe storm is seen approaching.
>   The motion is _____

17. Some members want to get more support for their motion.
>   The motion is _____

18. A member likes the motion to buy a computer but not at the named price.
>   The motion is _____

19. Debate on the motion shows much opposition to it.
>   The motion is _____

20. The assembly wants the matter investigated further.
>   The motion is _____

21. During the debate on a motion an urgent matter arose.
>   The motion is _____

22. The assembly wishes to debate the matter further.
>   The motion is _____

23. Members wish to await decision from a larger attendance.
>   The motion is _____

24. A member would like to offer another but similar motion.
>   The motion is _____

25. Members wish to have an expert come to the next meeting to advise on the purchase of some property.
>   The motion is _____

26. A member wants the Chair to control some member's disorderly conduct.
>   The motion is _____

LESSON 11
INCIDENTAL MOTIONS

"There is a class of motions in parliamentary procedure known as 'incidental motions,' so called because they are incidental to, or arise out of, a motion on which they have a bearing — as, for example, when a point of order is raised pertaining to a pending motion, or when information about it is asked for."

Demeter's Manual of Parliamentary Law and Procedure

LESSON OBJECTIVE

To learn the reason for and the use of incidental motions.

READING ASSIGNMENT

Robert pp. 247-293   **Demeter** pp. 120-152, 170-172
Sturgis pp. 16-17, 77-96 **Riddick** pp. 22, 56, 76, 82, 87, 119, 138-141,151, 172, 188, 208

LESSON MATERIAL

Incidental motions or requests usually relate to matters that are incidental to the conduct of the meeting.

Incidental motions have no rank but occur as the need arises. They are proposed when they logically pertain to any motion pending before the assembly, and they must be decided before action is taken on the main motion. Any motion proposing that the vote be taken in a specific way—by ballot or roll call—is an incidental motion that must be seconded, has no debate and is passed by a majority vote. Among other incidental motions are motions to close polls, to close nominations, to request permission to read papers and to be excused from duty. Following is an explanation of the most common incidental motions.

APPEAL

The motion to **Appeal** the ruling of the Chair permits the assembly to sustain or reverse the Chair's ruling, if members believe the Chair has ruled incorrectly.

1. After the Chair makes a ruling, any member, without recognition, may call, "I appeal the decision of the Chair." The motion must be seconded.

2. Appeals may not be made against parliamentary facts, law or the adopted rules of the society. Answers to questions of **Parliamentary Inquiry** or the announcement of a vote count may not be appealed. Items of this type represent the Chair's opinion or the statement of a fact and are not rulings subject to appeal. On the other hand, the Chair's ruling that a particular amendment is or is not germane to the main motion would be subject to appeal.

3. An appeal must be made immediately following the ruling that is being appealed. Decisions cannot be appealed following an intervening period of time.

4. Appeals are debatable if the pending motion is debatable. However, each individual member may speak only once on the appeal. The Chair, on the other hand, is permitted to speak first, defending the ruling, and then to speak a second time, after the others have finished, to refute the arguments against his position. The Chair may do this without leaving the Chair but may continue to preside throughout the whole procedure.

5. The decision on the appeal is by majority vote. In this case, a tie vote serves to sustain the Chair's decision, and the Chair's vote may serve to create the tie. There would be no need for the Chair to vote to break a tie, since the tie vote sustains the decision in any case.

The most difficult aspect of handling an **Appeal** is the process of taking a vote. An inexperienced Chair may be tempted to take a vote for and against the appeal, a procedure which would almost certainly throw the meeting into utter confusion. Instead, the Chair should put the motion in the affirmative: "Shall the ruling of the Chair be sustained? All in favor of sustaining the ruling, say 'Aye.' Those opposed, say 'No.'"

The Chair should make every attempt to assure that rulings are proper to avoid the necessity of these appeals. Several alternatives are available:

1. A recess could be taken before the ruling for the Chair to seek accurate information.
2. The Chair could ask for the advice of the parliamentarian, but the ultimate ruling must be made by the Chair, never by the parliamentarian.
3. The Chair could submit the problem to a vote of the assembly, in which case the majority would decide and there would be no ruling by the Chair subject to appeal.

But if the Chair rules, a member appeals and the assembly then decides against the Chair, he should accept the assembly's opinion in good grace and continue with the meeting in harmony with the majority decision.

THE QUESTION CONSIDERED INFORMALLY

When members of an assembly wish to have a discussion before agreeing to the wording of a main motion, or when a proposal is already pending but members need greater freedom in regard to the rules of debate, a motion for **Informal Consideration** is in order. This motion cannot interrupt a speaker. It requires a second, is not debatable or amendable and requires a majority vote. **Robert,** however, considers this motion a form of **Refer to Committee** and permits discussion of the motion. Other authorities consider it an incidental motion.

When such a motion is adopted, the rules of debate are relaxed. The length and number of speeches, the number of turns to speak, and the restriction as to the particular area under discussion are unlimited. The Chair continues to preside, as in a committee, and sees to it that the discussion continues in good order, recognizing those who wish to speak and permitting only one to speak at a time. The secretary should keep minutes of any decision that is made.

When formal rules of debate are again desired, two actions may be used to end the informal consideration. A motion to return to the regular procedure, to the regular rules of debate, may be made, seconded and passed by majority vote. If the group has been considering a previously stated main motion informally, the final disposition of that motion also automatically returns the group to the regular rules of debate.

OBJECT TO CONSIDERATION

This objection may be raised against any original main motion which a member considers so contentious or inflammatory that it should not be discussed at all, let alone voted on by this organization. Perhaps the main motion is outside the purposes of the society or is of such a sectarian nature, with discriminatory aspects, that it should be thrown out immediately. As soon as this motion is stated, without waiting to be recognized and even interrupting a speaker, the member may rise and say, "I object to the consideration of this question." No second is required, and the objection forces the Chair to submit the admission of the question to the vote of the assembly.

Upon hearing such an objection, members are naturally tempted to ask the reason. In this regard, parliamentary authorities differ. All agree that the motion is not debatable, since discussion would open up the very areas the objection intends to avoid. **Robert** would put the objection to an immediate vote. Others would permit a brief summary statement as to the reason for the objection.

The objection may only be made in regard to new matters which have never been before the assembly before. One cannot object to an incidental main motion or to communications received from a superior body of the organization. The objection must also be raised immediately, before any discussion has begun. Since the Chair is often the one most aware of the sensitive nature of a proposal, the Chair himself may raise the objection and put it to a vote.

Taking the vote on such an objection may result in much confusion. If members are asked to vote on objections, they will rarely be clear as to the proper procedure to indicate their preferences. Rather, members should be asked to vote on the consideration of the new main motion: Shall this question be considered? The Chair should ask, "Those in favor of considering the motion to ..., please rise. Thank you, be seated. Those opposed to considering the motion, please rise. Thank you, be seated." The counted vote is necessary because two-thirds must oppose the consideration of the main motion before it is thrown out and the objection sustained. If fewer than two-thirds oppose the consideration, the group goes ahead to discuss the new main motion. Under these circumstances, no motion to reconsider is in order. If two-thirds or more oppose the consideration, the main motion is disregarded, as though it had never been made. However, at a later time the motion to **Reconsider** may be used to overcome the effects of this negative vote and to bring the main motion before the group.

This motion is used when the assembly wishes to suspend an adopted rule temporarily in order to accomplish some specific goal. Often it is used to alter the order of business. It may be made at any time when it is needed, but a member may not interrupt a speaker and must gain the floor to offer it. The motion requires a second and is not debatable or amendable. If it is made in order to permit the introduction of another motion, the maker of that motion should be recognized immediately upon the adoption of the suspension.

The vote needed to **Suspend the Rules** depends on the nature of the rule to be suspended.

1. An ordinary custom of the group, not related to parliamentary procedure, may be suspended by a simple majority vote. For example, the organization may have a rule that smoking is not permitted during the business meeting.

2. Rules of parliamentary procedure may only be suspended by a two-thirds vote. For example, the group may suspend rules in order to vary the agenda and take up a motion out of its proper order.

3. The bylaws of the organization or the provisions of its charter may never be suspended, even by unanimous vote.

4. Rules that protect the rights of absentees cannot be suspended. For example, a rule requiring previous notice to the members that certain action will be taken at the meeting assures absentees that the action will not be taken since they were not notified. Such a rule could not be suspended at the meeting in an attempt to take this action.

5. Also, in general, any rule that protects a minority of a specific size cannot be suspended in the face of a negative vote equal to or larger than that minority.

Requests are incidental motions usually resolved without a vote and ordered by the Chair if no one objects. A **Request** to consider a complex motion section by section, for example, would usually be viewed by all as a helpful suggestion under the circumstances and one immediately adopted by the Chair. If an objection is made, the request is handled as a motion, requiring a second and a majority vote. As an incidental motion, it would not be debatable or amendable. Other requests might include demands that the assembly be divided for voting purposes, a request for the division of a motion or for the withdrawal of a motion, points of information and parliamentary inquiries.

CONSIDERATION BY PARAGRAPH OR SERIATIM

This request seeks to consider a long or complex motion or resolution in its natural parts. Technically, to consider seriatim (pronounced "see-ree-**ate**-im") is an incidental motion that may not interrupt a speaker, requires a second, is amendable but not debatable and is decided by a majority vote. However, it is often treated as a request and is approved by *general consent*. If the main motion is obviously long, consisting of several parts or paragraphs, the Chair may on his own authority proceed to handle the motion in this fashion.

The procedure is for someone to read the first paragraph or section of the motion. The reader could be the individual moving the adoption of the resolution, the secretary, or perhaps even the Chair himself. That paragraph or section is then open to discussion and amendment. In the same manner, succeeding parts are open to discussion and amendment until the entire resolution has been examined. The Chair then opens the entire motion to further amendment. Finally, the vote is taken on the adoption of the total resolution.

DIVISION OF A QUESTION

The division of a motion or resolution differs from **Seriatim** consideration in that a separate vote is taken on each part of the divided motion. Considering seriatim pertains only to the discussion (and perhaps amendment) of one section at a time. A divided resolution, however, is treated like two or more separate motions.

The possibility of dividing a resolution depends on the nature of the resolution at hand. At times a resolution may consist of several parts, each independent of the others and each treating an entirely different subject. The situation could arise, for example, from a committee report containing separate recommendations treating different subjects. The motion to adopt this report would place all of these separate resolutions before the assembly. In this case, any individual member has the right to request a division of the motion, and the Chair is then obligated to take each separate resolution, one at a time, and treat it like an independent motion, open for discussion, possible amendment and finally a vote to adopt or to reject.

At other times, the resolution offered may have several independent parts but all related to the same subject. The parts must be independent in the sense that the adoption or rejection of any one part will not affect the others. In this case, the formal incidental motion to divide the question would be in order. The motion cannot interrupt a speaker; the member must gain the floor to offer it. A second is required, and the motion is amendable but not debatable. An amendment could be offered to change the manner in which the motion is divided. A majority vote is needed to pass the motion, and this decision cannot be reconsidered. If the motion is passed, the main motion is divided, and each part is treated like an independent motion.

The third situation involves a long and complex motion of many parts, but the parts are interdependent. If one part is rejected, it would make nonsense of the remaining parts. In this case, the motion cannot be divided at all. The best procedure for the assembly, then, would be to consider the motion **Seriatim**, discussing each section in turn but taking only one vote on the adoption of the entire motion.

In all these cases, the request for **Division of the Question** would come while the main motion is pending. When this request or motion comes, the Chair should either rule on whether or not the motion can be divided or submit this decision to the vote of the assembly. If the Chair rules, his decision would be subject to appeal.

DIVISION OF ASSEMBLY

When a voice vote (Aye and No) is taken on any motion and the result is in doubt, any one member has the right to be assured that the result has been properly determined. The member asserts this right by simply calling "Division" at the time the vote was taken, even after the Chair has announced the result of the vote. The member may interrupt the Chair in order to make this demand. It requires no second, no discussion and no vote. When a vote is close, the Chair may be tentative in announcing the result, saying, "The 'Ayes' seem to have it," then pausing to give any member the opportunity to call for a division before finally saying, "The 'Ayes' have it, and the motion is carried."

When the demand for a division is made, the Chair must respond by taking the vote again, this time in a manner that makes the result more obvious. Usually he will ask those in favor and then those opposed to stand. A show of hands could be equally effective in a very small group, but **Robert** insists that only a rising vote can meet the demand for a division. If the vote is at all close, the Chair would be well advised to repeat the vote by having members rise, even if no member has called for a division. The Chair also has the authority to count the rising vote, even though the call for a division does not technically force such a count. The wisest procedure would probably be for the Chair to count the affirmative votes while the members are standing. Then, when the negative vote is taken, the Chair can decide to count, if the result seems close, or not to count, if the result is obvious to all, those standing in the negative being far fewer than the affirmative vote previously counted. No individual member has the power to force the Chair to count a vote, but a member can offer a motion that the vote be counted. Such a motion must be seconded, and a majority vote would force the Chair to repeat the rising vote and to count the voters as they stand.

The procedure for counting a vote sometimes presents difficulties, particularly in large groups. The Chair may appoint tellers to assist, sometimes dividing the room into sections with a teller given charge over each section. Another procedure is the "serpentine" count. The members standing are asked to count off, one at a time—1-2-3-4-5-etc. moving from the front of the room to the back. As each member counts, he resumes his seat. The number counted by the last member to resume his seat is thus the total vote for that side. When the motion being voted requires a two-thirds vote, the Chair simply doubles the number of those voting "no." If the number voting "Yes" equals or exceeds the "No" vote doubled, the motion passes by the necessary two-thirds.

PARLIAMENTARY INQUIRY OR POINT OF INFORMATION

These requests may be made at any time the information desired is significant. A **Parliamentary Inquiry** is directed to the Chair and asks about rules of parliamentary procedure as they are related to the business at hand. If the question relates to a matter requiring immediate attention, it would be in order even when another member has the floor. If an immediate answer is not necessary, the Chair may wait until the speaker finishes before giving a reply. This request may not be used to raise hypothetical questions. The Chair's reply gives an opinion, not a ruling; thus it is not subject to appeal.

The **Point of Information** may also be raised when another member has the floor, but in this case the member speaking is asked whether he will yield for a question. If he does, the time consumed is taken from his speaking time. If the speaker will not yield, the question must wait until he finishes. Whenever the question is asked, the information desired should be provided, either by the Chair, by the speaker or by whatever officer or member has the information. The **Point of Information** is sometimes used as a subtle means of pointing out an error or raising a counter argument, but it must always be phrased as a question.

A **Parliamentary inquiry** and a **Point of Information** are requests and not motions. They require no seconds, are not debatable or amendable and no vote is taken on them.

A member may rise to a **Point of Order** when he believes that there has been a violation of rules or an error in procedure. For example, points of order may be raised on the Chair's neglect to ask for debate on a debatable motion or to take the negative vote on a question. Since the violation or error must not continue, the member should raise the **Point of Order** immediately, at the time of the violation. The member rises and, not waiting for recognition, says, "I rise to a point of order." The Chair must then ask the member to "State your point." The member then indicates the nature of the violation which he believes has taken place.

The **Point of Order** may interrupt a speaker, requires no second, is not debatable or amendable and requires no vote. Instead, the Chair immediately rules on the point raised. If the Chair agrees that an error was committed, he says, "Your point is well taken," and he proceeds immediately to correct the error. On the other hand, if the Chair disagrees, he says, "Your point is not well taken." The Chair should then explain why he disagrees, and he should continue with the business at hand. No vote is taken, but these rulings by the Chair would be subject to an appeal.

Instead of ruling, the Chair may submit the question to the assembly for decision. For example, suppose the **Point of Order** is raised that a proposed amendment to the main motion is not germane. The Chair is in doubt, so he asks the assembly to decide. "All those who believe the amendment to be germane, say 'Aye.' All those who believe the amendment is not germane, say 'No.'" The Chair then announces the result of the vote and proceeds accordingly. No appeal against the decision of the assembly is possible.

The request to **Withdraw** a motion must be viewed in terms of the point at which this request is made. Putting a motion before a group involves several distinct steps. First, a member rises, addresses the Chair and is recognized. The member then states the motion. Someone seconds the motion. Finally, the Chair repeats the motion and opens it for discussion. At any point in this procedure the member may have a change of mind and ask to withdraw or to modify the motion.

The initial statement of the motion by the Chair is the critical moment in the whole process. Prior to that statement, the motion is the property of the member offering it. He may withdraw it or revise it in any way he wishes; the motion belongs to him. A motion withdrawn at that point would simply be disregarded and not even mentioned in the minutes. Presumably the one seconding the motion could, if he liked the idea, gain the floor and offer the motion himself, gaining a second from someone else. If the motion is restated at this point, the Chair should be certain that the revised motion has a second and that his own statement of the motion incorporates the revision.

Once the Chair has stated the motion, however, the situation changes radically. Now the motion no longer belongs to the one who originated it. The motion is now the property of the assembly. It cannot be withdrawn, nor can it be changed without the approval of the assembly. At this point the member's wish to **Withdraw** the motion is no longer a simple request but becomes an incidental motion requiring assembly approval. Usually this approval is given by *general consent,* but if anyone objects, a formal vote becomes necessary. A proposal to change the wording of the motion would be the subsidiary motion to **Amend,** requiring a second, being open to discussion and amendment and requiring a majority vote.

A motion may be withdrawn, with the consent of the assembly, at any time prior to the actual vote on that motion. If the discussion of the motion indicates major problems, anyone may ask whether the maker is willing to withdraw it. If the maker agrees, the Chair states the question on the withdrawal, and the approval of the assembly removes the motion, just as if it had never been made. Both legally and psychologically there is a difference between withdrawal and defeat of a motion. Legally, the former is as though the motion never existed, and the motion could be renewed later in the same meeting. Psychologically, voluntary withdrawal is different from outright defeat. Ordinarily a withdrawn motion is not even mentioned in the minutes of the meeting unless some action on the motion requires mention. For example, a motion postponed from one meeting to the next and then withdrawn at the second meeting would require mention in the minutes. The record of the first meeting would include the motion to postpone, so the record of the second meeting must include the fact of the withdrawal in order for all to be aware of the disposal of the original motion.

The incidental motion to **Withdraw** cannot interrupt a speaker, requires a second when made as a formal motion by the person asking permission, is not debatable or amendable and takes a majority vote. Usually, however, permission to withdraw is given by *unanimous* *consent.* If a main motion is withdrawn, any incidental or subsidiary motions that adhere to it are also automatically withdrawn and are no longer before the assembly.

One of the basic principles governing any democratic group is that the majority rules; that is, the will of the majority is the will of the group. The process of voting is simply the method by which the will of the majority is determined. A related principle has to do with the secrecy of the ballot. That is, the true will of the majority is only determined when each individual is free to express an opinion apart from any outside influence or fear of reprisal. This freedom may only be achieved when that opinion is expressed anonymously in a secret ballot. Thus the bylaws of many organizations require that voting be done by secret ballot, particularly in situations involving personalities, such as elections. If the bylaws specify such a requirement, no incidental motion to change or suspend the requirement in a particular case would be in order.

Ballot votes take time, however, so most groups are willing to sacrifice secrecy for expediency. Ordinary motions are passed when the majority indicates assent by saying "Aye." (Notice that the vote is "Aye" and not the pronoun "I." "Aye" simply means "yes.") This would be the normal voice vote. While this method is customary, it may not be the best method to take the vote in all circumstances. Thus incidental motions to specify other methods of voting may be in order.

The members should be free to select any fair method of voting that does not violate the bylaws. A motion would be in order to take the vote by ballot or by roll call. Even after a voice vote has been completed and a rising vote demanded by the call for "division," a member might move to have the rising vote counted. All such motions would take precedence over the motion on which the assembly is voting. The member offering a motion pertaining to voting must gain the floor, and a second is also necessary. Such a motion is not debatable, but it could be amended. A majority vote would pass the motion.

TO CLOSE OR REOPEN THE POLLS

When a vote is being taken by ballot and all have apparently voted, the Chair would ordinarily declare the polls closed. However, a formal motion to **Declare the Polls Closed** is also possible, although it should not be permitted before all who wish to vote have been able to do so.

The motion to **Reopen the Polls** is more common. Perhaps late members come in after the polls have been closed, and these people also wish to vote. The assembly can grant them permission by this incidental motion.

Both of these motions must be seconded, and neither may interrupt a speaker. Neither is debatable, but both may be amended, most frequently in regard to the time when the polls are to be closed or reopened. The motion to **Close the Polls,** since it infringes on the right to vote, requires a two-thirds vote. The motion to **Reopen the Polls** restores the right to vote, so it may be passed by a simple majority.

MOTIONS RELATED TO NOMINATIONS

The bylaws of most organizations specify the way in which candidates for office are nominated. However, the bylaws may not cover a problem such as electing members for an ad hoc committee, or the bylaws may not mention nominations at all. In this case, the assembly is free to choose the method of nomination that it desires. At the time of the election, the incidental motion to **Prescribe the Method of Nominating** would be in order. A number of possibilities present themselves: nominations by the Chair, by a nominating committee, by the members in the general meeting, by a nominating ballot. A member could gain the floor and offer the motion that nominations be carried out by any one of these methods. Such a motion would require a second. It could not be discussed, but it might be amended. A majority vote would pass it.

If nominations are being offered by the members in general meeting, someone might wish to limit the number of nominees by moving the **Close of Nominations.** This motion interferes with the basic right of making nominations, and it is rarely needed. The Chair's chief responsibility is to see that everyone is given the opportunity to nominate. Even when nominations are done by the Chair himself or by a committee, additional opportunities for nominations from the floor should be given. Then, when no one wishes to offer further nominations, the Chair simply declares the nominations closed. The motion to **Close Nominations** would not be in order until all members have had a reasonable opportunity in which to make nominations, and it certainly should not be permitted to interrupt a member who is making a nomination. If a member gains the floor and offers this motion, it requires a second. It would not be open to discussion, although it might be amended, perhaps in regard to the time when nominations are to close. Since it interferes with the basic right to nominate, a two-thirds vote would be necessary to pass it.

If nominations are closed, either by declaration of the Chair or by a formal motion, an incidental motion to **Reopen Nominations** would still be possible. This motion should be treated in much the same way as the motion to **Close Nominations.** It cannot interrupt a speaker, requires a second and cannot be debated, although an amendment in regard to time would be possible. Since it restores a basic right, a simple majority vote would pass it.

┌─ **Review Quiz** ─────────────────────────────┐

LESSON 11: INCIDENTAL MOTIONS

In the blank preceding each statement, write the motion called for.

1._____   To verify a vote too close to call.

2._____   To correct an error in procedure.

3._____   To require the group rather than the Chair to decide on an issue.

4._____   To insist that the organization cannot debate an unsuitable motion.

5._____   To separate the parts of a main motion.

6._____   To request permission to ask the speaker a question.

7._____   To find the exact wording of the main motion under debate.

8. _____ To tell a speaker that his debate
                            is not germane.

9. _____ To relax the rules of debate.

10. _____ To remove the motion before a
                            vote on it.

11. _____ To ask for a specific list of
                            expenditures.

12. _____ To ask for a vote required to
                            adopt.

13. _____ To discuss a motion with several
                            independent parts.

14. _____ To prevent any discussion on
                            a motion.

15. _____ To reverse the Chair's ruling.

16. _____ To change the order of
                            business.

LESSON 12
RESTORATORY MOTIONS
CHANGING PREVIOUS DECISIONS

"Frequently, decisions made in a deliberative body must be referred to again. Members sometimes need to review a decision made too hastily, or when a changed situation, new developments, or additional information prompts the need to reexamine the adopted issue."

Riddick Butcher, *Riddick's Rules of Procedure*

LESSON OBJECTIVE

To learn that restoratory motions may change adopted main motions, return any motion to its prior status or allow for renewal of discussion and action.

READING ASSIGNMENT

Robert pp. 294-338
Sturgis pp. 28-29, 33-41

Demeter pp. 48, 152-170
Riddick pp. 41-43, 83, 165-167, 173-174

LESSON MATERIAL

Sometimes a group wishes to change its mind or have the opportunity to change its mind. Members have the right to "rethink" a situation if a decision was made too hastily or if an action was inappropriate because of faulty or insufficient information.

Certain motions restore consideration of a motion already acted upon. **Demeter** calls such motions "restoratory" motions. They are: **Amend a Motion Already Adopted, Discharge a Committee, Reconsider, Rescind** and **Take From the Table** (resume consideration). In reality, they are main motions proposed when no business is pending. Since business cannot be interrupted constantly by indecisive members, restoratory motions must be treated according to procedural rules.

AMEND A MOTION ALREADY ADOPTED

This motion is used when the intent is to alter a part or to substitute for the original main motion. It restores discussion on the original motion.

Only that part of the motion not yet acted upon can be amended, since action taken as a result of the original motion presumably could not be undone. Neither can a motion be changed if notification has been given to the parties concerned with that motion. If this motion to amend applies to amending special rules, it requires previous notice and a two-thirds vote or a majority vote of the entire membership.

The following rules govern this motion:

1. Can only be moved when no business is pending.
2. Requires a second.
3. Is debatable.
4. Is amendable.
5. Requires a two-thirds vote without notice, a majority vote with notice or a majority of the entire membership.

TO DISCHARGE A COMMITTEE

A motion to **Discharge a Committee** is in order if the committee has failed to report or to perform its assigned tasks, or if the assembly wishes to drop the matter or to take action itself on the subject assigned to the committee.

When a special (ad hoc) committee gives its final report, no motion is required to discharge it; the discharge is automatic.

The motion cannot interrupt a speaker, requires a second and is debatable but not amendable. It requires a majority vote with notice, a two-thirds vote without notice, or a majority vote of the entire membership.

RESCIND

Rescind is used to countermand, or to nullify, an adopted order. Common sense tells us that it is too late to **Rescind** after action dictated by the main motion has already taken place. Previous notice of the intent to offer this motion may be given at one meeting, with the motion itself being offered at the following meeting.

The motion to **Rescind** takes precedence over nothing but may be made at any time that a main motion would be in order. It is usually proposed when it is too late to move to **Reconsider** the decision the assembly wants to change. **Sturgis** says it may only be applied to the main motion.

If previous notice has been given, the motion may be adopted by majority vote. However, any change proposed that exceeds the scope of the earlier announcement would require a two-thirds vote to adopt. If the motion to **Rescind** or to **Amend a Motion Already Adopted** applies to a bylaw, no change would be in order that is greater than the change stated in the previous notice that was given.

The following rules govern this motion:

1. Cannot interrupt a speaker.
2. Requires a second.
3. Is debatable, opening the main motion to debate.
4. Is amendable.
5. Requires a two-thirds vote without notice or a majority vote with notice.
6. May be reconsidered if the vote is in the negative.

RESCIND AND EXPUNGE

This is a form of the motion to **Rescind.** When an organization regrets having done something that has already been entered in the minutes and later wants to express strong disapproval of the action, it should use this form, a member offering the motion to **Rescind and Expunge** from the minutes. Passing the motion would record strong condemnation of the previous action.

Because minutes (the official record) must always reflect precisely what was done, the expunged portion should be marked with a single line drawn through or around the offending words. These should not be erased, blotted or cut out, since the record must show exactly what was ordered expunged. A note is then added, "Rescinded and Expunged by order of the assembly." This note should be signed by the secretary and dated. Some authorities ask that the president also sign the note. The expunged portion of the minutes is never published.

The motion:

1. Requires a second.
2. Is debatable.
3. Is amendable.
4. Requires an affirmative vote of the majority of the entire membership.

A separate motion to condemn previous action taken is in order if the assembly has already rescinded the action. **Robert** recommends this procedure, first a motion to **Rescind** the action, then a separate resolution condemning the action that has been rescinded.

TAKE FROM THE TABLE

A motion that has been laid on the table remains there, unless by a motion to do so it is taken from the table during the same session or the next session of a group meeting quarterly or more often. If the motion is not taken from the table before the end of that next session, the motion expires.

A motion taken from the table must be in the same form as when it was laid on the table, including any adhering motions. Adhering motions to **Refer to Committee,** to **Amend** or to **Postpone Indefinitely** are taken up in their turn, just as though the motion had never been put aside. A pending motion to **Postpone Definitely** would also be taken up, provided that the delay involved in tabling the main motion had not made nonsense of the motion to postpone.

If the original motion is taken from the table on the same day that it went to the table, those who had exhausted their right to speak would not be permitted to participate in the discussion. However, if the motion came off the table on the next day, these speaking rights would be renewed, and all could participate once more. The rules pertaining to adopted motions to limit or to end discussion are slightly different. If the **Previous Question** has been ordered or a motion to **Limit Debate** adopted, those restrictions would still apply when the main question is removed from the table, even at an adjourned meeting taking place the next day. Only if the motion is taken from the table at the next session are these restrictions on free debate considered to be exhausted and disregarded.

A motion taken from the table can be laid on the table again if other business interrupts.

The motion:

1. Cannot interrupt a speaker.
2. Requires a second.
3. Is not debatable.
4. Is not amendable.
5. Requires a majority vote.

Adoption of the motion to **Reconsider** suspends all action on the main motion except on matters already implemented. It must be moved on the same day or the next day as the motion to which it applies. *Making* the motion takes precedence over any other motion, *but not the consideration of it.* Making the motion is in order at any time, with the highest precedence, since the group may need to stop any action about to be taken under the original motion. The actual discussion and vote on the motion to **Reconsider** has the precedence of the motion to which it applies. Thus the motion may be made at one point in the meeting, but the motion might be called up for discussion and vote much later in the same or the next session.

Robert says that the motion may only be made by one who voted on the prevailing side on the original motion, which protects the majority against dilatory use by a defeated minority, but he permits others to persuade someone who did vote on the winning side to make the motion by giving reasons for moving to **Reconsider.** Many other parliamentary authorities believe the motion may be made by any member, reasoning that no member should be penalized for the way the member votes. This opinion has been validated in the courts.

RECONSIDER
AND ENTER ON
THE MINUTES

This motion should only be permitted if the bylaws or standing rules of the organization allow for it. **Sturgis** simply says, "When this motion is made, it should be ruled out of order."

The motion to **Reconsider and Enter on the Minutes** must be proposed on the same day on which the motion acted upon was proposed, but the motion may not be called up, if seconded, until at least the next day. Once called, it is treated like any motion to reconsider. The motion cannot be moved at the last business meeting of the session in an organization that does not have regular sessions as often as quarterly.

The following rules apply:

1. Can interrupt business.
2. Must be made by one voting on the prevailing side **(Robert).**
3. Requires a second.
4. Cannot be called up on the day on which it was made.
5. Once called up, is treated like the motion to **Reconsider.**

RATIFY

This motion, if adopted, endorses action taken at a meeting where no quorum was present or when the action taken by a committee was beyond the scope of its responsibilities. If the endorsement (ratification) is not provided, those who took the action are fully responsible for the results. The motion to **Ratify** is presented at the first meeting where a quorum is present. It is debatable and amendable and requires a majority vote.

RENEW

There is no specified motion to renew. Any defeated or withdrawn motion may be offered again at a time later than the same session. A renewed motion usually is proposed in different language or form, supported by better information or offered when more supporters of the motion might be present, in the hope that the outcome of the vote will be different.

Review Quiz #1

LESSON 12:   RESTORATORY MOTIONS
CHANGING PREVIOUS DECISIONS

COMPARISON OF RECONSIDER AND RESCIND

Fill in the following chart.

Comparison	Reconsider	Rescind
When Proposed:		
Precedence:		
How Proposed:		
Action Taken:		
Vote Required:		
Effect:		
Special Consideration:		

┌─ **Review Quiz #2** ──────────────────────────────┐
└──┘

LESSON 12: RESTORATORY MOTIONS
CHANGING PREVIOUS DECISIONS

1.   What is the status of a motion taken from the table?

_____

_____

2.   When can a motion be taken from the table?

_____

_____

3.   What is the difference between **Amend Something Previously Adopted** and **Rescind?**

_____

_____

4.   When can a member move to **Rescind?**

_____

_____

5.   What vote is required to **Rescind?**

_____

_____

6.   What restriction does **Reconsider** place on a motion?

_____

_____

7.   What is unique about the motion to **Reconsider?**

_____

_____

8.   What is the effect of adopting the motion **to Discharge a Committee?**

_____

_____

9.   Which of these motions may require previous notice?

_____

_____

10. What is the purpose of **Rescind and Expunge?**

_____

_____

11. What is the potential abuse of the motion to **Reconsider and Enter on the Minutes?**

_____

_____

12. What can a member do if he did not vote on the prevailing side?

_____

_____

13. What motions may not be **Reconsidered** or **Rescinded?**

_____

_____

14. Is **Reconsider** a debatable motion?

_____

_____

15. What does the Chair do if **Reconsider** is not called up?

_____

_____

16. How is **Reconsider** handled in committee?

_____

_____

17. Does adopting **Reconsider** adopt the main motion also?

_____

_____

18. What is the result if **Reconsider** is lost?

_____

_____

19. What is the effect of adopting the motion to **Rescind?**

_____

_____

20. What is the effect of adopting the motion to **Reconsider?**

_____

_____

┌─**Review Quiz #3** ──────────────────────────────────────┐
└──┘

LESSON 12:   RESTORATORY MOTIONS
CHANGING PREVIOUS DECISIONS

Select the best answer.

1. A motion was set aside temporarily, *laid on the table*, with no provision for its later consideration. At the next meeting, a motion is in order to:

   a. **Take From the Table**
   b. **Rescind**
   c. **Reconsider**
   d. **Amend a Previously Adopted Motion**

2. A society adopted a resolution to exclude from membership any applicants who had a Latin heritage. Sometime later, the society wished to broaden its views and wanted to remove this ruling from the record. Action could be taken to:

   a. **Rescind** the ruling
   b. **Rescind and Expunge from the Minutes**
   c. **Reconsider** the motion on exclusion
   d. propose a new main motion

3. A member interrupted business to move to **Reconsider** the vote on an adopted motion to:

   a. get attention officially
   b. confuse the members
   c. clear the record of previous action
   d. stop action being taken on the previously adopted motion

4. A special committee failed to report on its assignment. The assembly may:

   a. consider the assignment itself without the report
   b. forget the matter altogether
   c. move to **Discharge the Committee**
   d. **Refer** the matter to another committee

5. Which motion is used to return a motion to consideration by the assembly that was set aside temporarily?

   a. **Postpone Indefinitely**
   b. **Object to Consideration**
   c. **Take From the Table**
   d. **Refer to Committee**

6. The motion to **Rescind** is applied to:

   a. a resignation that has been accepted
   b. a vote on a motion adopted six months ago
   c. an election to membership, the person notified
   d. a motion adopted on the same day, which a member has moved to **Reconsider**

7. An assembly adopted a motion to give a scholarship for accomplishment in mathematics. Before action was taken, the society wished to change the scholarship from mathematics to science. Which of the following is in order?

   a. It is too late to propose another motion.
   b. Motion should be **Rescinded.**
   c. The vote on the motion should be **Reconsidered.**
   d. A member moves to **Amend a Previously Adopted Motion.**

8. A member wanted to give further consideration to the vote adopted last spring that dues of associate members be half that of regular members. The motion is:

   a. to **Reconsider**
   b. to **Amend Something Previously Adopted**
   c. to **Lay on the Table**
   d. to **Rescind**

LESSON 13
THE PRESIDING OFFICER
PRESIDENT - CHAIRMAN

"As presiding officer the president is the leader and representative of the entire assembly. Respect for his position is respect for the organization. The president must maintain firm control of the meetings, yet always must act primarily as the 'first servant of the assembly.' "

Alice Sturgis, *Standard Code of Parliamentary Procedure*

LESSON OBJECTIVE

To recognize the characteristics of a good presiding officer, the special circumstances that arise and how a presiding officer deals with each.

READING ASSIGNMENT

Robert pp. 20-24, 438-456
Sturgis pp. 153-156

Demeter pp. 39-46, 250-252
Riddick pp. 40-41, 125-126, 145-146

LESSON MATERIAL

An efficient leader, be it as a president or Chair, needs to be:

1. Confident, knowing procedural rules and how to use them.
2. Impartial during debate, insuring fair play to both sides.
3. Efficient, moving without hesitation through the order of business.
4. Helpful, assisting members to exercise their rights, making tactful suggestions.
5. Correct, insisting upon decorum but flexible enough to use good judgment when it becomes necessary to adapt to special needs.

A good leader needs skill in human relations. When presiding, the Chair is responsible for protecting the rights of the members and assisting them in the exercise of those rights.

As an administrator, the president needs to understand what motivates members, anticipate problems, set a goal for the administration and be familiar with the organization's bylaws and basic parliamentary procedures. At all times, he is responsible for preserving order; he should act quickly at the first sign of trouble and keep the members working together harmoniously. The president is accountable for the success of the organization, and needs to supervise all aspects of the organization—organize, plan and initiate activities.

The Chair's presiding skills should reflect balanced judgment, impartiality, patience in answering questions, firm control, tact and diplomacy. **Sturgis** states, "Just as a judge exercises wide discretion in a courtroom, the presiding officer should exercise wide discretion in a meeting. He is not a robot, limited to mechanical responses, but must meet each situation with flexibility of judgment, common sense, and fairness to all members—acting always impartially and in good faith."

As a meeting progresses, the Chair must concentrate on the progress of debate, showing keen perception in sorting out misunderstandings, identifying dilatory tactics, stating information when no other member knows the same facts, discouraging the member who tries to dominate and encouraging the shy member. The Chair should encourage and stimulate discussion, giving both sides an equal opportunity to express their views. The Chair must respond decisively but not defensively. With a sense of humor, a ready smile when appropriate and firm guidance coupled with self-control, the presiding officer can encourage all sides as he gets the job done.

The Chair must pace the progress of the meeting. The group should not be allowed to bog down nor to grow into a ratifying body rather than a deliberative body. To offset such tendencies, the Chair should preside skillfully as he does the following:

1. Calls the meeting to order on time, quorum being present.
2. Helps a member rephrase a confusing motion.
3. States a motion clearly, accurately.
4. Repeats the motion before putting it to a vote.
5. Rules promptly on procedural matters.
6. Pays close attention to the discussion.
7. Clarifies and explains obscure points.
8. Takes the vote correctly.
9. Announces the result of the vote audibly.
10. Appoints committee members with discretion when required to do so.

The Chair can increase respect and give guidance in decorum when required to do so by:

1. Properly recognizing the member entitled to speak.
2. Being alert to recognize those who properly seek the floor.
3. Ignoring those who seek the floor incorrectly.
4. Providing each member who desires it, a first turn in debate.
5. Alternating recognition of speakers from affirmative and negative as far as possible.
6. Preventing impatient members from closing debate too soon.
7. Protecting speakers from noise and disruption.
8. Using testimony from experts on the pending subject.
9. Insisting on language in the third person to eliminate personalities.
10. Applying disciplinary measures with a firm, controlled manner. The Chair may judge when to ignore irrelevant remarks and when to enforce rigidity of rules. If in doubt, the Chair may ask the assembly to decide.

┌─ **PRACTICE EXERCISE** ─────────────────────────────┐
└───┘

LESSON 13: THE PRESIDING OFFICER
PRESIDENT - CHAIRMAN

Act out the following situations.

1.   Stating motions and putting motions to a vote

Member: Mr. Chairman.

CHAIR: The Chair recognizes _____.

Member: I move that _____.

Member: Second.

CHAIR: (being positive that the motion is clearly stated)
It has been moved and seconded that _____
_____. Is there any discussion?
(Hearing no discussion, the Chair will put the
motion to a vote.) Those in favor of the motion
to _____, say "Aye." Those opposed,
say "No." The Ayes have it and the motion is
carried. The next business in order is _____
_____ (or) Is there any further new
business?

2.   Guiding the assembly

Member: Mr. Chairman.

CHAIR: The Chair recognizes _____.

Member: I move that our delegates be instructed to support
the proposed amendment at the state convention.

Member: I second the motion.

CHAIR: It has been moved and seconded that our delegates
be instructed to support the proposed amendment
at the State Convention. Is there any discussion?

Member: Mr. Chairman.

CHAIR: The Chair recognizes _____.

Member: Is it in order to ask a question at this time?

CHAIR: Please state your question and the Chair will decide.

3. Recognition by the Chair

Member #1: Mr. Chairman.

Member #2: Mr. Chairman.

Member #3: Mr. Chairman.

CHAIR: The Chair can recognize but one member at a time. The Chair recognizes member
_____
since the Chair believes member _____ sought recognition first.

Member _____ discusses the motion.

Member #2: Mr. Chairman.

Member #3: Mr. Chairman.

Member #4: Mr. Chairman.

CHAIR: The Chair will not overlook anyone. Please be patient. You will be recognized in turn.

4. Members refusing to come to order (standing in the aisle)

CHAIR: The members will come to order. (Tap gavel firmly.)

Members: (Continue to talk and fail to be seated.)

CHAIR: (Using the gavel very firmly, again.) The members will be seated. There shall be no business until there is order and all are seated. (Stand erect and wait for quiet.) Thank you. We will now proceed.

5. **Ruling on a proposed amendment**

Member: I move to amend the motion by adding the words "and Mr. Brown."

CHAIR: The Chair is in doubt as to the relevancy of the amendment and will ask the assembly to decide. Those who wish to declare the amendment germane, say "Aye." Those who believe it is not germane, say "No."

The Noes have it and the amendment is not germane. The motion now before you is

_____ .

6. **Helping member phrase a motion**

Member: Madam Chairman.

CHAIR: The Chair recognizes _____ .

Member: Madam Chairman, I think we ought to come to some decision about raising dues five dollars a year.

CHAIR: The bylaws do not require previous notice for a raise in dues. Does the member wish to say, "I move that dues be raised five dollars a year?" (The member replies, "Yes." It is discussed, and voted upon and adopted.)

7. **Curtailing the members from speaking off the question**

CHAIR: The Chair asks the member to confine his remarks to the pending question.

Member continues as before.

CHAIR: Sir, your remarks are out of order, not germane. Please speak to the subject or the Chair will ask you to be seated. We are working on a time schedule.

8.   Inquiry on a nondebatable item

CHAIR: It has been moved and seconded that the motion be *laid on the table*. (Member rises.) For what purpose does the member rise?

Member: Mr. Chairman. I move the *previous question*.

CHAIR: The motion is not in order at this time. It has a lower order of precedence (rank) than *lay on the table*. If the immediately pending motion to *lay on the table* is lost, the Chair will again recognize the member.

9.   Taking a vote that might be questioned

CHAIR: All those in favor of the motion to _____ _____ say "Aye." All those opposed to the motion, say "No." The Chair is in doubt. Will as many as are in favor of the motion please rise. (Members rise.) Be seated. As many as are opposed, please rise. (Members rise) Be seated. The "Ayes" appear to have it (pause). The "Ayes" have it, and the motion is adopted.

10.   In reply to a point of information (A member has made a motion with very unclear intent.)

Member: *Point of information*, Madam Chairman.

CHAIR: State your point.

Member: Does the passage of this motion mean we have to be involved in candidate approval from now on?

CHAIR: It is not clear to the Chair what the substance of the motion is. Would the speaker (proposer) please explain the intent of this motion?

LIST OF DO'S AND DON'TS FOR PRESIDENTS

Do's

1. Do call the meeting to order promptly.
2. Do preserve order at all times.
3. Do insist that the rules of debate be observed.
4. Do entertain one piece of business at a time.
5. Do insure full and free discussion.
6. Do see that the will of the majority is preserved.
7. Do protect the rights of the minority.
8. Do take a vote properly.
9. Do keep a quorum present.
10. Do read mail and distribute information promptly.
11. Do encourage members to take an active part.
12. Do keep your temper.
13. Do use *general consent* whenever possible.
14. Do quit running things when your term of office is over.

Don'ts

1. Don't do all the talking because you can do it better.
2. Don't try to impose your will.
3. Don't use your office for personal gain.
4. Don't change everything because you are the boss.
5. Don't be smug about frictionless meetings. Was there progress?
6. Don't use the pronoun "I."
7. Don't refer to "my club, my board," but rather "our club, our board."
8. Don't be pedantic about parliamentary law on every occasion.
9. Don't "turn the meeting over." Present or call upon another person to occupy the Chair or the next person to lead the program.
10. Don't permit exceptions to bylaws.
11. Don't just do the same things better. Do better things.
12. Don't let the meeting drag. Expedite.

┌─**Review Quiz #1** ─────────────────────────┐

LESSON 13: THE PRESIDING OFFICER
PRESIDENT - CHAIRMAN

1. Explain what the Chair should say when, at the close of a meeting, several members asked, "How did you feel about having our next convention in Hawaii? During the meeting we couldn't get a clue as to your opinion."

2. Tell what the Chair should have said, instead of pounding the gavel furiously and shouting, "Hey, sit down. Come to order. You are acting like a bunch of kids. Stop yakking and let's get the show on the road."

3. Tell what the Chair should do and say when heckled by a group of dissenters.

4. What should the Chair do during energetic discussion when a bored member from the fourth row audibly remarks, "I move that we send these members to the Energy Department which could probably use all that hot air."

5. What are the Chair's (or president's) voting rights?

6. What should the Chair say when several members rise and address the Chair at the same time?

7. When should the Chair use the gavel?

8. What should the Chair say after the vote is taken?

9. What are at least two important attributes that the Chair (presiding officer) should possess?

10. What are some responsibilities of a president as an administrator?

┌─Review Quiz #2 ─────────────────────────────────┐

LESSON 13:   THE PRESIDING OFFICER
PRESIDENT - CHAIRMAN

Decide whether the Chair (presiding officer) may or may not take these actions. Mark "Y" for yes or "N" for no.

_____Announce unfinished business

_____Close debate

_____Order a vote by ballot

_____Close nominations

_____Declare a close vote unanimous

_____Validate voting results

_____Preside at committee of the whole

_____Conduct business in absence of a quorum

_____Assume motion to adopt auditor's report

_____Rule a motion out of order

_____Preside at own election

_____Preside when ex officio

_____Order secretary to note offensive remarks

_____Depart from adopted agenda

_____Call an offender to order

_____Appoint a temporary chairman

_____Be counted in committee quorum

_____Vote twice on a proposition

_____Assume office immediately

_____Order a bylaw revision

_____Order a counted vote

_____Move to adopt own recommendation

_____Be ex officio member of all committees

_____Appoint the parliamentarian

_____Take a vote on an assumed motion

_____Adjourn the meeting

_____Take a vote on an unseconded motion

_____Assume full authority to make rulings

_____Refuse recognition to the floor

LESSON 14
DEBATE

"An organization conducts meetings primarily to provide an opportunity to consider proposals and make concurrent decisions about the proposition under consideration. The basic principle of parliamentary procedure is that such consideration called debate, be free, full, and vigorous."

Riddick Butcher, *Riddick's Rules of Procedure*

LESSON OBJECTIVE

To understand the meaning and purpose of the goals of debate in parliamentary procedure.

READING ASSIGNMENT

Robert pp. 380-394   Demeter pp. 28-32
Sturgis pp. 114-121   Riddick pp. 71-79

LESSON MATERIAL

THE MEANING OF DEBATE

One of the most important basic principles of parliamentary procedure is that of full and free *debate* or *discussion* of all substantive issues that may come before the assembly.

Although *debate* and *discussion* are often used interchangeably in meetings, **Debate** is the oral communication that is applied to the passage or defeat of a substantive motion. Some have described debate as a two-sided propositional argument.

Discussion, more technically perceived, is the less formal oral communication that best characterizes the verbal exchange in small groups such as committees. The object of discussion is to develop a recommendation or proposal for debate before the assembly.

THE GOAL
OF DEBATE

John Stuart Mill reminds us that it is the clash of opposing ideas that gives truth the chance to emerge. It is the clash of informed and caring minds that leads to wise decisions. So we debate a motion, not just to be heard, but to enlighten, to advocate a position. Wise men often identify their debate as they begin: "Mr. Chairman, I rise to speak in favor of the motion before the house," or "Madam Chairman, I oppose the adoption of this motion now before us." A second critical goal of debate is member participation. Organizations are stronger because members are present and speaking. Participation in debate signals a concern for the best interests of the group. What any organization votes to do influences the status of all members. Those who assist in the decision-making process through enlightening debate have demonstrated allegiance to their organization. Commitment and strength go hand in hand.

THE USE
OF DEBATE

An able debater or discussant in a meeting is one who knows rules and has some contribution to make to the assembly's understanding of the topic or the proposal before the assembled members. Many motions may be debated, but not all. The substantive general main motion proposed by the finance committee to "increase member dues by two dollars a year" is fully debatable. Such a motion clearly invites members to affirm their support of this needed increase in dues or, in contrast, to speak against this added cost of membership in the organization. The membership must decide whether the increase is warranted. Vigorous, free and full debate in open meeting with most of the members participating (debating) is the best way to decide the issue of raising dues.

Some motions are not debatable, especially those that do not require a second or where debate would interfere with the immediate decision about the motion. A good example of a nondebatable motion is the motion to **Object to Consideration**. To debate whether to consider would effectively make the motion unnecessary.

Procedural motions such as **Previous Question** (vote immediately) are not debatable. Most authorities disallow debate on the motion to limit debate or recess because, again, debate would interfere with accomplishing the objectives of the motion. Some authorities, however, allow restricted debate limited to a comment or two at the discretion of the Chair and directed to the time stipulated in these motions.

On the question of limits to the rights of members to debate, fair play is the guiding principle. The proposer of the motion or the chairman of the committee from which the resolution came should have first opportunity to debate. No member should expect to speak a second time in a debate upon a specific motion as long as members who have not yet spoken desire to speak. A presiding officer should seek, as nearly as possible, to alternate speakers who favor and speakers opposed to the motion. The presiding officer must maintain the appearance of impartiality, since the Chair determines which members are to speak and sees that a balance of different opinions is entertained. Should the Chair have information needed to apprise the members of the issues related to a wise decision, the Chair may impartially clarify and explain.

If the Chair actually wishes to debate the question, however, the Chair calls the next officer in rank to preside during the rest of the debate on the motion and to conduct the final vote. **Decorum**—propriety and good taste—in debate is an important consideration. Recognition by the Chair of those who wish to speak is the first critical requirement. The speaker's remarks are to be relevant, or germane, to the immediately pending question.

In the motion to "increase membership dues by two dollars," relevant debate should focus on the advantages or disadvantages to the organization of an increase in dues. Any comment on the ineffectiveness of the treasurer in handling the organization's funds is irrelevant and in bad taste. Remarks to the effect that "a dues increase may assist us in paying our bills on time" are relevant and in good taste.

The presiding officer should be quick to caution or correct a member whose debate deteriorates to personalities or slander or simply wastes time. Debate helps the assembly to become informed on both sides of an issue, enabling it to make a wiser decision. It provides for a two-sided argument.

Debate is intentional group thinking. Speakers present their facts and opinions to support their advocacy or to oppose the proposition. To debate well, one must understand the problem, an understanding made possible by a presentation of facts and how they affect the issue. Use of "I think ..." or "I guess..." usually indicates ineffectual arguments.

Debate is conducted with formality and courtesy to help preserve order by keeping the exchanges impersonal. We debate a motion, not so much to be heard, but to enlighten and be enlightened.

An organization grows in strength when the members are present to participate by speaking (debating) and voting on the issues debated.

All main motions and amendments are fully debatable. Some motions have limited debate. For example, it would be foolish to permit debate on a motion to close debate.

Speakers in debate, after recognition from the Chair, may speak without interruption until their allowed time has expired.

Interruptions during debate can be legally made when they involve the rights of members and cannot wait, such as *points of order* or *questions of privilege*. The Chair may also interrupt a speaker for any infraction of the rules of decorum in debate.

Sometimes a comment from a speaker excites the need to question it at once. The member, on a **Point of Information**, can ask that question through the Chair. The Chair will ask the speaker if he is willing to respond at once, as the response will be deducted from his speaking time. The speaker may refuse or agree. If the answer is brief, the speaker often answers the question at once.

THE RULES OF DEBATE

- Members must be recognized by the Chair for the right to speak.
- No other member should be standing while the speaker has the floor.
- Each member must speak within the imposed time limit, unless granted an extension of time by the assembly.
- No motion may be debated until stated by the Chair.
- Debaters must observe proper decorum, using not personal names when speaking of others, but such terms as "the speaker on my right" or "the previous speaker."
- Personalities or motives of members may not be attacked, however vigorous the attack on the issue.
- All members are expected to observe the final decision of the assembly (majority rule).
- A member's strongest opinion is the vote he casts.

Although free and full debate is an important principle, circumstances may require some limitation to debate or even its termination. A very full agenda may require need to limit debate to a short time or to the number of speakers. To move the **Previous Question** (to vote now) terminates all debate if adopted. Note that because these motions deprive members of their rights, the vote required is a two-thirds majority.

THE CHAIR
IN DEBATE

The Chair:

- Has the right to recognize who is to speak.

- Has the responsibility to maintain orderly discussion by protecting the rights of speakers. Speakers have a right to demand such protection from the Chair.

- Has the responsibility to seek, as nearly as possible, alternate speakers for those who favor the motion as well as for those opposed to the motion.

- Has the responsibility to keep the action moving, not permitting any member to monopolize the discussion or prolong repetition of facts.

- Must see that discussion is germane, is relevant and does not wander from the issue.

- Has to keep the *procedure* of the debate from misuse, such as accepting motions to stop debate before there has been any. The Chair can explain the need for adequate information to obtain the right decision. Dilatory motions or delaying tactics should be controlled by the Chair.

- Should be quick to caution or correct a member whose debate deteriorates into criticism of personalities.

- Does not enter into debate to preserve impartiality but may do so on leaving the Chair while another officer presides, and does not return until the motion is resolved in some way.

- States the proposition clearly, takes the vote accurately and announces the result correctly.

MEMBERS IN DEBATE

- Every member has the right to share equally in discussion.

- No member should try to monopolize the discussion.

- The member who made the motion has first right to speak to it.

- Members should address all remarks to the presiding officer.

- Members should observe the rules of decorum in debate.

- Members should obey the legitimate orders of the Chair.

INFORMAL CONSIDERATION

A modification of debate occurs when the assembly moves to consider informally. This is a time-saving, practical method for making decisions by relaxing some of the formality as required in debate. The motion is usually adopted by *general consent*; if there is an objection to *general consent*, then it requires a majority vote. **Informal Consideration** places no limit on the number of turns to speak or the number of speeches a member is entitled to make, but all other rules of debate remain in effect. Once a decision is reached, the assembly automatically returns to the regular rules for debate. The decision made is entered in the minutes.

┌─Review Quiz #1 ──────────────────┐

LESSON 14: DEBATE

1. Assume that a motion to raise dues by 25 percent is pending. Try to create three reasons to defeat it. Two comments during debate should be ruled not in order as dilatory or lacking in decorum.

2. Open debate for five minutes on each:

   Abolishing capital punishment.

   The love of money is the root of all evil.

   All sports athletes should be tested for drug use.

   Subject selected by students.

Debate should be conducted formally. Motions to limit or end debate would be in order.

Review Quiz #2

LESSON 14: DEBATE

1. Define the principle of debatability.

_____

_____

_____

_____

2. Name three nondebatable motions.

_____

_____

_____

_____

3. How can the presiding officer enter debate?

_____

_____

_____

_____

4. What are the rules for decorum in debate?

_____

_____

_____

_____

5. What are dilatory tactics in debate?

_____

_____

_____

_____

6. Cite a basic goal achieved through debate.

_____

_____

_____

_____

_____

7. What is meant by "gaveling through"?

_____

_____

_____

_____

8. How may members interrupt a speaker?

_____

_____

_____

_____

9. Name some motions which help control debate.

_____

_____

_____

_____

10. How can one give an opinion on a pending motion without debating it?

_____

_____

_____

_____

LESSON 15
STRATEGY OF DEBATE

Persuasion: "To prevail and convince persons by advice, urging, reasons, inducements."

Strategy: "Skillful management in getting the better of an adversary."

American College Dictionary

LESSON OBJECTIVE

To understand the basic procedures that help win in debate.

READING ASSIGNMENT

Robert pp. 125, 154, 599-600   **Demeter** pp. 28, 29, 32
Sturgis pp. 9-10   **Riddick** pp. 76-79

LESSON MATERIAL

Debate is the civilized way to argue, the ultimate act of persuasion. It is the method used in courts of law, legislative bodies and deliberative societies and governed by rules of decorum (parliamentary law) to insure fair play at all times.

Among the understood courtesies of debate are the following:

1. Debate must be germane.
2. Personalities and motives are not brought under attack.
3. Only facts and provable statements are presented. Waste no time on hearsay.
4. Courtesy and good temper are maintained. Disagreements are handled agreeably.
5. Haste is avoided. Time is taken to examine facts and to evaluate areas of difference.

6. Recess should be called when fatigue threatens good judgment and lucid thinking.
7. Humor is used but never to embarrass or humiliate.

There are certain techniques and legitimate strategies that effective debaters use to help persuade their listeners. For example, a member planning to introduce a controversial motion at a coming meeting of her organization could take the following steps **before** the meeting begins:

1. Have the necessary facts in mind and at hand.
2. Have the motion ready in writing, correctly prepared.
3. Have lined up support of members who will attend the meeting.
4. Have parliamentary material available (bylaws, chart of motions, parliamentary authority).
5. Have additional illustrative anecdotes at hand.

Whenever a member knows ahead of time that a controversial motion will come before the assembly, perhaps because it was postponed from the previous meeting or because notice was given in the call for the coming meeting, the effective debater could follow similar steps in preparation, whether intending to pass or to defeat the motion in question.

During the meeting, the effective strategy for the member introducing the motion would be:

1. Ask for recognition by the Chair and state the motion promptly and clearly.
2. After stating the motion, hand a clearly written copy to the Chair and another to the secretary.
3. After the Chair has stated the motion and called for discussion, claim the floor and present a brief but clearly reasoned argument for an "Aye" vote on the question.
4. Use the **Point of Order** to stop any improper procedures being used against the motion.
5. Use the **Point of Information** to ask members speaking in opposition to yield for appropriate questions.
6. Speak promptly against any motion to **Postpone Indefinitely,** explaining why the main motion should be passed.
7. Don't permit the motion to **Lay on the Table** unless some emergency actually arises. If someone offers this motion, rise to a **Point of Information** to inquire about the nature of the emergency that makes this motion in order.

8. Graciously accept proper amendments when the opposition has a legitimate objection.
9. Oppose delaying tactics when the sentiment is in favor of the motion. Move to **Limit** or **End Debate** if the majority is clearly with you.
10. If the opposition appears to be in the majority, move to **Postpone Definitely** or to **Refer the Motion to a Committee.** Be sure to specify a committee that will be favorable to your position.
11. When a vote is taken, vote promptly, enthusiastically, firmly.
12. If you suspect that personalities are having an undue, negative influence, move for a **Vote by Secret Ballot.**
13. Be sincere and honest; and never "talk down" to others.

Much of the same advice would apply to the effective debater supporting a motion that another member has introduced.

The member opposing the motion could adopt such effective strategies as:

1. Obtain the floor as soon as possible and state objections clearly and concisely.
2. Use the **Point of Information** to get permission to put questions to the proponents of the motion, putting them on the defensive.
3. Move to **Postpone Indefinitely.**
4. Move to **Amend** the motion adversely, to encumber it.
5. If delay would work to the proponents' disadvantage, move to **Postpone Definitely, to Lay on the Table** or to **Refer to Committee.** Be certain that the committee named will be hostile to the motion. Remember that **Lay on the Table** is only in order when an emergency arises.
6. If sufficient members have left the room, raise the question of no quorum.
7. Move to **Recess** in order to caucus for more votes.
8. Move to **Adjourn** in order to prevent action during the present meeting.
9. If a personal influence may be favoring the motion, move for a **Vote by Secret Ballot.**
10. Vote promptly and emphatically. If you suspect that the vote will go against you, you may wish to vote "Aye" with the prevailing side. If the motion passes, you may then move to **Reconsider** before the motion is put into action.

Be careful in doing these things that your opposition is always seen to be sincere and reasonable. If you seem to be simply obnoxious, you may turn undecided members against your cause.

Either side should accept defeat gracefully. Those in favor of the proposition can renew it later with improved arguments, more facts and better information more convincingly presented. Those opposed to an adopted motion have the opportunity, either with a two-thirds vote or with notice and a majority vote, to rescind the motion.

Both sides should be aware of the need for a quorum and remain until adjournment. If too many of the winning side depart after their victory, the opposition can then move for reconsideration.

Courtesy, restraint, patience, good humor are winning factors. To be impatient, irritable, cantankerous are losing factors.

It is acceptable procedure to use legitimate techniques to influence and persuade others to your opinion. The following are additional strategic actions to win votes:

1. Prepare arguments in advance. Do the research; assemble supporting facts.
2. Prepare the proposition to be psychologically attractive. Believe in it.
3. Have more information on hand than you may need. Don't get caught short.
4. Look at the controversy from your opponents' viewpoint. What are the usual arguments that they may be expected to advance? What facts will they have to support these arguments? Prepare counter arguments. Question the facts. Find other authorities to cite in support of your position.
5. Speak enthusiastically, audibly, pleasantly. Be certain those in the back row can hear. Control your speaking rate; don't let the pressures of the moment trap you into speaking so rapidly that you are difficult to understand.
6. Keep to the issue. Be germane.
7. Don't repeat yourself unnecessarily.
8. Be willing to acknowledge an opponent's good points. Be generous with praise.
9. Be patient, courteous, pleasant.
10. Conclude by urging members to vote for your position.
11. Vote promptly.

If, in spite of your best efforts, you see that you are probably in the minority, don't give up. There are still alternatives.

1. Utilize the parliamentary alternatives remaining open to you. Move to **Postpone Indefinitely,** to **Amend,** to **Refer** to a committee favorable to you, to **Recess** to caucus and develop strategy, to **Postpone** or to **Adjourn** until a time when the members attending will likely be more favorable to your position. Shift your vote to the prevailing side so you may later move to **Reconsider.**

2. If you lose, do so gracefully. Try again later with better facts and improved wording of the motion.

3. Remember that the will of the majority is the policy of the group. As long as you are a member of the organization, and until the majority changes, it is also your policy, even though you did not favor it. Accept that position gracefully.

DEBATE
STRATEGY
SUMMARY

Using techniques to influence and persuade others to your beliefs is not unfair. It makes parliamentary procedure your servant. Having good intentions, while meritorious, is not enough. A good debater needs competence and skill to promote his beliefs fairly and successfully.

Remember

1. The motion may not be debated until stated by the Chair.
2. Debate the issue, not the motives.
3. Debate and vote against an issue you believe is wrong.
4. Keep your temper; if lost, the cause, too, is usually lost.
5. To be controversial is to be unpopular. Save argument for real need.

How

1. Prepare your motion to be psychologically attractive, well organized, to fill a need in line with the purposes of the society. Be logical.
2. Get support. Ask members of prestige or authority to speak for your motion. Believe in it sincerely yourself. On occasion, prepare a petition. Get those who agree with you to attend the meeting and provide for an enthusiastic second.

3. For debate, plan your speech in advance before securing the floor. Keep it brief, full of facts, with necessary explanations. Avoid tedious repetitions. Argue forcefully, but stick to the point. Keep it germane, relevant. Conclude with a clear statement of your position, pro or con, the action you support. Stop.

Win friends

1. Develop a reputation for sincerity, competence and honesty, one who holds unbiased opinions based on facts. Be friendly, never snobbish.
2. Be generous with praise, give credit where it is due. Charming manners disarm. Show good humor.
3. Acknowledge opponents' good points.

When speaking

1. Speak audibly, understandably, conversationally, pleasantly. Don't rush.
2. Appeal to human motives. Touch the emotions of your listeners. Develop a sense of timing.

When in danger

1. If your motion is in danger of being lost, try to salvage it. Accept compromise in a motion to **Amend,** or a motion to **Refer it to a Committee** for further study and clarification. Get good personnel on the committee.
2. Propose certain other motions: **Recess** to get more support, **Postpone** to a certain time until further facts or persons can be located or until emotions have cooled down or known adversaries will not be present in such strength. If the situation permits it, use the motion to **Lay on the Table.**
3. **Postpone Indefinitely** rather than risk a vote. Kill the motion and try again some other time in some other form.

Lose gracefully

If you must lose, plan to live to fight another day.

┌─PRACTICE EXERCISE────────────────────────────┐

Assign teams of two students each, one to support, the other to oppose a proposition. Allow time for preparation after you give the assignment. Then conduct a brief debate, one student taking five minutes to support the proposition, the other taking five minutes to oppose it. Follow proper parliamentary procedure, with the first student gaining the floor, introducing the proposition as a motion, and then the students being recognized to present their arguments. At the end, have the class vote, not on the proposition but as to the best preparation and presentation on the part of the speakers.

Topic suggestions:

1. To abolish the grading system for college courses.

2. To make all college tuition free.

3. To adopt a new national anthem.

4. To deport all illegal aliens.

5. To outlaw all experimentation on animals.

6. To conduct all examinations on the honor system.

7. To argue some local problem.

┌─ **Review Quiz** ──────────────────────────┐
└──┘

LESSON 15: STRATEGY OF DEBATE

Complete the sentences.

1.   When preparing to debate, be sure to

_____

_____

_____

_____

2.   To persuade others to your opinion, always

_____

_____

_____

_____

3.   When speaking as an adversary, be

_____

_____

_____

_____

4.   When the opponent is speaking,

_____

_____

_____

_____

5.   If debate gets heated, it is often wise to

_____

_____

_____

_____

6. To support your arguments, prepare with

_____

_____

_____

7. A member about to propose a subject for debate should

_____

_____

_____

8. Base your arguments on the psychological

_____

_____

_____

9. Confound your opponent by asking

_____

_____

_____

10. To save your position if losing,

_____

_____

_____

11. Remember that procedural motions are not

_____

_____

_____

12. After rising to speak, be sure to identify yourself and

_____

_____

_____

LESSON 16
QUORUM

"A quorum in an assembly is the number of members entitled to vote who must be present in order that business can be legally transacted."

Henry M. Robert, *Robert's Rules of Order Newly Revised*

LESSON OBJECTIVE

To learn what a quorum is and that a valid meeting requires previous notice and presence of a quorum.

READING ASSIGNMENT

Robert pp. 19-20, 339-345   **Demeter** pp. 148-152
Sturgis pp. 104-106, 231   **Riddick** pp. 161-163

LESSON MATERIAL

Quorum is the Latin word meaning "of whom." Quorum has been defined as the number of voting members who must be present at a properly called meeting in order for the action taken to be valid. Requiring the presence of a quorum prevents the too few from making decisions for the many.

A quorum should be realistic, not so large that a representative number cannot be obtained under difficult conditions nor so small that action taken fails to express adequately the wishes of the majority of members.

A quorum may be computed on the basis of the entire qualified membership (those entitled to vote), as a specific number (no matter what the size of the membership may be at the time) or as a percentage of the entire membership. Percentage is less advisable, because membership may fluctuate between meetings.

Common parliamentary law provides that if more than half of the members are present, the body is considered to be complete as though all the members were present.

HOW IS A QUORUM DETERMINED?

The size of the quorum is usually determined by the entire membership and stated in the bylaws. If no quorum has been provided, it is a majority of the membership. A quorum is determined by the number of members present, not the number present and voting. No matter how small the vote, if a quorum is present, the vote is valid.

Less than a quorum vote does not affect the presence of a quorum. Members who abstain from voting cannot alter the quorum count. Abstentions and blank ballots are sometimes counted merely to establish the presence of a quorum.

WHO IS COUNTED IN THE QUORUM?

All members qualified to vote are counted in the quorum. Nonmembers, or members who have been disqualified from voting for some reason, are not counted. If the presiding officer is a member, he is counted in the quorum.

Ex officio members who work as regular members are counted in the quorum, but if they are elected incidentally and are not required to attend meetings, they are not counted in the quorum.

WHO DETERMINES THE PRESENCE OF A QUORUM?

The Chair should be sure that a quorum is present before calling the meeting to order. The Chair states the presence of a quorum for entrance in the minutes. In the event of a possible lawsuit, that recorded statement would be proof that action taken at the meeting was taken with a quorum present.

Once the presence of a quorum is determined, it is presumed that a quorum is present throughout the meeting. If the presence of a quorum is challenged successfully—a situation occurs often called a "disappearing quorum"—the meeting is then adjourned or recessed.

The Chair may order a quorum count at any time, but any member who doubts the presence of a quorum, either before business begins or during the meeting, may rise, address the Chair and ask for a quorum count by saying, "I wish for a quorum count," or "I doubt the presence of a quorum." As a *point of order*, the question may interrupt business, but the challenge must be made at the time of doubt. (**Robert** says this challenge may not interrupt the speaker.) If action has already been taken, it is too late to make a *point of order* unless facts can be produced to prove the absence of a quorum. The Chair will rule on presence of the quorum, with or without a count, subject to appeal.

WHAT SPECIFIC QUORUM IS REQUIRED?

In boards or committees, which are definite bodies with required attendance, the quorum is a majority of its members unless provided otherwise in the bylaws.

Regular or special meetings of the membership require the same quorum, either a specific number or a percentage of the total membership. A quorum at a convention is a majority of the registered delegates and others qualified to vote, whether or not they are present in the assembly meeting, unless otherwise defined in the bylaws.

IF NO QUORUM IS PRESENT

When a meeting has been scheduled, but no quorum arrives, legally there can be no valid meeting. But some parliamentary authorities say that the meeting can be called to order as proof that the requirement to meet was met, if only to adjourn at once.

The absence of a quorum allows the **Motion to Adjourn** or to **Recess** to be made, in order to obtain a quorum or to move for an adjourned meeting.

Should the business be so urgent that it cannot wait until the next regular meeting, the assembly may, of necessity, meet and take action. The action must be ratified at the next meeting where a quorum is present before the decision becomes binding. If the action is not ratified, those who took action are responsible for any damage to the organization.

CHANGING A QUORUM

The proper method to change the quorum in the bylaws is to move to **Strike Out and Insert**, thus accomplishing two actions at the same time. It usually requires a two-thirds vote to change the quorum. The amendment procedures specified in the bylaws must be observed.

SPECIAL RULES
SUMMARY

A summary of special rules relating to quorum are show below.

1. Because so few members are required to be present, previous notice for each meeting is imperative. If the time of meeting is in the bylaws, no other previous notice is required unless it is a special meeting.
2. Quorum should be specified in the bylaws.
3. Quorum should be large enough to provide for expected attendance under unfavorable conditions.
4. Proportional quorums usually range from five percent to 10 percent.
5. A member disqualified from voting, such as for a conflict of interest, is not counted in the quorum during that item of business.
6. Members not in good standing (and not qualified to vote) are not counted in the quorum.
7. **Call of the House** is to provide for a quorum attendance as used in legislatures.
8. Quorum always refers to those present, not present and voting.
9. Proxy votes may not be counted in a quorum unless provided otherwise in the bylaws, or in the statutory law of the state in which the organization is incorporated.

┌─**Review Quiz #1** ─────────────────────────────┐

LESSON 16: QUORUM

1.   What is meant by a quorum?

_____

_____

_____

_____

2.   Why should a quorum be small in number?

_____

_____

_____

_____

3.   If the bylaws do not provide for a quorum, what is the quorum
      for:

      a mass meeting?

      _____

      _____

      a convention?

      _____

      _____

      a special meeting?

      _____

      _____

      a committee or board?

      _____

      _____

      an ordinary society?

      _____

      _____

4.   What action may be taken in absence of a quorum?

_____

_____

_____

_____

5.   Who is counted in a quorum?

_____

_____

_____

_____

6.   In a committee, what is the quorum of four; five; six; seven members?

_____

_____

_____

_____

7.   If there is less than a quorum vote, is the action valid?

_____

_____

_____

_____

8.   What is meant by a "disappearing" quorum?

_____

_____

_____

_____

LESSON 16: QUORUM

1. In a committee of 10, six were present, four were absent. Was a quorum present?

_____

_____

_____

_____

2. At a meeting scheduled to start at 2 p.m., the Chair called the meeting to order and announced that no quorum was present. What could be done?

_____

_____

_____

_____

3. At a regular meeting called to order at 8 p.m., there was no quorum. The Chair opened the meeting, provided the opening ritual and then gave the members an informative talk about the progress of the organization. Was the Chair correct in doing this?

_____

_____

_____

_____

4. During a business meeting a member noticed that a quorum was no longer present. What could he do?

_____

_____

_____

_____

5. A committee of 15 met. After deliberation the vote was five "yes," six "no," one abstention. Explain the result.

    _____

    _____

    _____

    _____

6. A committee of 12 took a vote, three "yes," two "no," one abstention. Comment.

    _____

    _____

    _____

    _____

7. Seven members out of a committee of 10 met. Vote was three "yes," two "no," two abstentions. Comment.

    _____

    _____

    _____

    _____

8. During a business meeting it was determined that a quorum was no longer present. An important piece of business needed to be decided upon. Can this need be fulfilled? Comment.

    _____

    _____

    _____

    _____

LESSON 17
MINUTES

"Minutes are the official record of action taken in a deliberative society—the proceedings of the business, what was done but not what was said."

Riddick Butcher, *Riddick's Rules of Procedure*

LESSON OBJECTIVE

To learn about the contents, writing and importance of minutes.

READING ASSIGNMENT

Robert pp. 458-466   **Demeter** pp. 21-25
Sturgis pp. 188-192   **Riddick** pp. 113-116

LESSON MATERIAL

Minutes are the official and historical record of actions taken by the assembly. Only the action as proposed and disposed is recorded in the minutes; none of the debate is included unless the minutes are published.

Minutes record only action taken. Remarks and debate are never entered in the minutes unless a motion was adopted to do so. Minutes should be accurate, up-to-date, and written in parliamentary language. They should record only what was done, not what was said.

Minutes of the meetings of an organization belong to the society and can be made available to the members for reference. (Board minutes are not read to the general assembly and are approved by the board.)

Minutes of the previous meeting are read for approval or correction at each regular meeting, which approval the Chair usually determines by *general consent*.

For easy reference, minutes should be written in outline form, not in narrative style. Each item or new subject begins a new paragraph.

Minutes are usually approved and corrected by *general consent*. The Chair may assume the motion to approve the minutes and declare them approved, with no objection. Corrections are treated in the same manner. If there is an objection, a vote is taken. A majority vote is required. Minutes may also be corrected at a later time, provided proof of the error has been submitted, by use of the motion to **Amend Something Previously Adopted**.

The secretary reads the minutes of the previous meeting, not the "last meeting." The secretary signs the minutes with name and title. After approval, the minutes may be cosigned by the president.

Minutes should contain the following:

1. Kind of meeting, regular or special, name of society, date, time the meeting was called to order, and place—if different from the regular one—and the presence of a quorum.
2. Who presided (use full name and title) and who took the minutes (name and title in final signature).
3. Disposition of previous minutes.
4. All main motions in exact words as stated by the Chair with the full name of the proposer—not the seconder—whether adopted or rejected.
5. All other motions on which a vote was taken.
6. All *points of order* and *appeals*, including the Chair's reason for the ruling and the result of the vote on appeal.
7. All notices of motions to be made in the future (previous notice).
8. All counted votes for each side.
9. Treasurer's statement, including amount on hand at the previous meeting, receipts, disbursements and amount on hand at the current meeting (in totals only).
10. Reports of other officers, including full name and title of the reporting officer, and name of the report, if any—not the report itself.
11. Reports of committees, standing and then special (ad hoc), including the full name of the reporting member and the name of the committee or its assignment. (The report itself is placed on file, and recommendations are treated as main motions.)
12. Names of members appointed to special (ad hoc) committees, together with the name of the committee and its purpose.

13. Important announcements pertaining to the whole society.
14. The name of the speaker or title of speech program or panel, for historical references. (Optional, according to custom.)
15. Hour of adjournment.
16. Signature and title of the recording secretary or, in the secretary's absence, that of the secretary pro tem.

The presence of a quorum may be announced by the presiding officer at the call to order and so entered in the minutes.

Minutes of a special meeting are read for approval at the next regular meeting or, as in convention, are approved by a minutes committee. Minutes are read and approved at an adjourned meeting.

If the reading of minutes has been deferred until a later meeting or to a later time in the same meeting, the reading must be done for approval or correction at that later time.

Printed and distributed minutes need not be read orally, although certain portions may be read on request. The Chair asks for approval of the minutes as distributed.

The president can help the secretary by announcing, in order, each item of business clearly, identifying each speaker or proposer, and stating the motions accurately and clearly. The president should require all lengthy or complex motions to be submitted in writing and should provide the secretary with a copy of those motions and any printed or written materials to be used during the meeting.

The president should require an advance copy of the minutes before they are read to the assembly.

Once minutes are entered in the minutes book, they are never to be erased or obliterated. If the membership wishes to undo some past action, the motion to **Rescind and Expunge** is in order. If adopted, the secretary circles or crosses out the portion of the minutes to be expunged and writes in the left margin, "Expunged by order of the assembly" with the date, and signs the notation together with the president. That action is not referred to or read again.

Review Quiz #1

LESSON 17: MINUTES

1.   Why are minutes kept?

_____

_____

2.   Why should minutes be approved?

_____

_____

3.   Can minutes be corrected after they have been approved?

_____

_____

4.   How should motions be entered in the minutes?

_____

_____

5.   May members read and see a minutes book?

_____

_____

6.   Who approves board minutes?

_____

_____

Review Quiz #2

LESSON 17: MINUTES

Number in proper order information contained in the minutes from opening of meeting to close.

_____ Who presided

_____ Kind of meeting

_____ Disposition of previous minutes

_____ Name of society

_____ Date, time, place

_____ All points of order and appeals

_____ Hour of adjournment

_____ All main motions as stated by the Chair

_____ All notices of motions to be made

_____ Signature of who took the minutes

┌─ **Review Quiz #3** ─────────────────────────────┐

LESSON 17: MINUTES

Mark "T" for True or "F" for False for each statement and explain why statements labeled "F" are incorrect.

_____ 1. Counted votes should always be recorded.

_____ 2. All proposals should be entered whether or not they have been stated by the Chair.

_____ 3. A member may request to have a dissenting vote entered in the minutes.

_____ 4. The president may order insertion in the minutes of something not considered at the meeting.

_____ 5. Minutes may be corrected at any date.

_____ 6. Minutes of a regular meeting are read at a special meeting.

_____ 7. Uncounted votes may be entered in the minutes as "unanimous."

┌─ **Review Quiz #4** ─────────────────────────────┐

LESSON 17: MINUTES

List at least five items that should NOT be recorded in the minutes.

_____

_____

_____

_____

_____

_____

LESSON 18
FINANCES

"Every organization, large or small, should establish and maintain an appropriate accounting system for its funds."

Alice Sturgis, *Standard Code of Parliamentary Procedure*

⌐ LESSON OBJECTIVE

To show the necessity for well-kept records of income and expenditure of an organization.

⌐ READING ASSIGNMENT

Robert pp. 451-452, 467-470, 580
Sturgis pp. 178, 203-205

Demeter p. 253

Riddick pp. 25-26, 95-96, 171-172

⌐ LESSON MATERIAL

All viable organizations need funds with which to operate and carry out their purpose. Budgets must be able to compensate for the unforeseen, must be realistic and attainable. A budget must be prepared having considered needs, plans and expectations. A financial accounting should be accurate and appropriate. A budget is the first requirement.

CONTENTS OF BUDGETS

Budgets should not exceed anticipated income. Income budgets consist of expected possible sources of income such as dues, special fees, sales, conference fees, fund-raising projects, donations. Expense budgets would include a review of the previous year's expenses, and requests, including supporting arguments for committee expenses, and operating costs.

Bylaws and standing rules should be referred to for financial obligations such as donations, president's expenses, awards, programs and training sessions.

Minutes of the previous year should indicate approved projects requiring funds for the coming year.

No items of expense should be overlooked.

Items obtained gratis should be noted, as this might not be permanent. If the adopted income is exceeded by the expenses, each item must be reduced, not necessarily pro rata, until the expenses aggregate no more than the expected income. This might require a reevaluation of the anticipated income. Within reason, it might be possible to dip into a reserve to fund a particular expense, but a group should never adopt a deficit budget which exceeds all reserves.

If an adjustment in the budget is required, it may be amended by striking out an amount from one item and inserting in another.

Budgets are proposed by the treasurer and other members appointed for that purpose. All past accounts should be in order before a new administration will assume the responsibility of handling organization funds.

The finance committee, with the treasurer, submits a budget to the assembly for its approval. The committee may advise on ways to help finance authorized projects. The committee may not buy or execute financial transactions, but may make recommendations.

PROTECTION

Careful watch should be kept over income and outgo. Receipts and disbursements should be recorded accurately and reported to the membership at its regular meetings. The budget as submitted may be adopted by a majority vote. It may be amended at any time by striking out an amount from one item and inserting it in another.

It is not possible to increase the budget unless additional revenue becomes available. Adoption of the budget does not permit the treasurer to pay bills automatically. Bills are submitted to the membership or board as stated in the bylaws, who authorize payment which is recorded in the minutes. If considerable funds are involved, the treasurer should be bonded.

Audit of the treasurer's books protects the society from fraud, misuse or manipulation of funds. The auditor verifies the accuracy of the treasurer's report or exposes errors. The auditor should be qualified to do the work. If the bylaws do not provide for an audit, any member may move to have the financial records audited, adopted by majority vote. Every organization should have a regular audit, usually done once a year and reported at the annual meeting.

The treasurer makes available to the auditor copies of bylaws, treasurer's books, adopted budget, vouchers, cancelled checks, receipts and any other financial memoranda such as copies of the minutes.

Bank deposits and checks issued and paid should balance. The balances should equal. Approval for payments should be checked. If there is a discrepancy in the records, the treasurer is responsible to explain.

AUDITOR'S REPORT

The auditor's report, carrying with it the report of the treasurer, is presented to the assembly. The Chair may assume the motion for approval and take the vote. A majority adopts.

Treasurer's Report
of the Community Service Society
For Year Ending
June 1, 19____

Cash Balance on Hand May 31, 19____ $1,000.00

Receipts (Name each item)

_____ $ _____

_____   _____

_____   _____

Total Receipts   800.00 $ 800.00
Total $1,800.00

Expenditures (Itemize)

_____   _____

_____   _____

_____   _____

Total Expenditures   600.00 $ 600.00

Cash Balance on Hand
May 31, 19____ $1,200.00

Total $1,800.00

                               John Doe, Treasurer

Audited and found to be correct.
(Names of Auditing Committee)
(Date of audit)

BUDGET

In establishing the proposed budget for the year, it is helpful to set up the financial format to include the previous year's budget and the previous year's actual income/expense in addition to indicating proposed budget for the current year. This provides a base for determining the efficiency and practicality of proposed budget amounts for the various line items of income and expense. Once established and approved, the operating budget should be reviewed on a monthly, or at least a quarterly, basis against actual current income and expense.

An easy-to-use format for this is indicated below:

19____ OPERATING BUDGET			
	19____ Budget	19____ Actual	Variance
INCOME	Can show on a	Can show on a	Indicate difference
List line items of income	yearly, quarterly or monthly	yearly, quarterly or monthly	between budget and actual to
TOTAL INCOME	basis	basis	provide review of financial operation
EXPENSES			
List line items of expense			
TOTAL EXPENSE			
EXCESS (DEFICIT)			

Review Quiz #1

LESSON 18: FINANCES

Finish these sentences.

1. Allocation of an organization's expenditure of funds is determined by _____

    _____

2. Two main items included in preparing a budget are

    _____

    _____

3. Adoption of a budget is authorized by _____

    _____

4. A budget may be amended if _____

    _____

    _____

5. An audit is valuable because _____

    _____

    _____

6. The treasurer's report is not submitted to vote because

    _____

    _____

7. Adoption of a budget does not permit the treasurer to

    _____

    _____

┌─**Review Quiz #2** ─────────────────────────────────┐

LESSON 18: FINANCES

Write a treasurer's monthly report.

LESSON 19
OFFICERS

"It is the duty of all officers to obey the bylaws and rules and to obey and execute all lawful orders of the body, else they betray their trust."

Demeter's Manual of Parliamentary Law and Procedure

LESSON OBJECTIVE

To learn the responsibilities and duties of elected officers.

READING ASSIGNMENT

Robert pp. 438-456   **Demeter** pp. 250-258
Sturgis pp. 153-165   **Riddick** pp. 124-130

LESSON MATERIAL

Officers should be elected who have qualities of competency, stability, integrity and concern. An organization may have as many officers as it needs or desires, so long as the officers' titles and duties are provided for in the bylaws. The bylaws should also specify how officers shall be elected or appointed, the term of office and number of terms, the qualifications for the office and how vacancies in the office should be filled. More than half a term of service is considered a term when filling vacancies or reelecting to office.

Officers, as members of the organization, have the same rights as regular members but with additional power to conduct the responsibilities of their offices.

PRESIDENT

The president has the dual role of:

1. **Presiding officer**, for which he has the authority to conduct all meetings of the society and board unless stated otherwise in the bylaws. He has the duty to preside impartially, to know and use correct procedural rules, to insist upon proper decorum in debate, to maintain order at all times, to rule on all *points of order*, to protect members' rights. He must take the vote and announce the result accurately. If the president or an officially designated substitute does not preside, the meeting is an irregular assembly and decisions are invalid.

2. **Administrator.** The president must set goals, plan for their implementation, supervise the organization's activities. Therefore, the president frequently serves as ex officio member of all committees, with the exception of the nominating committee.

The president listens to problems, offers advice, observes and is aware of the "hidden agenda" in order to insure the harmonious progress of the organization.

The president speaks for and represents the organization to the public and signs all necessary documents, as well as appointing members of committees as provided in the bylaws or by vote of the assembly.

VICE PRESIDENT

Because the vice president may be required to act for the president at any time, that person should possess the same qualities of competence as the president. A vice president should not "move up" automatically to the office of president.

When serving in the absence of the president, the vice president has all the powers and responsibilities of the president. However, the vice president cannot alter the rulings of the president, cannot fill vacancies, nor make appointments, and cannot serve ex officio for the president, unless he becomes the president in fact.

If there is more than one vice president, the officers should be numbered. Vice presidents accede to office in numerical order so that the vacancy occurs in the lowest office.

The vice president usually is assigned an important chairmanship or duty.

PRESIDENT-ELECT

This office should be created only for large organizations with widely scattered membership. It can exist only if provided in the bylaws, which should state specific responsibilities and limitations for the office. The president-elect should be chosen for the same qualifications required for the president.

Usually the president-elect automatically becomes the next president without ever being elected directly to that office. In addition, the president-elect assumes such other powers or authority as may be provided in the bylaws.

TREASURER

The treasurer holds a position of trust and is legally responsible for protecting the monies of the organization. If large sums are involved, the treasurer should be bonded.

The treasurer collects and disburses funds as directed, deposits money promptly in the bank of the organization's choice, keeps accurate financial records, helps prepare the budget, prepares tax forms and presents a report in detail for the audit at the annual meeting. During that meeting, the auditor's report, which contains the official verified report of the treasurer, is adopted. The motion to adopt the auditor's report may be assumed. It requires a majority vote, or it may be adopted by *general consent* without objection.

At each regular meeting, the treasurer presents a statement of the total amount on hand at the preceding meeting, receipts, disbursements and the amount on hand at the current meeting. A copy of that statement should be given to the secretary to insure accuracy in recording. No action should be taken on this report since it has not been verified.

SECRETARY

The position of secretary is the second most important of the elected positions. Along with the president, the secretary must be present in order for the meeting to be valid. (A presiding officer is necessary to conduct the meeting and a secretary to record action taken.) Some organizations call the secretary "clerk" or "recorder."

The secretary is a member of the board, serving there also as secretary. In the absence or tardiness of the president and vice-president, the secretary acts to call the meeting to order for the election of a presiding officer pro tem.

A secretary should qualify as one who can write grammatically and accurately, who has some knowledge of procedural rules. The secretary should transcribe notes promptly and neatly in the minutes book and be able to write an intelligent, informative, persuasive and tactful letter for the organization unless this assignment is allotted to a corresponding secretary.

A secretary must be responsible to:

1. Take minutes accurately, reading them in a clear, audible, pleasant voice.
2. Prepare the agenda, including all unfinished business and special orders.
3. Keep an accurate, up-to-date account of all proceedings (minutes) and send a copy to the president within a reasonable time in advance of the next meeting.
4. Keep records of all committee memberships, chairmen and committee reports.
5. Furnish committees with whatever documents or orders are required.
6. Furnish delegates with proper credentials and notify officers and chairmen of their appointments.
7. Keep an accurate membership roll.
8. Sign all copies of assembly decisions.
9. Send out all notices unless a corresponding secretary has been elected.
10. Be custodian of all records, rules, minutes and keep them readily accessible.

The secretary has the same right as any other member to participate in the business of the meeting but is usually too busy to exercise this right.

The secretary may cast the elective ballot only if provided for in the bylaws.

OTHER
OFFICERS

Other officers and their duties may be provided for in the bylaws. Such officers may include corresponding secretary, executive secretary, sergeant-at-arms, historian, and so on.

EXECUTIVE
SECRETARY
OR EXECUTIVE
DIRECTOR

This officer is often required in a very large organization, and usually serves as a general manager. This member is employed by the executive board, as stated in its bylaws or elected at a convention. The executive secretary serves by direction of the board, attends board meetings, does not have a vote on the board unless elected as a member of the board.

⌐Review Quiz #1

LESSON 19: OFFICERS

Complete the following sentences.

1.   Officers should be selected for

_____

_____

_____

_____

2.   Bylaws should contain the following requirements for office:

_____

_____

_____

_____

3.   A president has the duty and responsibility to

_____

_____

_____

_____

4.   As administrator, the president is responsible to

_____

_____

_____

_____

5.   As presiding officer, the president must know

_____

_____

_____

_____

6. The vice president should be highly qualified because

_____

_____

_____

_____

7. After the term of office of the president expires, the president-elect

_____

_____

_____

_____

8. The treasurer reports at each regular meeting on the financial condition of the society, but no

_____

_____

_____

_____

9. The most important role of the secretary is to

_____

_____

_____

_____

10. Officers required to be present for a meeting to be valid are

_____

_____

_____

_____

┌─ **Review Quiz #2** ───────────────────────────────┐

LESSON 19: OFFICERS

1.   What should be contained in bylaws relating to offices?

_____

_____

_____

2.   If there is more than one vice president, how is succession to
       office of president determined?

_____

_____

_____

3.   Why should a society provide for an annual audit?

_____

_____

_____

4.   What is the unusual feature in the election of the president-
       elect?

_____

_____

_____

5.   What officers are the legal representatives of the organization?

_____

_____

_____

_____

6. What is the chief responsibility of a secretary?

_____

_____

_____

_____

7. What is the chief responsibility of the treasurer?

_____

_____

_____

_____

8. Can the elected president delegate his duty to preside?

_____

_____

_____

_____

9. Can the treasurer issue checks for payment on his own authority?

_____

_____

_____

_____

10. What are the duties of a sergeant-at-arms?

_____

_____

_____

_____

LESSON 20
EXECUTIVE BOARD
BOARD OF DIRECTORS

"Members provide in the bylaws that a small elected group acting as the representatives of all the members shall carry on the work of the organization during the intervals between meetings of the membership."

Alice Sturgis, *Standard Code of Parliamentary Procedure*

LESSON OBJECTIVE

To learn the duties, powers and limitations of an executive board.

READING ASSIGNMENT

Robert pp. 471-479   Demeter pp. 269-273
Sturgis pp. 161-162, 173-174, 230   Riddick pp. 27-30

LESSON MATERIAL

Although membership is the final authority, executive boards or boards of directors are the power structure of the organization. The members are elected or appointed according to the bylaws to do the work for the membership between its meetings and to exercise routine management of the organization as defined in its bylaws.

COMPOSITION

Executive boards are usually composed of elected officers, chairmen of standing committees (in some organizations) and such others as are specified in the bylaws. Terms of office should be staggered so that some experienced members will be serving on the board at all times. An uneven number of members is preferable, to help avoid tie votes. Board members should be competent and experienced; they should be familiar with bylaws, customs, policies and procedural rules, or orientation to these items should be provided. Board members should be willing to work diligently and in good faith. Board members are considered officers of the organization.

DUTIES
AND POWERS

Boards formulate policies, correlate activities, discover problems, recommend solutions and carry out assignments from the membership. They prepare and usually control financial plans subject to membership approval and are responsible to adhere to the purposes of the organization. In general, board members should support the goals of the president. No board member, other than the president, has authority to speak for the board or to interpret board action. All decisions of the board must be the result of group action. Boards act for the entire organization when its meetings are not in session.

CONDUCT
OF BOARDS

Boards meet at regularly stated intervals. They may make their own rules if such rules do not conflict with parent bylaws or any laws. Formality of conduct is in ratio to the size of the board; the larger the board, the more formality is required.

No business is valid unless the meeting was properly called and a quorum present. The quorum of a board is the majority of its members, unless otherwise stated in the bylaws.

Rules of decorum must be observed, but there generally should be no limit to the turns of each member to speak and no motion is in order to limit or close debate. Boards must provide sufficient opportunity for full exploration of proposals and problems placed before them.

In small boards, informal consideration may precede actual proposals.

The chairman, if a member, may participate fully, to speak, to make motions and to vote.

The elected president and the secretary of the parent body serve on the board in the same capacity. Some corporate boards, however, elect a chairman, who presides and supersedes the position of president.

With the exception of the president and/or the chairman of the board, no board member has more authority than any other board member, and no individual assignment from a board member, or interpretation of board action, is valid unless authorized by the board. To be valid, all decisions of the board must be the result of group action.

A board member's vote, as with any member, should be withheld if there is a conflict of interest, unless full disclosure has been made and permission to vote granted.

Any board member is liable for action taken by the board unless that member recorded a dissenting vote prior to the action taken.

Adopted motions of the board remain in effect until completed or rescinded.

Unfinished business of an outgoing board is terminated with that administration.

Conducting board votes by means of mail or by telephone calls to individual board members is not valid voting unless teleconference voting has been approved in the bylaws and is properly conducted.

BOARD LIMITATIONS

Board members must take direction from the membership, which can amend or countermand action taken by the board.

A board cannot create offices, add to its membership, fill any vacancies, elect officers, punish members, except as provided in bylaws or charter.

Although boards may be given broad comprehensive powers, even full power to act in certain circumstances, no board may assume certain powers merely because those powers were not expressly prohibited in the bylaws.

No board may delegate its responsibilities; it may appoint subcommittees which answer to it but may not act for it.

Boards cannot concern themselves with issues outside the objects of the organization.

Boards usually should not meet during the regular business sessions of the organization except to carry out orders or to prepare a recommendation.

No board may encumber a succeeding board.

MINUTES OF THE BOARD

Proceedings of the board must be recorded accurately in the board minutes, read to and approved by the board. Board minutes may be read or read in part to the general assembly by board permission or by motion adopted by majority vote of the assembly to produce them.

The **managerial functions** of the board are to:

- Formulate policies, plan strategy, recommend.

- Appoint, supervise committees as bylaws direct.

- See that bylaws are kept up-to-date.

- Manage the financial plans, budget, insurance.

- Select the executive secretary, if any.

- Determine board rules and procedures.

- Implement plans and projects.

The **chairman of a board** should:

- Think positively.

- Keep informed.

- See problems in perspective.

- Be comfortable with opposing sides as necessary for good decision-making.

- Achieve decisions made on facts, not from hearsay.

THE EXECUTIVE COMMITTEE

The establishment of an executive committee must be provided for in the bylaws. The board may elect from among its own members a small committee, usually including the president and other officers. This committee meets to carry out board directives when the board is not in session. It reports to the board, which report is included in board minutes. The committee usually functions as authorized by the board to investigate and recommend on sensitive matters dealing with personnel, discipline, negotiations or property deals. It cannot rescind action taken by the board.

PROCEDURES IN SMALL BOARDS

In small boards (up to about 12 members), some of the formality that is necessary in a large assembly would hinder business. Therefore, the procedures governing such meetings are different from the rules that prevail in larger meetings, in the following respects:

1. Members are not required to obtain the floor (rise and be recognized) before making motions and speaking.
2. Motions need not be seconded.
3. There is no limit to the number of times a member can speak on a question.
4. Informal discussion of a subject is permitted while no motion is pending.
5. The Chair need not rise while putting questions to vote.
6. The Chair can speak in discussion without rising or leaving the Chair.
7. The Chair can make motions and vote on all questions.
8. Motions to close or limit debate **generally** should not be entertained in small boards.
9. There is no limitation as to **when** or as to the **number** of times reconsideration can be moved. *Reconsideration* can be moved, not only by one who voted on the winning (prevailing) side, but also by one who abstained or was absent. A two-thirds vote is required, unless all members who voted on the prevailing side are present or have received notification of the intention to move to **Reconsider**—in which case only a majority vote is required.

┌─ **PRACTICE EXERCISE** ────────────────────────┐

1.   In brief, how are board meetings conducted?

   _____

   _____

   _____

   _____

   _____

2.   Can any board member validly interpret board decisions?

   _____

   _____

   _____

   _____

   _____

3.   How is a board different from a deliberative society?

   _____

   _____

   _____

   _____

   _____

4.   How does the Chair participate in board meetings?

   _____

   _____

   _____

   _____

┌─**Review Quiz #1**─────────────────────────────┐

LESSON 20:   EXECUTIVE BOARD
BOARD OF DIRECTORS

1.   For what reason is an executive board created?

_____

_____

_____

_____

2.   What could be the composition of an executive board?

_____

_____

_____

_____

3.   What rules govern the conduct of a board?

_____

_____

_____

_____

4.   What are board responsibilities?

_____

_____

_____

_____

5.   Who is entitled to hear the minutes of the board?

_____

_____

_____

_____

6.   Are all board members equal in rank?

_____

_____

_____

_____

7.   Does a board have specific limitations?

_____

_____

_____

_____

8.   What happens to a motion adopted by the preceding board?

_____

_____

_____

_____

9.   What is an executive committee?

_____

_____

_____

_____

10.   Do boards have exclusive powers?

_____

_____

_____

_____

┌─ **Review Quiz #2** ──────────────────────┐

LESSON 20: EXECUTIVE BOARD
BOARD OF DIRECTORS

Mark "T" for True or "F" for False for each statement and explain why statements labeled "F" are incorrect.

___F___ 1. Boards resolve all problems for the assembly.

___T___ 2. Board rules for conducting its meetings must be in the bylaws.

___T___ 3. Board members can fill vacancies.

___T___ 4. Boards can act only when in actual session.

___T___ 5. Board minutes are confidential property of the board.

___T___ 6. Certain boards have autonomous control.

___F___ 7. A board reports its deliberations to the assembly.

___T___ 8. Motion adopted by previous boards remain until rescinded.

___T___ 9. Boards should recommend policies.

___F___ 10. The president as an ex officio member of the board is counted in the quorum.

___T___ 11. Board members should know the bylaws and rules of the organization.

___T___ 12. An executive committee is a board within a board.

F ___T___ 13. All board members have equal authority as members of the board.

___T___ 14. Unfinished business of the outgoing board terminates with that administration.

___F___ 15. A board member may vote even if he will gain personally while others do not.

_T_ 16. Action taken by a board becomes the liability of every member.

_F_ 17. Teleconferences may be conducted without authorization in the bylaws.

_T_ 18. An executive committee must be provided for in the bylaws.

_T_ 19. Boards meet regularly between meetings of the organization.

_T_ 20. All business of the board must be the result of group decision.

LESSON 21
MEMBERSHIP

"Members are essential to any organization. They provide the officers, workers, money, ideas and source of achievement."

Riddick Butcher, *Riddick's Rules of Procedure*

LESSON OBJECTIVE

To learn the rights and obligations of members.

READING ASSIGNMENT

Robert pp. 291-293, 371-384, 565-566

Demeter pp. 6-7, 28-30, 56

Sturgis pp. 210-216

Riddick pp. 109-111

LESSON MATERIAL

Members are the lifeblood of an organization, for without members there can be no work done, no money, no ideas, no achievement.

Members have ultimate control over a volunteer organization, for they make their own rules subject only to regulations from a parent organization, if any, and the local, state or national laws.

Members are obligated to observe their own adopted parliamentary authorities unless provisions have been made for their suspension.

Because bylaws are written to protect all members, no one member has special privileges over another member unless granted by the membership. The rights of members are protected under law, but only in relation to the rights of all members.

Membership is defined as having rights and obligations of participation in a society's activities according to the classification of membership set in the bylaws. Such classification may be: active, associate, honorary, student, family or organization. Bylaws should specify the rights of each class. Bylaws should also contain requirements for eligibility to membership, application and acceptance procedures, dues or any other required fees, provisions for resignation and causes for suspension or expulsion. A prospective member should read the bylaws of an organization before becoming a member.

Fundamentally, members have the right to do the following:

1. Attend meetings.
2. Propose business.
3. Speak for or against a proposition.
4. Vote or abstain from voting.
5. Nominate and be nominated for office.
6. Serve on committees.
7. Inspect official records, receive up-to-date copies of by-laws and adopted rules.
8. Resign.
9. Elect officers.
10. Have a trial, if accused, and a fair hearing.
11. Expect equitable treatment from members and officers.
12. Receive notices.
13. Enjoy the social functions of the organization.

To sustain these rights, members have the obligation to:

1. Qualify for membership.
2. Pay dues promptly.
3. Attend meetings and remain until adjournment.
4. Serve on committees.
5. Participate in decision-making.
6. Protect the good name of the society.
7. Abide by the decisions of the majority.
8. Obey the legitimate orders of the Chair and their own adopted rules.
9. Observe proper decorum during debate.
10. Increase the membership.
11. Learn procedural rules.
12. Become familiar with bylaws and other documents of authority adopted by the organization.
13. Keep informed of organization activities.
14. Choose well-qualified officers.

The organization has certain rights, among which are the following:

1. To discipline its members.
2. To suspend or expel its members by such processes as described in its bylaws or adopted authority.
3. To establish requirements for eligibility.
4. To determine dues and other assessment fees.
5. To write its own bylaws and rules.
6. To delegate authority to others, within legal limits.

Members have certain privileges:

1. To see or, better, to own a copy of the bylaws and standing rules.
2. To receive all notices.
3. To speak without interruption, unless it is authorized.
4. To appeal the Chair's ruling.
5. To change one's vote before the result is announced by the Chair (except by ballot vote).
6. To request one's minority vote to be recorded.

Motions that particularly affect members' rights and usually require a two-thirds vote are:

1. Adopt bylaws.
2. Amend something previously adopted.
3. Close nominations.
4. Object to consideration.
5. Rescind without previous notice.
6. Close debate.
7. Limit debate.
8. Suspend the rules.
9. Require a member to reveal his vote in order to propose a motion to reconsider (**Robert**).

┌─**Review Quiz** ─────────────────────────────┐

LESSON 21: MEMBERSHIP

1.   If in arrears for dues, may a member vote?

_____

_____

2.   May a member refuse to serve on a committee?

_____

_____

3.   May a member vote for himself?

_____

_____

4.   Under what conditions may membership be terminated?

_____

_____

5.   What is meant by an honorary member?

_____

_____

6.   May a member refuse to serve as an officer?

_____

_____

7.   May a member who has a direct personal or pecuniary interest in a proposition vote on it?

_____

_____

8. What is meant by "member in good standing"?

_____

_____

_____

9. List five rights of membership.

_____

_____

_____

10. List five obligations of membership.

_____

_____

_____

11. What should be included in the bylaws articles?

_____

_____

_____

12. Define membership.

_____

_____

_____

13. What are the rights of an ex officio member?

_____

_____

_____

14. Is a vote taken on a resignation?

_____

_____

_____

LESSON 22
COMMITTEES

"Through the use of committees the responsibilities of an organization are apportioned among its members."

Alice Sturgis, *Standard Code of Parliamentary Procedure*

LESSON OBJECTIVE

To learn the values, composition and responsibility of committees and how they function.

READING ASSIGNMENT

Robert pp. 479-492   **Demeter** pp. 269-278
Sturgis pp. 50-52, 166-172, 182-187   **Riddick** pp. 48-55, 167-168

LESSON MATERIAL

Committees are small groups, appointed or elected to do the work for many. Their importance should not be underestimated. Members, in committee, have the time and the patience to pursue their assignment. A society should not create a committee unless there is a valid reason for its existence. Committees are important in democratic decision-making, but their influence is not often realized except by those experienced in group processes.

The advantages of a small group allow a committee to work efficiently. The members can think together constructively and share the credit, since the orientation in committees is usually "we" and "us," not "I" and "me." Communication thrives in the informal conduct of a committee, as the group seeks answers and solutions and there is no winner or loser.

TYPES OF COMMITTEES

A **standing committee** is a permanent group. Members may be appointed or elected as established by the rules of the organization, and their duties and powers are generally specific. These committees often work independently of the parent organization, but they make progress reports from time to time as well as an annual report.

Usually the term of membership on a standing committee coincides with that of the officers' term of administration. Frequently the term is staggered so that only a part of the committee goes out of office at one time. It is considered wise to retain a nucleus of experienced persons on a permanent committee.

Although standing committees are usually provided for in the bylaws, a standing committee may exist by custom or common practice, such as a committee to purchase a gift for each retiring president and to attend to similar matters.

SPECIAL OR AD HOC COMMITTEE

A **special** or **ad hoc** (for this purpose only) **committee** is created for a particular purpose and continues in existence until the work is completed and a final report given, or it has been discharged by the assembly. No special committee should be created to do the work of an existing committee. A special committee is created for a designated purpose by a motion from the floor or as bylaws provide.

Special committees meet as often as required. If the work is complicated or the committee large, a secretary may be elected. Meetings should be called by the committee chairman, but if the chairman fails to do so, any two members of the committee may call the meeting, provided all members have been notified. Once the committee work is completed and the report prepared and signed by a majority of concurring members, the report is presented and the committee dissolves automatically (e.g., a nominating committee).

Special committees are created for one of three purposes: to investigate, to recommend action or to take action.

1. **To investigate**: An organization may need more information before it can intelligently consider what action should be taken in a particular situation. The group may assign to a committee the responsibility of gathering and reporting simple facts.

   For example, suppose that a club was considering holding a picnic but lacked information about where it should be held. A committee is assigned to investigate the various parks and picnic grounds available and to report the facts so that the club could consider the information and make a decision. Such a committee is an investigative or fact-finding committee. It merely reports facts, and the organization makes the decision.

2. **To recommend action**: The club may wish to give the committee the responsibility of making a decision, after investigation, and offering that decision to the club for adoption. Such a committee might be called an action-recommending committee. In this case the club would move to adopt the recommendations of the committee and, if passed, the decision of the committee would be carried out by the club. For example, the committee might be instructed to find a suitable place for a picnic, with further instructions concerning the necessary facilities such as softball diamond, picnic tables, swimming beach and cooking facilities. The committee would then be asked to recommend the place that it thinks would best suit the wishes of the club.

3. **To take action**: When a matter is referred to a committee with full power to act, the committee acts autonomously, but the society is responsible for and bound by the action taken by the committee.

   The club wishing to hold the picnic might assign to the committee the responsibility of deciding on a place and making all the necessary arrangements or contracts. On the other hand, the club may have decided on a place, but may instruct the committee to make all arrangements.

EXECUTIVE COMMITTEE

The executive committee must be provided for in the bylaws. The board may elect from among its own members a small committee, usually including the president and other officers. This committee meets to carry out board directives when the board is not in session. It reports to the board, with the report included in board minutes. The committee usually functions as authorized by the board to investigate and recommend on sensitive matters dealing with personnel, discipline, negotiations or property deals. It cannot rescind action taken by the board.

EX OFFICIO MEMBER

Occasionally a member is made a member of a committee by virtue of some office that she holds. Perhaps the treasurer, holding the office of treasurer, is made an ex officio member of the finance committee. "Ex officio" simply means "from office" or by virtue of office. This ex officio member would have all the rights and privileges of any committee member, including the right to speak and the right to vote. She would also be counted in determining the quorum. The exception here would be the president, who is often made an ex officio member of all committees except the nominating committee. In this case, the president would not be counted in the quorum.

Sometimes a nonmember of the society, one who is not under the authority of the organization, is made an ex officio member of a board or committee because of special talent or knowledge that she possesses or some office that she holds. This ex officio member would have all the rights of committee membership, including speaking, voting and making motions, but none of the obligations of membership. If such an ex officio member has no obligation to participate, she would not be counted in the quorum.

When an ex officio member no longer holds the office that entitles her to committee membership, her membership automatically ends.

COMPOSITION OF COMMITTEES

A committee may consist of any number of persons, but usually those committees created for action should consist of a small number of members in favor of the action. A member who is not in favor of the action should be replaced.

Those committees created for investigation should be fairly large and composed of members representing conflicting points of view. The value of such a committee is reduced if varying points of view are not represented. A committee should have an uneven number of members in order to avoid a deadlock or tie.

A committee is a miniature assembly, but it is not bound by all the same rules. It has more freedom and less formality, yet it is restricted to the duties as stated in the bylaws or the instructions from the parent body. The committee must follow those instructions and concern itself only with matters referred to it. Committee officers are always a chairman, often a secretary and rarely a vice chairman or treasurer, usually chosen by the committee.

SELECTION OF
COMMITTEE
MEMBERS

Great care should be taken in selecting a committee. If possible, persons who are interested in the matter, knowledgeable about the matter and willing to do the work should be selected.

There are several ways of selecting committee members. Each has its disadvantages:

1. **Volunteering** may supply an insufficient number or too many, both of which situations can be embarrassing. Some members who volunteer are not aware of their inadequacy for service on the particular committee. Others volunteer only to become listed on the committee and have no intention of giving service.

2. **Elections** often become popularity contests, and the majority point of view is frequently the only one represented.

3. **Appointments** require time, effort and good judgment if done correctly, not on the spur of the moment during a meeting. Such appointments leave the Chair open to criticism. If done well, appointments are the most successful method, because they guarantee that:

   A fair representation of opinions and abilities can be secured, and a cross-section of membership consisting of age, sex and experience can be obtained.

Appointments can be made after the prospective members have discussed the responsibilities and the time involved and have given their consent to serve.

Absentee membership can be prevented, because it is easier to say "no" face to face if a person does not wish to serve.

Committee members may be **appointed** in the following ways:

1. The member moving to refer may use the qualified form and name the members of the committee, saying, "I move that this matter be referred to a committee of three consisting of Mr. A, Miss B, and Mr. C." If the motion is adopted, these three persons constitute the committee. If no chairman was specified, the first name by custom serves as chairman. Some authorities advise, however, that the first person named should serve as temporary chairman until the committee elects its own chairman.

2. The unqualified motion to refer may be amended by another member who qualifies it by adding the names. Therefore, the motion, "I move that this matter be referred to a committee of three," may be amended to add "and that they consist of Mr. A, as chairman, Miss B, and Mr. C." If both the main motion and the amendment are passed, the committee is named.

3. After an unqualified motion to refer has been adopted, a member may move that the committee consist of certain members, saying, "I move that the committee be Mr. C, as chairman, Miss B, and Mr. A." The motion is debatable and amendable.

4. The committee may be appointed by the Chair, if authorized by bylaws or by motion to do so. The motion might be as follows: "I move to refer the matter to a committee of three, appointed by the Chair."

Members may be **elected** in these ways:

1. The committee may be nominated by the Chair and elected by the assembly. If any names nominated by the Chair are not elected (by majority vote or general consent), the Chair must continue to make nominations until a full committee has been selected. Members may not nominate.

2. The committee may be both nominated and elected by the assembly. If the exact number of names nominated is the same as that needed to fill the committee, no vote is necessary, and the Chair may declare that those nominated are elected as members of the committee. If more than enough names are nominated, the names are voted on in order of nomination until enough receive a majority vote. Both affirmative and negative votes are taken on each name to determine which names receive a majority. The remaining names are ignored.

CONDUCT OF
COMMITTEES

Committees have no inherent powers, only those assigned to them by the assembly.

The assembly may appoint certain members as ex officio members, who have rights but no obligations.

The assembly may discharge the committee before it completes its final assignment or makes its final report.

Committees are subordinate to the power that created them; therefore, they cannot add to or subtract from the membership or fill vacancies. Committees may meet as often as necessary if a quorum (majority of committee) is present.

Committee business is usually conducted informally. There is no time limit on debate and no limit to the number of times a member may speak, although only one member may speak at a time. No motion to close debate is in order. A motion adopted may be reconsidered as often as required, and reconsideration may be moved by any member. (**Robert** qualifies that by adding "any member who has not voted in opposition.")

The committee may make its own rules as long as those rules do not conflict with the laws of the organization.

Subcommittees may be appointed from among the committee members.

Hearings may be held, where nonmembers may be invited to give expert opinion or advice. These persons usually may not remain for the committee's deliberations.

PROBLEM-SOLVING IN COMMITTEES

A committee takes five essential steps in arriving at a decision:

1. Identifying the problem, considering questions relating to who, what, where and why.
2. Agreeing on the criteria by which solutions will be weighed and considered, in light of the available resources such as people, time and money.
3. Proposing possible solutions by using such methods as brain-storming (being creative but not critical at the time of idea presentation) to bring numerous ideas before the group.
4. Selecting the best solution or solutions by analyzing the alternatives, balancing the benefits and considering possible circumstances. The solutions should be measured by the criteria previously agreed upon.
5. Writing up the report so that it will be understood by those not serving on the committee. The rationale for the decisions should be given. Usually this rationale consists of a statement like the following: "Because of A, B and C, therefore D."

COMMITTEE CHAIRMAN

A committee chairman should always be an active participant but should never dominate the group. Besides knowing procedural rules, the chairman should be able to work closely with people in a friendly, courteous, unhurried manner. Although informal discussion should be permitted, the chairman should observe decorum and ensure that all decisions are majority decisions.

A committee chairman has definite responsibilities:

1. To select a time convenient for all and to give adequate notice.
2. To select and secure a comfortable and quiet meeting place where interruptions will be minimal.
3. To supervise and keep in touch with each member.
4. To start on time, a quorum present, with no wait for stragglers.
5. To open with statements outlining the assignment and proposing methods for solutions and have copies of all necessary documents, motions and assignments.
6. To provide ample discussion with provisions for note-taking and preparation of the final report.
7. To ensure that all members may enter discussion fully and freely.

8. To plan for another meeting as necessary, ensuring that each member undertakes duties to prepare for it.
9. To close on a positive note, reviewing progress and thanking the group for participation.

Often the committee fails because of its leader. Among the negative types of leaders are the following:

1. The "policeman," who looks at the chairman function primarily as one of keeping order. This type of leader expects to discipline the members and is conscious of position and authority. The "policeman" answers questions with finality as the group boss.
2. The "we-must-get-results" chairman, who is afraid that the group will not act swiftly enough. This type has little faith in the group's ability to think and has a prepared agenda from which there may be no departure. Such a chairman frequently forces the group to accept a product that is the chairman's and not that of the group.
3. The "good fellow," who believes that since two heads are better than one, seven heads must be even better. This leader believes that letting the group talk and talk will somehow get the task done. The "good fellow" has no ability to supervise, inspire and direct a group.

Besides incompetent leadership, committees often fail for these reasons:

1. Holding irregular or insufficient meetings without adequate advance notice.
2. Poor attendance.
3. Poor attitude about the value of the assignment.
4. Inadequate instructions.
5. Unrepresentative selection of members.
6. Lack of quiet, comfortable, relaxed atmosphere or environment.

ADVANTAGES OF COMMITTEES

1. They perform an important useful function, as described in the definition of a committee, as they apportion work among the members.
2. They are powerful tools to facilitate the transaction of business.
3. They shorten assembly meetings as they work on matters of importance but often of little interest to the general membership.

4. They provide for potential leadership, keep members interested, provide training in cooperation and participation, develop a sense of belonging on a team and sharing responsibility for action and decisions taken.
5. They provide time for research, fair deliberation, adequate consideration, attention to details.
6. They can work with less distraction, in more privacy.
7. They can utilize the expertise of selected members who may advise or explain.
8. They can, through informality and more intimacy, learn to empathize better with opposing opinions.
9. They provide a sense of self-identity through the contributions of service. Self-esteem can be enhanced.

DISADVANTAGES OF COMMITTEES

1. Personality conflicts become more noticeable in small groups.
2. Too many committees lead to too many divisions of opinion.
3. If given "full power," the control of the assembly is weakened.
4. Policy-making may become fragmented.
5. Duplication of effort may be increased.
6. Those created with no specific duties or purpose lead to apathy and nonattendance.

Review Quiz #1

LESSON 22: COMMITTEES

1. Demonstrate three methods of giving instructions to a committee.

2. List:

   a. Advantages of a committee.

   _____

   b. How a committee may be created.

   _____

   c. How committee business is conducted.

   _____

   d. Five responsibilities of a committee chairman.

   _____

┌─ **Review Quiz #2** ──────────────────────────────────┐
└──┘

LESSON 22: COMMITTEES

Mark "T" for True or "F" for False for each statement and explain why statements labeled "F" are incorrect.

_____	1.	Motions out of committee require a second.
_____	2.	Incompetent committees may be discharged.
_____	3.	Committees can be established by inference or custom.
_____	4.	A committee of one is legal.
_____	5.	Ex officio members have the same rights as regular members.
_____	6.	A committee may add to its group (if motion to create does not restrict).
_____	7.	A motion to reconsider may be moved an unlimited number of times in committees.
_____	8.	Volunteers make the best committee members.
_____	9.	A committee may determine its quorum.
_____	10.	Presidents are counted in the quorum of a committee.
_____	11.	Committees are created to perform three kinds of service.
_____	12.	A committee with "full powers" may act autonomously.

_____ 13. Special committees must be discharged after their final report.

_____ 14. The president must choose the committee chairman.

_____ 15. An executive committee acts as a board within a board.

_____ 16. Ad hoc committees are created by the president.

_____ 17. Committees may hold hearings of nonmembers.

_____ 18. A committee chairman may engage actively in partisan discussion.

┌─ **Review Quiz #3** ──────────────────────────┐
└──┘

LESSON 22: COMMITTEES

Discuss the following questions which could help expedite meetings.

1. Should committees keep minutes?

_____

_____

_____

_____

_____

2. How should the first committee meeting be organized?

_____

_____

_____

_____

_____

3. What is committee "brainstorming"?

_____

_____

_____

_____

_____

_____

4. What is known as the "Delphi Technique"?

_____

_____

_____

_____

_____

5. How can the Chair prevent any developing conflict?

_____

_____

_____

_____

_____

6. What is the best way to make committee decisions?

_____

_____

_____

_____

_____

_____

LESSON 23
COMMITTEE REPORTS

"A report of a subordinate board or a committee is an official statement formally adopted by, and submitted in the name of, the reporting body, informing the parent assembly of action taken or recommended, or information obtained."

Henry M. Robert, *Robert's Rules of Order Newly Revised*

LESSON OBJECTIVE

To learn how to write committee reports.

READING ASSIGNMENT

Robert pp. 493-521   Demeter pp. 278-284
Sturgis pp. 175-180   Riddick pp. 169-172

LESSON MATERIAL

Reports are essential to an organization to apprise members of what is being done or was done and to keep the record straight.

Reports are usually prepared by the chairman by authority of the committee and signed by all concurring members.

Reports are written in the third person.

Reports should contain information only on what was referred to the committee.

Reports requesting or recommending action may include the action to be taken presented in a resolution.

A signature to a report may not be withdrawn, as the report represents the action of a committee, not the members within the committee.

FORMS OF COMMITTEE REPORTS

The forms used by committees in making their reports are almost as varied as the number of committees, but there are certain rules that should be followed when a written report is submitted. The usual report is made verbally, when no written report is necessary. But if the report contains recommendations, resolutions or any other material that should be included in the records of the society, a written report should be submitted.

When the written report is submitted, it should begin with the name of the committee, its purpose and the date it was appointed. If the report is to be detailed, it includes a description of the assignment and the work done such as facts found, conclusions made and recommendations. The report should end with the word **Signed**, which should be followed by the signatures of all concurring members of the committee. The chairman's name should be first, with no designation. If the committee authorizes the chairman to sign the report, the only signature that appears is followed by the word **Chairman**. Committee reports are understood to be the report of the majority of the committee. Resolutions or recommendations coming from the committee are not seconded since they are considered seconded through discussion in committee. Reports are dated in the minutes from the day of the report.

There are several kinds of committee reports, depending upon the type of committee:

1. **Report of Fact**: When a committee is charged with the responsibility of investigating a matter and gathering facts, it makes a report of fact without recommendations for action as follows:

   The committee reports that Clark Park has the necessary facilities for the Pinion Civic Society annual picnic.

   Signed,
   George Smith
   Helen Brown
   Harry Boyd

2. **Action Report**:   Frequently a committee is given the responsibility of exercising its judgment in arriving at a decision and carrying out whatever action results from that decision. For example, the Pinion Civic Society might give its committee full power to decide on a place for the picnic and to make the necessary arrangements. In this case, the committee would report as follows:

Pinion, Michigan
May 13, 19__

To the Pinion Civic Society:

The committee appointed May 6, 19__ to secure a suitable site for the annual picnic submits the following report:

The committee polled the members to determine the kind of facilities desired. This poll indicated that the members were interested in boating, swimming and softball and that the members want suitable cooking facilities and adequate picnic tables.

After investigation of the various park and recreation areas, the committee unanimously agreed that Clark Park was the most suitable to the desires of the society.

The committee then contacted the Department of Parks and Recreation and reserved sufficient space and equipment, including boats and softball equipment as well as tables and stoves.   The committee took the responsibility of signing the necessary forms required by the Department of Parks and Recreation.

Signed,
George Smith
Helen Brown
Harry Boyd

(Minority Report)

To the Pinion Civic Society:

A minority of the committee appointed on May 6, 19__ to investigate possible sites for holding the annual picnic submits the following report:

1. Clark Park has boating, fishing and swimming facilities. Adequate picnic tables and camp stoves with a supply of fuel are available. There are two softball diamonds and facilities for horseshoes and volleyball. It is located 25 miles from town and is usually crowded on weekends.

2. Jones Park has no water sports (swimming, boating, etc.). The picnic facilities are considerably better than at Clark Park, and Jones Park is located in a wooded area with opportunity for hiking. It has three softball diamonds, two volleyball courts and ample opportunity for horseshoe pitching. It is 10 miles from town.

The Committee Recommendation Is:

Whereas, It is true that Jones Park does not have water facilities; and

Whereas, Jones Park does have much better picnic facilities; and

Whereas, Jones Park offers facilities not available at Clark Park such as hiking, birdwatching and nature study; and

Whereas, Jones Park is located only 10 miles from town with excellent bus service; therefore, be it

Resolved, That the Pinion Civic Society hold its annual picnic at Jones Park.

Signed,
Walter Black
Mary McAndrews

Reporting

The usual reporting member of a committee is the chairman. If the committee has a secretary, it is sometimes preferable to have the secretary make the report because the records are more available and more familiar to him.

The reporting member reads the report or states the gist of it without reading it. If the report is of any length, a written copy should be handed to the secretary of the assembly to place on file. The report is received but need not be voted on for adoption.

Recommendations within the report, usually placed at the end of the report for convenience, are voted on.

Receiving a report out of the regular order of business is a suspension of rules and requires a two-thirds vote. If the motion is adopted, the Chair may state that if there is no objection the report will be heard. She may put it to a vote by asking the assembly, "Shall the report be received now?" The question is undebatable. The matter is usually settled by *general consent*, or two-thirds vote.

Adoption or Acceptance

When a committee report has been presented to the organization, it is said to have been "received." Unless action on its recommendations is moved, it is placed on file.

1. When the report contains only information or facts for the assembly, no action is taken on it.

2. If the committee has made a recommendation but has not placed it in the form of a motion, the proper form is to move to "adopt" the recommendation. The motion may be made by any member of the assembly.

3. If the resolution is in the form of a motion or resolution, the proper motion is to adopt the motion or resolution (as contained in the recommendation). If the motion to adopt is passed, it means that the assembly agrees to carry out the recommendation contained in the motion. The parent body need not adopt all the recommendations. It may amend some

or reject some. It may not add to the committee report, however, since it is not then the report of the committee.

Amending

When the report of a committee includes a recommendation for action, it should be accompanied by a motion to adopt the recommendation, which becomes an ordinary main motion. That motion may be amended in the same manner as any other main motion. If the matter was referred to the committee in the first place, objection to consideration of the motion may not be made since the matter was previously considered at the time it was referred. Any amendments that are applied or attached to the recommendation are acts of the assembly and are not a part of the committee's report.

The assembly has no right to change the report of the committee, but it does have the right to alter what it adopts. Therefore, if the picnic committee recommends that the society hold a picnic on July 4 at 3:30 p.m. and this recommendation is amended to change the time to 1 p.m., the minutes should clearly indicate that the recommendation of the committee was 3:30 p.m. The recommendation of the committee cannot be altered by the society. Since the time was amended to 1 p.m. by the society, this change should be indicated as an act of the society. The committee's report should be placed on file exactly as it was made. Any alterations in it made by the assembly should be indicated as such—usually by bracketing the alterations.

Minority Report

Frequently committee members disagree, and sometimes this disagreement is strong enough that the minority may wish to present a separate report. Immediately after the majority (committee) report has been received, a member of the minority rises to offer a minority report.

Parliamentary authorities differ on the right to present such a report. **Robert** says that permission to present such a report must be granted by the assembly, since it must be assumed that the assembly is interested in only the (majority) committee report. **Mason, Sturgis** and many others believe that no permission is required and that to hold a minority view is as natural and right as to speak in opposition to a motion. The courts support this opinion.

If and when the minority report has been presented and handed to the secretary, two possibilities are open:

1. A motion may be made to substitute the minority report for the committee report, a motion which is debatable and requires a majority vote.

2. If no motion to substitute is made, the report is simply considered a dissenting opinion offered for information and filed.

PRACTICE EXERCISE

1. Write a report of facts, recommending action.

2. Write a report of action taken.

┌─**Review Quiz** ─────────────────────────────┐

LESSON 23: COMMITTEE REPORTS

Mark "T" for True or "F" for False for each statement and explain why statements labeled "F" are incorrect.

_____ 1.   A committee report should be signed by a majority of the members.

_____ 2.   A two-thirds vote is required to receive a report out of the regular order of business.

_____ 3.   A motion may be made to substitute the minority for the majority report.

_____ 4.   There are several kinds of committee reports, depending on the type of committee.

_____ 5.   When a committee report contains only information, it is proper to move to adopt the report.

_____ 6.   The committee chairman is always the reporting member.

_____ 7.   A minority, according to **Robert**, has the right to be heard.

_____ 8.   Adopting a report endorses every word in the report.

_____ 9.   "Adopt," "accept," "agree" are equivalent terms.

_____ 10.   A motion is required to receive a report after it has been read.

LESSON 24
BYLAWS
PART I

Bylaws "are more in the nature of rules and regulations which have been adopted to govern and regulate the conduct of intra-organization affairs, and also constitute a contract between the corporation and its members."

George S. Hills, *Managing Corporate Meetings*

LESSON OBJECTIVE

To learn the basic fundamental articles that should be contained in bylaws and their importance.

READING ASSIGNMENT

Robert pp. 557-558, 564-592

Sturgis pp. 193-198

Demeter pp. 177-181, 193-199

Riddick pp. 31-36, 86-87

LESSON MATERIAL

When our Founding Fathers set out to establish "a more perfect Union," they felt the necessity of having a document that would define the structure of the federal government and its relationship to the states. The document prepared was the Constitution of the United States.

Similarly, most American organizations have formulated documents to establish the purpose of the organization and the basic rules under which it operates. Such a document (constitution—also known as bylaws) guides the organization over the years and serves as its legal document of authority. Constitutions properly belong to legislative bodies and are created by law. Modern parliamentarians use the term "bylaws" for the document governing voluntary organizations. Bylaws come into existence by action of the members of the organization. The term comes from the Middle English, "bi-lave," which means the guiding laws for a village.

Charters are separate documents. They take precedence over bylaws and should be written in concurrence with charter rules.

Bylaws refer to a single document that is usually composed of the following articles: Name, Purpose, Membership, Officers, Meetings, Board of Directors, Committees, Parliamentary Authority, Amendments. Other important articles may include the following: Finances, Nominations, Elections, Dissolution. To understand the functions of an organization before joining it, prospective members should read a copy of the bylaws. Once they have joined, as members they are legally bound by its bylaws.

Every organization must occasionally adapt to changing conditions by being able to make changes in its bylaws. However, to insure stability and to enable members to feel secure in the basic nature and function of the organization, the group should make sure that such changes are not easily made.

Bylaws relate to basic rules for how a society functions. They include what should be written and what provisions should be made for change. Writers of bylaws should beware of overloading the document with information that belongs elsewhere.

Many of the questions concerning input to bylaws will be answered in the group's adopted parliamentary authority. When the organization wishes to differ with these answers, the bylaws will state those exceptions.

Accuracy is essential in writing bylaws. The document should be thought out carefully, then stated clearly, concisely and completely, with correct grammar and punctuation. Pronouns should be avoided. Each sentence should be accurately structured, complete in itself. Any references to another sentence should be clear.

Bylaws and related documents should be in agreement. No articles of the bylaws should contain violations of any laws.

Items of a temporary nature, such as procedural rules, standing rules, order of business and special rules, should not be included. Such rules are contained in separate documents.

Adoption of a parliamentary authority as a guide may be sufficient for a small organization that has no bylaws.

The following items may be considered, depending upon the size and scope of the organization.

Article I - Name

1. Give the full, exact name of the organization, properly spelled and punctuated.
2. Avoid a name that attempts humor or gives limitations that the group may eventually outgrow.

Article II - Purpose (or Object)

1. Make sure that the purpose is general.
2. Express the purpose precisely in a single sentence or in a series, set off by semicolons.
3. Include any statements that forbid the group to distribute political propaganda or from influence-peddling (unless a political organization).
4. Word the purpose carefully and clearly. (This statement may be a policy statement, included with adopted policies.)

Article III - Membership

1. Include information about the classes of membership:

    a. The definition of the classes, such as "active," "associate," "honorary."
    b. The rights of each class, as well as the distinctions between classes and any limitations on dues, rights or privileges.
    c. Special requirements: Does the organization include corporations as members? Does it offer family memberships or joint memberships?

2. Include information about qualifications for membership:

    a. Whether membership is limited to those of a certain geographical area.
    b. Whether membership is forbidden to those belonging to a competing organization.
    c. Whether certain tests must be passed at certain levels before an individual is admitted. In certain classes of membership, one's credit rating or police record must be checked for conviction for a felony.

    d. Whether the prospective member is required to have a sponsor.

        Note: The society may not, by law, prohibit membership on the basis of such items as race, sex, ethnic background, age or religion if its membership is open to the general public.

3.   Include information about membership dues or fees:

    a. The application and initiation fee.
    b. How, when and to whom dues are payable.
    c. Whether fees vary for different classes of membership.
    d. Any procedures for placing application fees in escrow pending final action on acceptance into membership.
    e. The procedure that will be used to notify delinquent members.
    f. Whether there is a procedure for dropping members for nonpayment of dues; whether voting rights are retained by a member so dropped.
    g. Whether the organization has the power to assess members in addition to dues.

4.   Include information about the rights of members:

    a. A statement of rights and privileges.
    b. A statement of limitations.

5.   Include information about resignation of members:

    a. The procedure for termination of membership.
    b. The obligations due the organization when one's membership is terminated.

6.   Include information about the transfer of membership:

    a. Whether memberships may be sold.
    b. Whether a transfer requires approval of a board of directors or of the other members.

7.   Include information about termination of membership by expulsion.

Article IV - Officers

1. Outline positions of leadership, the positions of president and secretary being the required minimum:

   a. President.
   b. First and Second Vice President.
   c. President-Elect (not recommended except for very large organizations).
   d. Recording Secretary.
   e. Corresponding Secretary.
   f. Treasurer.
   g. Finance Secretary.
   h. Historian.
   i. Sergeant-at-Arms.

2. Include the duties of the officers, especially if those duties extend beyond the ones cited in the parliamentary authority:

   a. President: Presides, appoints committees, serves ex officio on committees (with the exception of the nominating committee), signs contracts, oversees affairs.
   b. Recording Secretary: Keeps minutes of meetings, has custody of documents.
   c. Corresponding Secretary: Keeps the membership roll, handles correspondence, sends out notices, keeps lists of members and their addresses, officers and their terms of office.
   d. Financial Secretary: Keeps accounts, prepares budgets, reports the financial status of the organization, sends out notices, collects dues.
   e. Treasurer: Has custody of funds and other valuables, supervises deposits, disburses funds as directed, prepares for audit.

3. State the procedures for nominating officers (although the statement may more properly be contained in a separate article):

   a. Nature and function of the nominating committee.
   b. Number of candidates required for each office.
   c. Person who nominates.
   d. Whether a nominating ballot or election ballot.
   e. Whether a nominee must make a prior commitment to serve.
   f. Time and method for reporting nominations.

4.   State the method of voting:

    a. Whether the group can dispense with the (secret) ballot if only one person is nominated for an office.
    b. Whether voting may be conducted by mail.
    c. Whether a plurality vote is sufficient to elect.

Any section dealing with nominations and elections should answer questions about voting such as the following:

1. Are the nominations for all offices completed and closed before the voting for office takes place, or may the nomination and voting for each office be completed one at a time in order to have defeated candidates for one office nominated for another?
2. What is the procedure if no candidate gets a majority vote? May candidates with low totals be eliminated from subsequent ballots? What procedure is used if one person is elected to two or more offices?
3. If an election is conducted by mail, would a plurality vote to elect be permitted?
4. May election by roll call be conducted?
5. Is voting by proxy permitted?
6. What is done if a group should adjourn before an election is completed?
7. When does the term of office begin? Note: Be careful of the wording of this section. For example:

    a. "These officers shall hold office for a term of _____ or until their successors are elected." (This means that any officer may be replaced, at any time, by the simple expedient of electing a successor.)
    b. "These officers shall hold office for a term of _____ and until their successors are elected." (This means that each officer is expected to serve a full term unless removed for cause, following due process.)

8. May an officer serve two or more consecutive terms? If the number of terms is limited, is a partial term counted?
9. How are vacancies in offices filled?

Article V - Meetings

1.   Specify the regular meeting date. The exact time is too specific
      and should be left for the standing rules. Often a qualifying
      phrase is inserted: "unless otherwise ordered by the society" or
      "unless otherwise ordered by the board" to provide for changes
      in particular meetings.

2.   Provide for an "annual meeting" for elections, annual reports;
      specify the total agenda for this meeting.

3.   Include the provisions for special meetings:

         a. The notice required.
         b. How far in advance the notice must be given.
         c. The information that should be included.
         d. How the notice is to be delivered.
         e. The person responsible for sending out the notice.
         f. Whether the notice may be given by telephone.
         g. Whether attendance at a regular meeting at which the
            special meeting was announced could constitute a waiver
            of notice.
         h. Whether members could be given the power to submit a
            written waiver of notice.
         i. The complete data to be included in notice of a special
            meeting, including place, date, time, subject matter, any
            specific proposals to come before the meeting and the
            required notice time.

            Note: Limits upon the notice time are important; otherwise
                  a letter that was lost in the mail might invalidate the
                  entire meeting.

4.   Clearly define a quorum as a number, a percent of the membership
      or both:

         a. Be sure the quorum is realistic.
         b. Take into consideration that an organization's membership
            may be reduced to the point where it can no longer assemble
            a quorum of members to amend its own bylaws.

5. Outline the voting procedures here or in an article on nomination and election:

    a. The required method of voting and how it will be conducted: ballot, roll call, mail ballot, proxy.
    b. Whether a majority is necessary or a plurality will elect.
    c. How a majority is defined: a majority of the total votes cast, a majority of the valid votes cast or a majority of the membership.
    d. Whether write-in votes will be permitted.
    e. When a vote or a ballot will be considered invalid.

Article VI - The Executive Board or Board of Directors

Bylaws provide for such a board, and a great variety of structures is possible. Some organizations have a standing committee of officers that may have certain powers to act for the organization between meetings of the total membership. Others have a board that effectively controls the whole organization, and this board may even have its own executive committee empowered to act for it between meetings, as provided in the bylaws.

1. Specify the composition of the board:

    a. Number of members.
    b. Qualifications for membership.
    c. How the members should be elected.
    d. Whether the board will have, as ex officio members, community leaders or skilled persons who are not members of the organization.

2. Specify the powers of the board, either by giving the board full power and authority (with the exceptions as specified) or by limiting any of the board's special or emergency powers, reserving all other authority to the memberships. Among the items that may be considered are:

    a. To accept or reject applications for membership.
    b. To establish membership dues or certain other fees.
    c. To review and terminate memberships for cause.
    d. To hire, supervise or discharge employees of the society.
    e. To review and terminate memberships for cause.
    f. To establish general policies.
    g. To establish special committees.

    h. To fill vacancies on the board until the next general election of officers.

    i. To enter into contracts to do the following:

       (1) Commit the resources of the organization to fulfill contracts.

       (2) Borrow funds.

       (3) Pledge assets of the organization in order to borrow funds.

       (4) Purchase, sell or lease property.

       (5) Issue shares of stock, tokens of membership, evidences of indebtedness and the like.

       (6) Represent the society in dealing with the public, with government agencies and with related organizations.

3. Deal with the election of members of the board if provisions are not included in articles on nominations and elections:

    a. How the officers are elected.

    b. What their term of office is.

    c. How vacancies are filled.

    d. Whether a board member who has served a portion of a term may be a candidate for election to a full term.

4. Specify the procedure for filling a vacancy:

    a. By appointment from the board itself, the new member serving until the next general election.

    b. By election from the assembly, if it meets frequently.

5. Outline the procedure for the recall or removal from office of a board member. The organization may rely upon its parliamentary authority, or it may wish to include its own provisions, such as:

    a. To deny the board the power to expel its own members.

    b. To specify the conditions that may result in recall.

    c. To specify the means by which a recall may be initiated.

    d. To outline the procedures to be followed in considering the recall, including an executive session (or closed session), due process, the chance for the accused to be notified in sufficient time and to respond to any charges made.

    e. To specify the vote needed to recall a board member.

6. Outline procedures for resignation that answer these questions:

   a. When should a resignation take effect? Must the time be specified in the resignation, or will it take effect when the resignation is received by the designated authority?
   b. May a resignation be withdrawn before it becomes final? If so, at what point may it be withdrawn?
   c. Are repeated absences from board meetings considered automatic resignations?

7. Cover the following points about board membership:

   a. May a board member be paid for duties performed? To what amount and on what authority may the member be paid?
   b. Could a board member be employed by the organization?
   c. May board members enjoy special benefits such as borrowing funds from the organization or having business dealings with the organization, either of which might constitute conflict of interest?

8. State details concerning the board:

   a. Whether the board may make its own rules, provided that they do not conflict with the organization's rules.
   b. Whether the board activities should be open to the members of the organization or whether the members may review the board's minutes.
   c. How the special meetings of the board are to be called.

Article VII - Committees

1. Outline all standing committees, with a section for each committee.

2. Provide for the establishment of additional standing committees.

3. Make clear all lines of responsibility. For example, is the committee responsible to the total organization or to the board?

4. Make provisions for creating special or ad hoc committees.

   Note: Special needs of the organization may be met by additional articles in the bylaws. An article on finances will deal with fiscal policies. It might include such details as the dates of the fiscal year, the need for records, auditing requirements, budgets, the bonding of officers and other matters of finance.

Article VIII - Parliamentary Authority

No set of bylaws is extensive enough to serve as a guide through all of the problems that an organization might face in its voluntary or corporate life. Some parliamentary authority is needed to govern the organization's affairs not covered by the bylaws:

A statement to designate this parliamentary authority may be as follows: "The rules contained in the current edition of _____ shall govern this society in all cases to which they are applicable and in which they are not inconsistent with these bylaws and any special rules of order that the society may adopt."

Some organizations prefer to state the parliamentary authority in the standing rules, where the right to suspension is assured.

Article IX - Amendment

Bylaws should outline the procedure for their own change and development over the years. Three subordinate areas are involved and should be covered in this article.

1. Specify how changes may be proposed and how they originate.

2. Explain what notice and information should be given the membership about proposed changes in their bylaws:

   a. When and how the notice is to be given.
   b. Whether the notice must be oral or written.
   c. When copies are to be distributed.

   Note: Be careful of the wording of this article. Notice given at **the** previous meeting is one thing; notice given at **a** previous meeting means something else and could cause a significant delay between the notice and the group's action.

3.   Outline the procedure for approving an amendment to the bylaws:

    a. At which meetings amendments may be considered.
    b. What kind of vote and how large a vote is required.

    Note: A wise procedure might require a two-thirds vote of approval from those present and voting, following proper notice.   Remember that although an executive board may be given the power of originating and circulating proposed amendments, they should never be able to make an actual change in the bylaws.

          Precise language is essential in all articles of the bylaws.   Many parliamentary authorities offer sample bylaws.   Those samples may be used as a guide, but ideally, bylaws should be written to fit the particular needs of the particular organization.

Review Quiz #1

LESSON 24: BYLAWS
PART I

Find answers from any of the reading assignment texts to the following
questions:

1. What limits should be placed on the powers of the executive board?

_____

_____

_____

2. What powers should be granted to the executive board?

_____

_____

_____

3. What information on standing committees should be placed in the
bylaws?

_____

_____

_____

4. What are the requirements to amend bylaws?

_____

_____

_____

5. Why may not the vote to adopt a bylaw be reconsidered?

_____

_____

_____

_____

6. How may adoption of a bylaw be delayed?

_____

_____

_____

_____

7. What action is required to dissolve an unincorporated society?

_____

_____

_____

_____

8. How may bylaws be suspended?

_____

_____

_____

_____

┌─**Review Quiz #2** ────────────────────────────────────┐

LESSON 24: BYLAWS
PART I

Mark "T" for True or "F" for False for each statement and explain why statements labeled "F" are incorrect.

_____ 1. A basic right of members is the right to participate in amending the bylaws.

_____ 2. Only officers of the board should have the power to call a special meeting.

_____ 3. Only an executive board should recommend bylaw amendments.

_____ 4. A quorum should always be expressed as a percentage of membership.

_____ 5. Meeting dates are too precise to specify in bylaws.

_____ 6. A plurality of votes could elect if bylaws so specify.

_____ 7. Dissolution of a not-for-profit organization may disperse its assets to its members.

_____ 8. Borrowing money is a power reserved for the members and not delegated to the board of directors.

LESSON 25
BYLAWS
PART II

"Good bylaws alone do not make an effective organization; they are an outline of its structure. However, suitable bylaws are necessary to enable an organization to function well."

Alice Sturgis, *Standard Code of Parliamentary Procedure*

LESSON OBJECTIVE

To become familiar with some of the details needed to prepare us to maintain up-to-date bylaws.

READING ASSIGNMENT

Robert pp. 559-564
Sturgis pp. 198-202

Demeter pp. 182-199
Riddick pp. 36-38, 89-90

LESSON MATERIAL

The opening articles of the bylaws define the nature of the organization. Anyone familiar with them would know the name and purpose of the organization, the membership that comprises its body and the officers who provide its leadership. However, none of this is meaningful unless the organization also functions. The following discussion of the bylaws may serve to outline and to guide the organization's activities.

An organization must compose for itself in a unified document the important rules by which it is to govern itself.

DRAFTING ORIGINAL BYLAWS

Drafting original bylaws should be done by a committee of competent people concerned in the creation of a new organization, because this document will be of utmost importance and should be as nearly correct as possible to conform to the purposes that brought about the desire to create a new organization.

The committee should be large enough to include those concerned—who have special interest in the organization, who can compose well using proper language and good grammar. The services of a parliamentarian would be invaluable. If the group plans to incorporate at some time in the future, an attorney may be needed. Once prepared, the final draft should be agreed to by a majority of the committee before it is presented to the group for consideration.

Adopted bylaws become a legal document. Therefore, there must be no misunderstanding of what was agreed to. They must have only one interpretation. This requires precise vocabulary, sentence structure and punctuation. If some rules permit exceptions, those should be noted.

Bylaws, today, are best written in outline form in preference to narrative style. This provides for more rapid reference to the articles contained in them. Verbosity and repetition should be avoided.

AMENDING BYLAWS

On occasion there arises a need to alter an adopted bylaw, such as a change in the dues structure or membership requirements.

Usually an amendment is proposed by the board or a committee, the first to see a need for the change, but any member may propose an amendment also. (Bylaws should provide how the document may be amended.) It should require previous notice (to protect absentees) and usually a two-thirds vote to adopt.

The proposed amendment to a bylaw may itself be amended, which requires a majority vote. Amendments must be germane to the original bylaw and must apply directly to that part to be amended. Any form of amendment is in order.

An amendment is best considered when the proposed amendment is stated, together with the existing bylaw, and a statement given as to the reason for the proposed change. No amendments to a pending proposed amendment are in order which propose a change greater or less than that of the existing bylaw. As an example: The existing bylaw requires dues of five dollars. The proposed amendment is to raise the dues to $10. It is not in order to amend the amendment to an amount less than five dollars or more than $10.

An amendment, if adopted, goes into effect immediately unless it is provided otherwise.

A bylaw revision must be authorized by the assembly or as provided for in the bylaws. If it has been ordered, it means that any or all parts of the existing bylaws may be altered or an entirely new set of bylaws may be submitted.

A revision committee may be appointed or elected and should have the same qualifications stated for those creating new bylaws.

Adoption of the formation of this committee is considered previous notice. The committee is authorized to proceed without submitting further notice on each individual amendment to be submitted.

When the committee holds hearings, members may have the opportunity to submit and to justify suggested changes.

When the committee has completed its assignment, it gives notice as to when the proposals will be considered by the assembly. This is generally made a special order. Copies should be prepared for the members.

Each proposed article is read by the chairman, article by article, the difference between old and new explained and the effect of any change. As each will be considered one at a time, the assembly may propose amendments, if germane, and adopt by majority vote.

After each article is adopted by majority vote, the presiding officer puts the vote on the entire revision. This requires a two-thirds vote, unless otherwise provided for. According to **Robert,** the new bylaws go into effect immediately. Original bylaws may not be amended or considered during a revision.

After each article in the revision has been explained, discussed and possibly refined by amendment, the entire revision would be open to further discussion. Then the presiding officer would put the vote on the adoption of the entire revision. Ordinarily (following **Robert**), the same two-thirds vote necessary for the adoption of an amendment to the bylaws would be necessary for adopting a revision to the bylaws.

DISSOLUTION

Because of IRS requirements, a provision for dissolution should be included to protect the assets of the society. Not-for-profit, tax-exempt organizations cannot distribute profits to their members in the form of dividends, and cannot distribute the assets to their members during the life of the organization or upon its dissolution.

If the society is incorporated, it dissolves under the laws of incorporation; if not incorporated, it dissolves by adoption of a resolution to do so, including how any assets may be disposed of. It is a motion to rescind the bylaws.

POLICIES

Policies define the organization's philosophies, its guiding principles. Adoption of them is binding on the organization as much as bylaws, although easier changed. Policies are adopted to determine the action of the group when it meets problems requiring a decision. Once adopted, policies become the standard for judging and deciding all new proposals in like situations.

Policies should not be included in bylaws because of possible frequent changes, but they should be kept with all other documents of authority.

┌─**Review Quiz #1** ─────────────────────────────┐

LESSON 25: BYLAWS
PART II

Find the answers in one of the texts given as the reading assignment.

1. List the sections dealing with membership that might be found in bylaws for a large, highly organized society.

_____

_____

_____

2. If the group is to specify the rights of members, what specific rights might be listed?

_____

_____

_____

3. List, in order of rank, the officers that a large, highly organized society might have.

_____

_____

_____

4. How does a recording secretary differ from a corresponding secretary?

_____

_____

_____

5. How does the financial secretary differ from the treasurer?

_____

_____

_____

┌─ **Review Quiz #2** ────────────────────────────┐
└───┘

LESSON 25: BYLAWS
PART II

From the reading assignment, insert the missing word.

1. In practice today, constitution and bylaws are a _____ document.

2. Bylaws define the primary _____ of an organization.

3. A member should be familiar with bylaws if she looks forward to

    _____

4. Bylaws on members' rights bear on those present and

    _____ .

5. Bylaws may sometimes be subject to rules of a _____ body.

6. Bylaws should be made no more _____ than necessary.

7. Writing bylaws places a demand on clarity and _____

    _____

8. Each sentence should be impossible to quote out of

    _____ .

9. Specifications in bylaws should not be unnecessarily

    _____ .

10. Articles are designated by _____ numerals, sections by _____ numerals.

11. Provisions of a temporary nature should not be _____ in the bylaws.

12. The use of a _____ is recommended when drafting bylaws.

13. Subordinate units should not adopt provisions that have _____ application.

14. Conditions may be prefaced with " _____ ."

15. No proposed amendment to an existing bylaw provision is in order which proposes a change _____ or _____ than the range covered by the existing bylaw and the proposed amendment to it.

16. An amendment becomes a part of the bylaws _____ upon adoption.

17. An amendment to the bylaws may have a _____ as to when it shall take effect.

┌─Review Quiz #3 ──────────────────────────────┐
└──┘

LESSON 25: BYLAWS
PART II

Mark "T" for True or "F" for False for each statement and explain why statements labeled "F" are incorrect.

_____ 1.   The bylaws should be more difficult to change than the constitution.

_____ 2.   The term "bylaws" is derived from the Middle English term for laws governing a village.

_____ 3.   Matters of parliamentary procedure should be excluded from the bylaws.

_____ 4.   Major divisions of the bylaws are designated by Roman numerals.

_____ 5.   The name of the organization is a good place for humor and clever turns of the language.

_____ 6.   Bylaws should clearly spell out racial, sexual and religious qualifications for membership.

_____ 7.   Membership applications should not require the applicant's social security number.

_____ 8.   Fees or dues are too specific to be covered in the bylaws.

_____ 9.   A particular bylaw may be suspended by a motion to suspend the rules.

_____ 10. Honorary memberships are given for life unless a time limit is specified.

_____ 11. Any organization has the power to expel a member without a hearing.

_____ 12. All organizations should have at least a president and a secretary.

_____ 13. The president should serve as ex officio member of all committees.

_____ 14. The corresponding secretary keeps minutes of the meetings.

_____ 15. The financial secretary prepares the budget.

LESSON 26
STANDING RULES

Standing rules "are related to details of the administration of a society rather than to parliamentary procedure and . . . can be adopted or changed upon the same conditions as any ordinary act of the society."

Henry M. Robert, *Robert's Rules of Order Newly Revised*

LESSON OBJECTIVE

To learn the need for and the value of standing rules.

READING ASSIGNMENT

Robert pp. 17-18, 74, 612-618   Demeter pp. 181
Sturgis pp. 199-202   Riddick pp. 90-91, 141-142,
                                                184-186

LESSON MATERIAL

Standing rules are adopted by an organization as the needs arise to provide procedures unique to the organization. According to **Demeter**, standing rules are previously adopted main motions that have a continuing effect and remain so until amended or rescinded. **Demeter** also explains that custom has the effect of a standing rule, which may be discontinued by a two-thirds vote without notice. Standing rules are kept separate from bylaws so that any one of them can be suspended by a two-thirds vote for the duration of a meeting but no longer. Although standing rules may not conflict with bylaws, they may vary from the rules in the adopted parliamentary authority.

Each new session, as at a convention, may adopt its own set of standing rules. Convention standing rules are usually referred to as rules of procedure. They require a two-thirds vote to adopt if they contain any rules that of themselves require a two-thirds vote. Such rules are generally voted on in their entirety, but any single rule may be voted on or amended by a majority vote, if a two-thirds vote is not required.

Most organizations adopt a set of standing rules that apply to each meeting and continue from meeting to meeting. Standing rules are adopted by a majority vote and are amended and rescinded by the same vote. However, **Robert** requires a two-thirds vote if the rules are suspended or rescinded without notice.

If a rule is adopted at a meeting with the intent that it apply to that meeting only, it is a **special rule**, not a standing rule. If the intent is for the rule to remain in effect until rescinded, it is a standing rule. Standing rules are kept separate from bylaws but are filed with them. Standing rules may be proposed at any time when no business is pending.

DOCUMENTS OF AUTHORITY

Documents of authority for an organization are charter, bylaws, standing rules, special orders (which contain customs, policies, precedents), in that order of importance.

Policies, or platforms, are not standing rules but are adopted by an organization setting forth its views, customs or plans. These usually relate to rights, codes or standards to be used by the organization as a guiding code. Sometimes they are unwritten, but understood as custom. Care should be taken that policies or customs do not become an embarrassment to the organization. Custom has the status of a standing rule. Policies are usually prepared in a resolution. "Believing" may be used in the preamble instead of "Whereas." Policy defines belief or philosophy, and such resolutions, if adopted, are as binding on the organization as bylaws. Policies can be amended or rescinded by a majority vote, with notice. Without notice, the motion to rescind requires a two-thirds vote.

Example of standing rules are as follows:

1. All voters must present their membership badges before obtaining a ballot.
2. Smokers must sit in the rear of the assembly.
3. No literature may be distributed during a meeting without permission of the president (or the assembly).
4. Bylaw amendment proposals must be submitted in writing to the bylaws committee 30 days before proposal to the assembly.
5. Speakers must use the microphone when debating.
6. Past presidents may be luncheon guests at any organization luncheons.

7. All standing committee chairmen shall submit a report in writing at the annual meeting.

8. The annual meeting shall be a luncheon meeting. Arrangements shall be provided by the house committee.

9. Nomination speeches may be no longer than two minutes, and there shall be no more than two speeches per candidate.

10. Debate shall be limited to three minutes per speaker.

PRACTICE EXERCISE

Prepare a set of 10 standing rules which must be procedural. Adopt each one separately, or en bloc, by majority vote. (**Robert** requires a two-thirds vote to adopt the whole set.)

┌─**Review Quiz #1** ─────────────────────────┐

LESSON 26: STANDING RULES

1. What is the difference between a standing rule and a bylaw?

_____

_____

_____

_____

2. How long do standing rules remain in force?

_____

_____

_____

_____

3. What rules may be superseded by standing rules?

_____

_____

_____

_____

4. When may standing rules be proposed?

_____

_____

_____

_____

5. How is such a set of rules adopted?

_____

_____

_____

_____

6. Is it necessary to adopt a set of standing rules for each meeting?

_____

_____

_____

_____

7. Why should an agenda be placed in the standing rules?

_____

_____

_____

_____

8. Why should standing rules be separate from bylaws?

_____

_____

_____

_____

9. How do customs differ from standing rules?

_____

_____

_____

_____

10. Why might an organization desire to adopt a formal set of policies?

_____

_____

_____

11. How do policies differ from standing rules?

_____

_____

_____

_____

LESSON 27
VOTING METHODS

"The decision of a deliberative body can be made only by the taking of a vote at a meeting. The fact that members have individually expressed opinions on a question is not a decision of the body and is of no effect."

Paul Mason, *Manual of Legislative Procedure*

LESSON OBJECTIVE

To learn the common methods by which votes may be taken and what number of votes is required.

READING ASSIGNMENT

Robert pp. 43-52, 276-280, 395-421

Sturgis pp. 122-139

Demeter pp. 32-38, 133-135, 170, 309-310

Riddick pp. 197-208, 155-156

LESSON MATERIAL

The right to vote is not included in the Constitution of the United States. It is a privilege and an obligation. Any member of a society refusing to vote sanctions the actions of those who do vote.

Any deliberative body may determine its own method of voting unless the bylaws state that a certain method must be used. Bylaws should define who may vote and provide for any exceptions. No member may have more than one vote regardless of the number of positions held. Members who will receive personal gains not in common with other members should not vote, although any member may vote for himself for office. With the exception of ballot voting, members may change their votes until the results are announced. (When the voting is by ballot, no changes may be made after the ballot leaves the voter's hands.) No member may take the floor to explain his vote, and only the Chair has authority to verify and declare the voting results. All counted votes are recorded. The assembly makes the final decision when voting methods or the result of the voting is in question. Abstentions diminish the necessary requirement to obtain a majority. Abstentions are not counted, except to determine the presence of a quorum. In summary:

No member may be compelled to vote.

No member may have more than one vote, regardless of the number of positions held.

No member may "explain" her vote; that is, no debating is allowed after debate has been closed.

The assembly makes the final decision if any votes are questioned.

When a vote is taken a second time, as in division of assembly, debate cannot be resumed except by unanimous consent.

Each voting method is suited to a particular situation. The common methods of voting are as follows:

1. **Voice Vote** - This vote is taken orally, "Aye" and "No." The Chair decides the outcome by saying, "The Ayes have it," or "The Noes have it."

2. **Show of Hands** - If the result of a voice vote seems close, the Chair may require a show of hands, which makes the result more apparent. This method may be used in a small group when a two-thirds vote is required.

3. **Standing Vote** - This vote is used, when a two-thirds vote is needed, as the best way to get an accurate count. The Chair may order it, or any member may move to take a standing vote (**Division of Assembly**). If the result still appears doubtful, the Chair can take a counted vote, on her own initiative, or any member may move that a counted vote be taken. If the vote is to be taken immediately, the Chair will appoint tellers or have the members count off, a method called a serpentine vote. Affirmatives are counted first in a standing vote.

4. **Ballot Vote** - This method is the most democratic, since it provides secrecy and protection from the intimidation of revealing one's vote. Bylaws should establish when and how ballot voting is to be used (usually for election of officers).

Prior to the vote, however, any member may move to take a vote by ballot when it appears to be wise to avoid revealing members' votes or when public opinion on an issue could put some voters at a disadvantage. Ballots must be properly prepared, and a private polling place and a ballot box should be provided. Tellers should be appointed by the Chair to handle the voting and to count the ballots. All counted votes are entered in the minutes.

5. **Write-in Vote** - Unless prohibited in the bylaws, write-in votes may be written on ballots or mail-ins when the candidate's name has not been entered on the ballot. Ballots should provide a space for write-in candidates after each nominee for the office to be filled.

6. **Roll Call Vote** - This form of voting must be established in the bylaws or by a motion from the floor prior to taking the vote. It is often called "Yea and Nay" voting. Its purpose is to reveal each member's vote, which will be recorded in the minutes. Roll call is used mostly in legislatures, where citizens believe that they have a right to know how their elected representatives voted. Without special electronic equipment, roll call voting is time-consuming.

In a roll call, each member's name is called alphabetically. The member responds with his vote, "Yea" or "Nay," which is recorded next to his name. Those who abstain reply "Here" or "Present." The president votes last and usually only if it will affect the result. The secretary repeats each vote, at which time any voter may change his vote. After a tally, the Chair announces the result, and the entire roll is entered in the minutes.

In the case of a tie vote, the motion or election is lost because a majority vote was not obtained. If the Chair has not already voted but desires to do so, his vote may be cast to break a tie by a majority of one. If the vote resulted in a majority of one, the Chair may opt to make a tie, thus defeating the motion by changing the result of the election. Usually the Chair refrains from voting.

Unless the Chair has strong sentiment in favor of a particular motion receiving a tie vote, it is politic for the Chair to refrain from voting since, either way, half of the voters will be in opposition to him. The Chair's vote is sometimes called a "casting" vote.

7. **Plurality Vote** - A vote of one or more than the number received by any other candidate or issue in a group of three or more. Because it adopts by less than a majority, a plurality vote should not be used to elect officers. It may be used only if provided for in the bylaws or standing rules, or if a motion to do so is made prior to the vote. It is usually used to elect a series of names, as in appointing a committee.

8. **Proxy Vote** - Gives one member the power of attorney to vote in the place of another member. It is not permitted unless the bylaws or the charter permit it. Absentee members may not vote except by proxy, when such a vote is authorized.

9. **Preferential Voting** - Refers to a number of voting procedures used when there are three or more alternatives and the group does not wish to spend the time in taking repeated votes until one candidate attains a majority. In an election, for example, the voters might be asked to rank all nominees in order of preference, their first choice receiving a "1," the second choice a "2," and so on. The ballots would then be collected, and the tellers would place them in piles, one pile for each candidate, according to the first choice indicated on each ballot. If no one receives a majority vote on the basis of this distribution, the tellers would pick up the smallest pile of ballots and redistribute them according to the second choice listed on each of these ballots. This redistribution procedure would continue until one pile of ballots represented a majority of the total votes cast in the election, and that candidate would be declared elected. Preferential voting is often used when the balloting must be conducted by mail. It gives a more representative result than a plurality vote, although it is not a substitute for the normal method of repeated balloting to obtain a true majority. Preferential voting may only be used if the bylaws permit it.

10. **Cumulative Voting** - Provides for the grouping of votes for one nominee when several are on the ballot. For example, suppose that a committee of three is to be elected, but the ballot lists six names. The members are instructed to vote for three. Cumulative voting would permit one member to cast all three votes for one nominee, ignoring the others. The procedure would obviously increase the chances of that one individual being on the committee, but the voter would have given up her influence in regard to the selection of the other two. Cumulative voting is only possible when the bylaws permit it.

11. **Bullet Voting** - This is a procedure similar to cumulative voting, but one that is perfectly proper unless the bylaws forbid it. In this case, the member might also have three votes to cast for the three nominees to be elected to the committee. Instead, the member casts only one vote for her first choice and refuses to use the other two votes at all. Again, the bullet vote increases the chances for election of the nominee receiving the vote, but the voter has given up her influence in regard to the selection of the other two. Since members normally have the right to abstain from voting, a ballot listing only one choice instead of three would ordinarily be legal.

12. **Mail Balloting** - Must be authorized in the bylaws and is used if a vote of the full membership might be required on important issues. It is expensive and time-consuming and has little value except in organizations with a large and widely scattered membership. The details for handling a mail ballot should be stated in the standing rules, for the vote may be conducted as a secret ballot or not, and special procedures would be necessary to insure secrecy.

Remember, every member has the duty to vote but also the right to abstain. Abstentions diminish the number required to obtain a majority of those present and voting. They are not counted except to determine the presence of a quorum. Silence at this point indicates *general consent.*

A vote of **unanimous consent** or **general consent** is sometimes used for routine or inconsequential matters to save time. It simply means that all are in agreement, so no formal vote is necessary. Rules of procedure are designed to protect the minority, and when all agree, no real minority exists to be protected. Thus the formal steps of taking an "Aye" and "No" vote would not be necessary. To obtain unanimous consent, the Chair usually says, "If there is no objection ..." or "Is there any objection?" If anyone objects, the agreement is not unanimous, and a formal vote must be taken. Sometimes in elections where a ballot vote is not required, a defeated candidate or her representative may offer a courtesy motion to make the vote unanimous for the victorious candidate, to indicate the solid support of the assembly for the one just elected. Again, any objection would defeat this motion.

If the bylaws require that an election or any other vote be conducted by ballot, however, the **general consent** procedure cannot be used. The purpose of the ballot is to assure the secrecy of the vote. Anyone objecting would be revealing her vote and would thus be deprived of her right to privacy. Even the courtesy motion to make an election unanimous would be out of order when the bylaws require a ballot election, unless that courtesy motion itself were voted by a ballot vote. Then too, one negative ballot would defeat the motion.

Majority votes are usually required to validate decisions made by an assembly. The majority vote required is usually over half of the legal votes cast; otherwise, what constitutes a majority must be defined in the bylaws. The majority may be defined as a majority of those present and voting, a majority of the entire membership, a majority of a quorum or a majority of members in good standing. **Robert** counts illegal votes cast by legal voters in the majority vote.

A two-thirds vote is thought by some to protect action taken by requiring a greater majority whenever vested rights of members might be imperiled. Yet many times this requirement works in reverse, since a vote by one-third plus one can allow the minority to control the voting result. A two-thirds vote should be taken as a compromise between the rights of the members and rights of the assembly. Members may be asked to stand while voting, or may vote by a show of hands in small groups where all members can be seen by the presiding officer.

┌─ **Review Quiz #1** ─────────────────────────────┐
└──┘

LESSON 27: VOTING METHODS

1. What is meant by a majority vote?

_____

_____

_____

2. What is a plurality vote?

_____

_____

_____

3. What is a division of the assembly?

_____

_____

_____

4. What is the danger implicit in a two-thirds vote?

_____

_____

_____

5. Fifteen board members were present. A motion was pending. The vote taken: 12 Yes; 0 No; 3 Abstentions. Is this a unanimous vote?

_____

_____

_____

6. At an election with only one candidate for office, it was moved to take a vote by "acclamation." Explain.

_____

_____

_____

7.   Should the Chair call for abstentions when calling for a voice vote?

_____

_____

_____

8.   Can a member change his vote?

_____

_____

_____

9.   How may a counted vote be obtained?

_____

_____

_____

10.   If bylaws require a ballot vote and there is only one candidate, can the ballot vote be suspended?

_____

_____

_____

11.   If tellers report more than one candidate received a majority vote, is anyone elected?

_____

_____

_____

12.   If tellers report that no one received a majority vote, is anyone elected?

_____

_____

_____

┌─ **Review Quiz #2** ─────────────────────────────┐
└──┘

LESSON 27: VOTING METHODS

Write answers in the blanks and complete the solution.

GENERAL RULE: The Chair should vote only when the Chair's vote will change the final result.

SITUATION: Two-thirds vote required.
                  Vote is 20 yes, 11 no.

SOLUTION: A. **Without** the Chair voting:

1.   The total number of votes cast is _____

2.   The number of votes required for the motion to pass is _____

3.   Therefore, in the original voting, the motion is _____

B. **With** the Chair voting:

1.   The total number of votes cast is _____

2.   The number of votes required for the motion to pass is

      _____

3.   Therefore, if the Chair votes **for** the motion, the motion is

      _____

4.   Therefore, if the Chair votes **against** the motion, the motion is

      _____

RESULT:

Will an affirmative vote by the Chair change the final result? _____

Will a negative vote by the Chair change the final result?   _____

ADVICE:

If you were the parliamentarian advising the Chair, what would be your advice?

_____

LESSON 28
NOMINATIONS

"To nominate is to propose someone—presumably a well-qualified member—to fill a position for a particular office."

Riddick Butcher, *Riddick's Rules of Procedure*

LESSON OBJECTIVE

To learn the fundamental principles of the nominating process and how to put the principles into practice.

READING ASSIGNMENT

Robert pp. 422-430, 540-541, 567-568   **Demeter** pp. 238-241
Sturgis pp. 140-146   **Riddick** pp. 120-123

LESSON MATERIAL

To "nominate" is to propose someone as being suitable for election to an office. The procedures that we use in nominations probably had their origins in ancient Greece.

For some types of organizations, the nomination procedure may be specified by law (e.g., state legislative assemblies, public boards and commissions, city councils). In other organizations, the procedure used in selecting those who are thought to be suitable for elective office is either specified in the bylaws or established by custom.

If neither custom nor bylaws provide an established procedure, the organization should look to its adopted parliamentary authority, adapt the procedure therein to one suited to its needs, and then make the procedure a part of its rules. For organizations with no designated parliamentary authority, any well-recognized authority may be used.

NOMINATIONS

Generally, nominations and elections fall within the new business portion of the agenda as a special order. The six methods most often used in making nominations are listed below:

1. **Nomination by the Chair** - Usually this procedure is used only at the organizational meeting of a new group or at a mass meeting where the group's procedures are yet to be established. For established groups, nominations are preferably made by members other than the Chair.

2. **Nomination from the floor** - This is probably the most common method of making nominations and is always in order unless prohibited in the bylaws. Under this procedure, members are recognized by the Chair for the purpose of suggesting the names of those suitable to hold an office. Each member is entitled to propose a nomination without being recognized by the Chair. No second is required. Nominations from the floor always come after the report of the nominating committee, if there is one. A member may nominate only one candidate at a time.

3. **Nomination by committee** - This procedure is an adaptation of floor nominations, in which a committee meets to develop a list of nominees. This committee is usually elected from the membership, and its size, duties and method of selection are provided for in the bylaws. Its main advantage is that of saving time, for in many organizations some research must be done in order to determine which members have the best qualifications and can work together. The nominating committee can interview nominees and obtain their consent to serve. It can also arrange for proportionate representation.

When the nominations are to be presented, the committee makes its report to the members. Following the report, the members may make additional nominations from the floor.

4. **Nomination by ballot** - This is another adaptation of floor nominations in which each member may make a secret nomination by using the written ballot. In this method, ballots are distributed or mailed, and each member writes the name of a person who is suitable for the office to be filled. Members not wishing to make a nomination may return a blank ballot. Each member nominated will be a candidate for election.

This system has some advantages. First, it allows nominations to be made secretly. It also reveals the sentiment of the group, for some members may receive several nominations.

A disadvantage of this method is that there is no control over the number of nominees. It is possible that every member—or none of the members—will be nominated under this system. There can be no further nominations from the floor since each member has already had an opportunity to nominate.

5. **Nomination by mail** - This method is a variation of nomination by ballot in which the ballots are mailed to the members. The method is often used when members are widely dispersed. In some cases, such as in large organizations, nominations are made by mail, and members are notified of the results when they receive the list of nominees. The notification is followed by a meeting at which the election is held. This method allows members some time to review the list of nominees. Many national organizations conduct elections at an annual convention, after nominations have been completed by mail.

6. **Nomination by petition** - This method may be used only if provided for in bylaws which prescribe how the nominations should be handled, how many signatures are required and how many candidates may be endorsed. The bylaws would also list the date and place for filing the petition and how offices are to be designated.

Those involved in any of the methods of nomination should be aware of these important facts:

1. A nominee is one who has been named for office. A candidate is one who seeks office.
2. Methods for nomination should be included in an organization's bylaws.
3. Members of the nominating committee may be nominated for office.
4. The president should not be a member of the nominating committee.
5. Before placing a name in nomination, the person doing the nominating should secure the nominee's consent to serve if elected.
6. A member may be nominated to more than one office but usually should not serve in more than one office. Bylaws may not permit it.
7. Nominations do not require seconds, but seconding speeches may be allowed as endorsing statements.

8. Nominations may be debated. Members may explain their nominee's qualifications for office.

9. A member already serving in office and who has been nominated to fill another position need not resign from that office until the election result is announced. The member may then choose which office to fill. The resulting vacancy causes an incomplete election, and nominations must be reopened to fill the vacant position.

CLOSING NOMINATIONS

After all names have been placed in nomination and no one rises to present more, the Chair may declare the nominations closed. Any member may move to close nominations, a motion that is amendable but not debatable and requires a two-thirds vote. Nominations may be reopened by a majority vote or by *general consent.*

REPORT OF NOMINATING COMMITTEE

At the time specified, the Chair calls for the report of the nominating committee. The chairman of the nominating committee reads the committee report and hands it to the presiding officer, who rereads it and declares those names placed in nomination. This declaration makes the nominations official.

The report may be similar to the following:

The committee then presents the following slate:

For President, John Paul Jones
For Vice-President, Betsy Ross
For Secretary, Clara Barton
For Treasurer, John Adams

Signed, by all concurring members

Nancy Smith
William Black
Greta Green
Lori White
Thomas Gold

At the conclusion of the nominating committee's report, the committee is automatically discharged. The committee may be revived if further nominations are needed.

┌─PRACTICE EXERCISE─────────────────┐

The students, either in groups, or as a class, will do the following:

1. Assume that this class is a newly organized group that will meet monthly and will need a president, a secretary and a treasurer. Officers are to be elected at next month's meeting. Using parliamentary procedure, select a temporary presiding officer and adopt, by majority vote, a nominating procedure.

2. Write a report of the nominating committee. Nominate three officers and five directors.

┌─**Review Quiz** ─────────────────────────────────┐

LESSON 28: NOMINATIONS

1. Who may nominate? Who may be nominated?

_____

_____

2. Why do committees present a slate of only one name for each office?

_____

_____

_____

3. To what extent are nominations debatable?

_____

_____

_____

4. Why are nominations sometimes seconded?

_____

_____

_____

5. What is the value of nominating procedures?

_____

_____

_____

6. Name the five methods of nomination.

_____

_____

_____

7. If a nominating report is published, must it be repeated at the election meeting?

_____

_____

_____

8. When can the Chair nominate?

_____

_____

_____

9. May a member be nominated to serve in more than one office?

_____

_____

_____

10. Should a nominating committee be appointed by the Chair? Explain.

_____

_____

_____

11. Give an advantage and a disadvantage of nomination from the floor, by ballot, by committee.

_____

_____

_____

12. What provisions should be in bylaws regarding nominations?

_____

_____

_____

13. Why are there no nominations from the floor after a nominating ballot?

_____

_____

_____

14. With a single slate, and no further nominations from the floor, may a member move to close nominations and that the slate be elected?

_____

_____

_____

15. If a minority on the nominating committee cannot make a report, what recourse do they have?

_____

_____

_____

16. If a nominating committee of five is instructed to report and one member of the committee resigns, what becomes of the report?

17. May a member of the nominating committee be nominated?

18. When bylaws provide for a nominating committee but say nothing about nominations from the floor, does the Chair call for them?

19. How many nominations may a member make?

20. Why is no action taken on a nominating committee report?

21. What specific information should be required from each nominee?

22. What are the advantages of:

a) Completing nominations for all offices at the same time?

b) For nomination for each office, one at a time?

LESSON 29
ELECTIONS

"The process of nominating and electing officers is vital to every organization, because the abilities and talents of the leaders largely determine the achievements of the group."

Alice Sturgis, *Standard Code of Parliamentary Procedure*

LESSON OBJECTIVE

To learn the fundamental principles of the election process and how to put the principles into practice.

READING ASSIGNMENT

Robert pp. 430-437   **Demeter** pp. 242-250, 315-317
Sturgis pp. 146-152   **Riddick** pp. 92-93

LESSON MATERIAL

To "elect" is to select by vote someone to serve in an office. The procedures that we use in elections probably had their origins in ancient Greece.

For some types of organizations, election procedures may be specified by law (e.g., state legislative assemblies, public boards and commissions, city councils). For other organizations, the procedure used in selecting those who are to serve as elected officers is either specified in the bylaws or established by custom.

If neither custom nor bylaws provide an established procedure, the organization should look to its parliamentary authority, adapt the procedure therein to one suited to its needs, and then make the procedure a part of its bylaws. For organizations with no designated parliamentary authority, any recognized parliamentary authority may be used.

There is a variety of methods of voting for candidates who have been nominated. These include secret ballot, voice vote and roll call voting. In this lesson, we shall deal with voting by ballot since it is the most satisfactory method in contested elections.

There are some **general principles** that should govern all elections. First, an appropriate nomination procedure must precede the election. All members should have prior notice that the election is to be held. They should also be made aware of the procedure to be followed. In addition, the election procedure should specify the percentage of votes needed in order for a candidate to be elected. This number is usually a majority, but some groups may have reason to require a different number, such as a plurality or a two-thirds majority. If the required number of votes is not obtained on the first ballot, additional balloting will be needed.

Elections are held either during meetings, between meetings, in a series or through the mail. Ballots should never be distributed along a row of *seated* members. Privacy, which is the purpose of balloting, is then lost. When the voting is by ballot, the Chair appoints tellers to prepare and distribute the ballots and to provide a polling place where members may vote in private. At the specified time, the Chair declares the polls open, and members (after the Chair declares a recess) proceed to cast their ballots. At the specified time, or after the Chair ascertains that all who wish to vote have voted, the Chair declares the polls closed. The tellers proceed to count the ballots. When the tally is concluded, the Chair asks for the report, which is signed by the tellers. The chairman reads the report, which may be as follows:

Report of the Tellers' Committee

Number of votes cast

Number of votes necessary for election _____ (majority)

For the office of

President -- Mrs. A. _____votes

Mr. D. _____votes

and so on.

The chairman of the tellers then hands the report to the presiding officer, who rereads the report and declares those receiving the majority votes as elected to office, a verification of election to office. The secretary includes in the minutes this official announcement, which records all counted votes.

When elections are held during meetings, the procedure to be followed in the marking and tabulation of the ballots should have certain characteristics. Tellers distribute an authentic ballot to every member present who is entitled to vote. The presiding officer is also a member and, therefore, has the right to vote. Members may abstain from voting, either publicly (by not taking a ballot) or secretly (by returning a blank ballot). Also, it must be possible for ballots to be marked in such a way as to preserve the secret nature of ballot voting.

If time permits, ballots should be deposited in a ballot box and counted by officially appointed tellers and appointed inspectors. Public balloting and counting guarantee the reliability of the outcome. Each member should have the opportunity to request a recount of the ballots. Ballots should not be destroyed until all members are satisfied that the balloting has been correctly reported and that the announced results are an accurate reflection of the vote count. Ballots may be kept in a box, sealed publicly by the secretary until a specified time. If balloting has not been challenged, a motion is in order to destroy the ballots.

Those involved in the election process should be aware of these important facts:

1. All counted votes must be recorded in the minutes.
2. If the voters distrust the announced result of the balloting, the challenge must be made promptly.
3. If voters are satisfied with the results of the election, the Chair may order the ballots to be destroyed.
4. Elections require a majority vote of members present and voting, a quorum being present.
5. In elections, if more than one nominee receives a majority vote, positions are filled by those receiving the greatest number of votes, as in filling blanks.
6. No election should be by plurality, unless for three or more members, as for a board or committee.
7. Members who have not been nominated may be voted for by a write-in vote, unless bylaws prohibit this.
8. The Chair and the tellers may vote.

It is sometimes necessary for elections to be conducted through the mail. In such cases, either an officer (usually the secretary) or a committee has the responsibility of distributing and tabulating the ballots. Herein lies an awkward problem. If the election is conducted through the mail, members are not present during the tabulation of the votes. They must trust those in charge to conduct an honest election. Therefore, if an election is conducted through the mail, it is especially important that the bylaws include procedures that lend credibility to the election. Many national organizations retain outside accounting firms to conduct mail elections.

Balloting is conducted according to bylaws. One method is to vote for a complete slate at one time on a single ballot. Another method is to vote for each office, one at a time, thus providing the opportunity for a defeated nominee in one office to run for another office.

Teller is the name for those in an election committee appointed to prepare ballots, distribute them to eligible voters, collect and count them accurately and prepare a report. Ballot counting may be expedited, such as having one teller read the vote cast for an office, another verify the correctness of the reading and a third record the vote. Votes can be tallied in groups of five. If the final tally does not match that of each teller, a recount should be taken. Any member has the right to be present during the counting. Votes in error, that cannot affect the result, do not require a re-ballot.

Legal ballots that are voted - If there is an error on a ballot in voting for one nominee, the vote for the remaining officers is legal.

- Misspelling or use of "✓" instead of "x" is valid if the intent is clear.

- In voting for a group of officers, as in committee, fewer votes than required are cast.

Ballots are invalid - If they are blank or votes are cast for ineligible persons. If more votes are cast than members entitled to vote, a vote must be retaken.

1. Votes may be cast for any eligible member as a write-in, if bylaws do not prohibit it.
2. In a re-ballot, all nominees' names remain on the ballot; none is dropped.
3. Nominee may run for more than one office sequentially, not simultaneously, unless bylaws permit holding two offices, as in secretary-treasurer.
4. It is not in order to move to make a vote unanimous when it was not.

5. If voting results are to be challenged, it must be done promptly.

6. Elections should be conducted early in the meeting to provide time for a possible re-ballot.

7. Election to office becomes effective as soon as the nominee has been notified, after consent to serve or at a time provided in the bylaws.

Acclamation - If only one member is nominated and a ballot is not required, with no objection the Chair may announce the nominee elected by acclamation.

Secretary Casting a Ballot - A majority of one may be used if bylaws do not require a ballot. The secretary casts the ballot for the assembly if a motion to do so is adopted, and the Chair declares the result of the vote.

Roll Call vote is required when the voter's choice is required to be recorded. As each voter's name is called, the vote made is recorded by the secretary next to the voter's name. If a voter wishes to abstain, the call is "Present" or "Here." This record is necessary to prove a quorum was present. The Chair votes last if his vote can affect the result.

Voice Vote is a poor way to elect officers, as the right to privacy of one's vote has been eliminated. This method applies principally to mass meetings or when a single candidate has been unopposed and bylaws do not require "ballot vote."

Cumulative Vote - This method entitles the voter to cast more than one vote, in order of preference, for the same list of candidates. The tallied votes are a cumulation of votes to determine a majority. There are several methods to do this. For example, each voter is allocated as many votes as there are persons to be voted upon and is permitted to cast all the votes for one person or distribute the votes among as many candidates as the vote chooses. Such voting is used in large organizations and must be defined in their bylaws. Because it violates the principle of one man/one vote, this method of voting is not widely used.

PRACTICE EXERCISE

Demonstrate the following:

Assume the class is an organized group that meets monthly. Elections are in order for a president, a secretary and a treasurer. Nominations have been completed.

Using parliamentary procedure, adopt an election procedure.

Prepare a tellers' report.

---- Review Quiz --

LESSON 29: ELECTIONS

1. What does it mean to "elect"?

    _____

    _____

    _____

    _____

2. Where should the group look to find the election procedure to be used?

    _____

    _____

    _____

    _____

3. What election procedure is generally used to select an officer from a slate of properly nominated candidates?

    _____

    _____

    _____

    _____

4. Must a person be nominated in order to be elected?

    _____

    _____

    _____

    _____

5. What advantage does a ballot vote provide for a voter?

    _____

    _____

    _____

    _____

6. What are the usual qualifications for voters?

_____

_____

_____

7. When may election by acclamation be used?

_____

_____

_____

8. How may polls be opened and closed?

_____

_____

_____

9. When does the president vote?

_____

_____

_____

10. Does installation have legal status for accession to office?

_____

_____

_____

11. Who may **not** vote?

_____

_____

_____

12. What happens when, in voting for a board, more than one nominee receives a majority vote?

_____

_____

_____

13. If no nominee receives a majority vote on the first ballot, how is the election determined?

_____

_____

_____

_____

14. How may a "dark horse" become elected?

_____

_____

_____

_____

15. What are the usual procedures for taking votes?

_____

_____

_____

_____

16. What are "absentee ballots"?

_____

_____

_____

_____

17. If a member elected for a one-year term holds office for more than half the term, is he eligible for reelection?

_____

_____

_____

_____

18. What is meant by ballot vote?

_____

_____

_____

_____

LESSON 30
THE "PROFESSIONAL" PARLIAMENTARIAN

"The parliamentarian should be qualified as an expert in parliamentary law and have knowledge of the rules applying to a specific society so that his or her opinions, if accepted, will be highly regarded, even in court."

Riddick Butcher, *Riddick's Rules of Procedure*

LESSON OBJECTIVE

To understand the proper role of the parliamentarian. To learn how to prepare for and serve as a parliamentarian.

READING ASSIGNMENT

Robert pp. 456-458, 550   **Demeter** pp. 253-254
Sturgis pp. 219-220   **Riddick** pp. 136-138

LESSON MATERIAL

The professional parliamentarian serves at the request of the Chair. Some organizations appoint or elect a parliamentarian from their own membership. This person is seldom a "professional." If a professional parliamentarian is employed by the president, the organization pays the fee for service.

There are two misconceptions about the role of the parliamentarian:

1. One is that the parliamentarian may give a "ruling." However, the proper role of the parliamentarian is to advise, not to rule. Only the Chair rules on matters of procedure. Except in complex situations, the organization should not hear the voice of the parliamentarian. To preserve impartiality, a professional parliamentarian, if a member of the organization, should give up the right of speaking or voting.

2. A second misconception is that the parliamentarian serves **only** the Chair. Attendant to this misconception is the image of the parliamentarian as one whose job is limited to solving

problems or serving as a hired gun to wipe out any opposition to the president. The proper role of the parliamentarian is to **prevent** problems. The parliamentarian fulfills this role by serving the Chair but also by being available to other members of the organization.

An assembly of delegates is a unique body. The Chair wants to create an atmosphere of movement, of progress, of getting things done. Each time the Chair has to stop to consult with the parliamentarian, the Chair risks breaking—and thus losing—that atmosphere. Once the mood is broken, it is difficult to reclaim. Therefore, the good parliamentarian does more than wait to be asked an opinion, always keeping at least one step ahead of the meeting and ready to alert the Chair to an impending problem. Like the ghostwriter to the public speaker, the parliamentarian works to direct all attention and credit to the Chair. In effect, the role of the parliamentarian is to make the presiding officer look good.

The effective parliamentarian knows that the best way to advise and serve the Chair is to advise and serve every member so that questions and problems are answered and solved without interrupting the business of the assembly.

The parliamentarian should understand parliamentary law, the rules of the organization and the procedures that the officers must use to conduct the meeting. Specifically, the parliamentarian should have access to the organization's bylaws, standing rules and policies, and should recognize authorities on parliamentary procedure, including that one adopted by the organization, in order to respond effectively.

For example, does the adoption or rejection of any proposed bylaw amendment affect any other proposed bylaw amendment? If the Chair repeatedly stops the business of the convention to find the answers to such questions, it is a sign that the leadership has not done its homework.

Also, the parliamentarian should meet with the president to establish an unobtrusive system of communication.

The qualities of a good professional parliamentarian are as follows:

1. Deep knowledge and understanding of the principles of parliamentary law and procedures.
2. Broad knowledge of several editions of recognized parliamentary authorities. (Note: Not every organization chooses **Robert** as its authority.)
3. Ability to adapt quickly to the needs of the organization and its practices.
4. Ability to remain calm and emotionally disassociated from the merits of the subjects being debated.
5. Patience to endure calmly during meetings any minor breaches of the rules and customs that cannot affect the result and to advise only when requested, or when the result might be affected.
6. Ability to preside at a meeting, regardless of its size or the complexities involved, should an invitation be issued to take the Chair, which must be agreed to by the assembly. (Parliamentarians should not assume the role of presiding officer except in very unusual circumstances or when the parliamentarian is employed as a presiding officer as part of his duties.)
7. A knowledge of the difference in rules for various kinds of organizations, such as voluntary, corporate or governmental.
8. An ability to write parliamentary opinions clearly and succinctly so that the opinions may stand up in court should a trial ensue.

The following example illustrates a typical situation in which a parliamentarian might have to work and explain what should be done prior to the actual meeting:

Imagine that you have been invited by the R. & S. Neighborhood Association to serve as parliamentarian at its monthly meetings. Because of the president's lack of knowledge of the standard practices, you may get the invitation on short notice. Hence you will need to do a quick study of Neighborhood's documents.

You may or may not get an invitation to meet with the officers in advance, although the association will profit if you do. Get acquainted with the officers and discuss what their plans are.

At the outset, consider the personality of each of the persons with whom you are working. Does the president appear to be a calm yet forceful person, who can "take charge"? Does the president appear to have the support of the other officers? If so, presiding should be easier and the work of the parliamentarian minimal.

On the other hand, if the president seems to be timid or indecisive, or to lack the respect of the other officers, you, as parliamentarian, may have to take a more active part in the meeting. Little time will be available for you to consult **Robert** or other sources if necessary, during such a meeting.

You should be prepared to answer numerous pre-meeting questions (being careful not to appear to take sides), to greet former acquaintances, and to attend to the last-minute details that so often arise.

Your kit of tools should include a copy of the adopted parliamentary authority, bylaws and standing rules of the organization, a parliamentary procedure chart of motions for quick reference to the rules, a writing pad, adequate supply of pens and pencils, and a stopwatch (in case you are asked to keep time). You may also need to supply a gavel in case the president does not have one.

With preparation for the meeting completed, time to call the meeting to order will have arrived. You ought to have been in your seat (preferably next to the president) for 15 to 30 minutes in advance. That time will have allowed you to compose yourself, to arrange the materials you have brought to use and to observe the general appearance of the attendees and the preparations for seating the membership for the counting of votes (standing and written). You may need to suggest rearrangement of the officers' seating, placing of microphones and lights, and ventilation of the room. This early attendance also permits time to answer parliamentary questions from any member, should it be needed.

Remember that:

- A parliamentarian advises only.
- Attention called to errors in proceedings is done as inconspicuously as possible, and only when they will affect the result. Nit-picking is not effective.
- The best procedure is to meet with the board and/or the president prior to the meeting.

- Only on involved matters is the parliamentarian called upon to explain the procedural problem to the assembly.
- Advocacy of issues is not the concern of the parliamentarian, but how to proceed correctly to resolve them.
- A parliamentarian gives an opinion, but need not explain it unless necessary. A ruling is never given by the parliamentarian.
- A parliamentarian must be able to reconcile conflicting principles and rules that may confuse a particular situation.
- Questions to the parliamentarian are addressed through the Chair, who may opt to answer them as presiding officer.
- A parliamentarian **never** advises on a legal matter.

WRITING
OPINIONS

Often a phone call or a letter will come from a worried member or officer of an organization that has been having parliamentary problems. The inquirer will request an opinion for the group. A parliamentarian should be wary of giving glib answers until having gleaned as much information as possible. Getting that information may involve having the questioner write a full description of the problem and include the organization's pertinent documents, such as constitution, bylaws, standing rules and minutes, for first-hand information about what the problem involves. Only after a careful study will the parliamentarian be able to write a worthwhile and accurate opinion.

Opinions differ about whether or not sources should be cited in an opinion. **Sturgis's** *Standard Code of Parliamentary Procedure* asserts that the writer's reputation as a professional parliamentarian should be sufficient.

In brief, for a written opinion:

1. Write down the question or, better yet, get it in writing from the questioner.
2. From dialogue with the questioner, write down information received.
3. Get facts and rules. Ask for copy of pertinent minutes, bylaws, other organization rules and the name of the adopted parliamentary authority.
4. Research your answer and analyze the problem.
5. After listing possible solutions, arrive at a conclusion.
6. Write your reply, stating the problem, the facts as you understand them and a concise opinion.
7. Support your opinion with facts (optional) and authorities (also optional).

┌─ **Review Quiz #1** ────────────────────────────────────┐

LESSON 30: THE "PROFESSIONAL" PARLIAMENTARIAN

1. What is the professional parliamentarian?

_____

_____

_____

_____

_____

2. What personal characteristics should a parliamentarian have if one
   is to serve effectively?

_____

_____

_____

_____

_____

3. Under whose direction does a parliamentarian serve in a meeting?

_____

_____

_____

_____

_____

4. What are some of the ways in which a parliamentarian may be
   called upon to serve?

_____

_____

_____

_____

_____

5. How should a parliamentarian decide whether to charge a fee, and
   if so, how much?

   _____

   _____

   _____

   _____

   _____

6. When should a parliamentarian offer unsolicited advice?

   _____

   _____

   _____

   _____

   _____

7. How does the parliamentarian answer inquiries from the floor?

   _____

   _____

   _____

   _____

   _____

8. What and when is the main work done by a parliamentarian?

   _____

   _____

   _____

   _____

   _____

Review Quiz #2

LESSON 30: THE "PROFESSIONAL" PARLIAMENTARIAN

Write what you would advise or what you would do if faced with the following problems:

1. An organization of which I am treasurer held a meeting without proper notice going to all members. I was ordered to pay certain bills; what should I do? The president stated as he called the meeting to order: "We have enough members present for a quorum."

   _____

   _____

   _____

   _____

2. A controversy has arisen in an organization, and your questioner is reluctant to give you such information as the name of the organization or a copy of its documents, relying instead on a "what if?" type of question. You may need to turn down the request for an opinion, even if it means the loss of a fee. Explain that, like a lawyer, physician or other professional, you cannot give sound advice without sufficient knowledge of the problem.

   _____

   _____

   _____

   _____

3. I represent a national organization. Our executive secretary has been in office ever since we organized. Now the executive secretary tries to dominate all business matters, regardless of how we vote. What can we do?

   _____

   _____

   _____

   _____

LESSON 31
DISCIPLINE

"Every association has an inherent right to expect members to conduct themselves in a manner that will be a credit to the organization."

Riddick Butcher, *Riddick's Rules of Procedure*

LESSON OBJECTIVE

To learn some methods whereby meetings may be kept under orderly control.

READING ASSIGNMENT

Robert pp. 638-657   **Demeter** pp. 171, 259-269
Sturgis pp. 164-165, 213-215   **Riddick** pp. 83-86, 193-194

LESSON MATERIAL

Every society has the legal right to quiet, orderly disposal of lawful business. Rules are made to be enforced, but good sense realizes that strict adherence to rules can sometimes create unnecessary confusion. Flexibility, at the right time, can alleviate the problem.

Opposition is a right of membership, **not** a disturbance, as long as it remains within the bounds of courtesy and consideration. Members have the right of free speech, with restraint, and the right to be heard. Confrontations should be avoided or derailed to avoid encouraging difficult personalities. Debates should not be permitted to belabor the issue. The Chair must keep debate moving ahead. Comments of dissenters should not be taken personally, nor should the situation become personalized.

The best prevention against disturbances is to **be prepared**. The bylaws should be well written and adhered to. Procedural rules should be used properly. The Chair should be alert to anticipate potential troubles. Consulting in advance of a meeting with the parliamentarian or other experts is a wise precaution. The Chair should know the issues to be considered and the main thrust of arguments to be debated.

There are several **causes of disturbances**, such as:

- An unfair or incompetent presiding officer.
- Lack of adherence to bylaws and rules of decorum.
- Inability to apply or interpret rules correctly.
- Failure to define and clarify rules.
- Perplexing personalities who may exhibit antisocial behavior.

Ranges of disturbance develop from:

- Mild infraction of rules to riot and violence.
- Use of debate to deliberately confound through abusive strategy.
- Heckling.
- Actions outside of meetings that interfere with the work of the organization.

THE PRESIDING OFFICER'S DUTIES

Good leadership, under stress, improves morale and increases productivity.

The law defines the duty of the presiding officer. It is to preserve order while transacting business, because the presiding officer is, as **George Hills** says, "endowed by law to conduct the affairs and maintain order, and act in full capacity of every facet of the conduct of the meeting."

The Chair must control the meeting and has the responsibility of enforcing discipline.

A discourtesy to the Chair is a discourtesy to the assembly, because the Chair represents the members. No disturber should be permitted to gain the advantage.

While presiding, it helps if the Chair:

- Uses common sense, patience, tact.
- Presides with composure, dignity and self-control and **never** resorts to sarcasm.
- Rejects motions or comments not made in good faith, and those that are dilatory.

- Uses humor as a safety valve to blow off steam.
- Raps the gavel to stop proceedings, announcing that business will not continue until all are quiet and in their seats. Waits.
- Insists on enforcing the rules.
- Permits only legal interruptions.
- Turns off the microphone, if there is one, in extreme cases, or even adjourns the meeting.

The Chair can defend a ruling that is appealed.

The Chair, in extreme circumstances, can "name" an offender, the name to be entered in the minutes.

The Chair may **not** punish; but may ask the assembly to order the offender to leave or move to censure.

Members can avoid parliamentary criticism if they:

- Obey the rules of decorum, speaking only **after** they have been recognized by the Chair.
- Obey the legitimate orders of the Chair.
- Use the proper motions to express disapproval, such as appeal, recess, object to consideration, etc.
- Abide by the organization's documents of authority.
- Accept the rule of the majority vote.
- Recognize that members have the right to a trial, if accused.
- Remember that members can be censured (a warning expressing indignation), which is entered in the minutes.

Offenses that may require more drastic steps, such as cases of alleged serious misconduct, require a resolution to create a committee to make a confidential investigation of the charges against the offender. If the findings of the committee substantiate the charge of misconduct, the accused is given the opportunity to privately rectify the situation.

If the accused does not privately rectify the situation, the committee reports its findings of misconduct (in executive session), and a trial is set, also in executive session. The accused must be given previous notice of time and place and has the right to have an attorney present; witnesses are allowed for both sides. The accused will be tried on the charges against him to determine guilt or innocence.

The vote must be by ballot. If the findings result favorably for the accused, the committee must report an exoneration. A two-thirds vote is required for expulsion. The reasons for expelling a member must not be publicized.

Courts have ruled that:

- Freedom of speech presupposes civility and good behavior, and that it may not be an instrument for abuse or incitement to violence.

- Less importance will be given to parliamentary forms than to the decisions themselves, but the courts will brook no injustice superinduced by neglect of established forms.

- If a decision is not made in clear terms that are reasonably incapable of more than one meaning, it will be construed to give that meaning which least interferes with the rights and liberty of individuals (Roman Law, Dutch Law, English Law).

MISCONDUCT OF PRESIDING OFFICER

A member may move for a vote of confidence (support of), or of no confidence (in opposition) for the acts of the presiding officer (Chair or president). Either motion may be made and both usually require a majority vote for adoption, unless the rules of the organization provide otherwise. A motion for a no confidence vote essentially puts the presiding officer on notice that some members disagree with the behavior, policies and acts of the Chair while presiding. If a stronger action against the Chair's conduct is needed, the motion to censure or even preferring charges may be considered. Misconduct while in the Chair usually relates to partiality and favoritism, unfair play, neglect of duties, failure to recognize members and valid motions, and much more. If the Chair will not recognize (entertain) the motion to censure, the vice president or the maker of the motion to censure may state the question and put it to a vote.

┌─ **Review Quiz** ────────────────────────┐

LESSON 31: DISCIPLINE

1. Is a vote of confidence a motion?

_____

_____

_____

_____

2. What does a motion to censure mean?

_____

_____

_____

_____

3. May the offender vote on the motion to censure?

_____

_____

_____

_____

4. If an offender persists in misconduct or in violating rules, what happens?

_____

_____

_____

_____

5. If the accused is found guilty, why should results of the trial be kept private?

_____

_____

_____

_____

6.   In what sort of meeting is a trial conducted?

_____

_____

_____

_____

7.   Can members be on trial for misconduct outside the organization?

_____

_____

_____

_____

8.   What vote is required for expulsion?

_____

_____

_____

_____

9.   Is hearsay permitted?

_____

_____

_____

_____

10.   Once elected, may officers be removed from office?

_____

_____

_____

_____

11. What sort of conduct is subject to disciplinary action?

_____

_____

_____

_____

12. To what extent may members disagree with the Chair's rulings?

_____

_____

_____

_____

13. What authority empowers the Chair to control the meeting?

_____

_____

_____

_____

14. How may the Chair control a disturber?

_____

_____

_____

_____

15. How do courts define freedom of speech?

_____

_____

_____

_____

LESSON 32
CONVENTIONS

"Conventions provide a showcase for members to display their parliamentary talents, achievements and enterprise."

Riddick Butcher, *Riddick's Rules of Procedure*

LESSON OBJECTIVE

To learn the architecture of how conventions are constructed, planned and processed.

READING ASSIGNMENT

Robert pp. 6-7, 593-637   Demeter pp. 291-297
Sturgis pp. 181-187   Riddick pp. 58-70, 79-81

LESSON MATERIAL

WHAT IS A CONVENTION?

1. A convention is an assembly of delegates chosen to represent constituent units who deliberate and hold voting rights.
2. A convention is a meeting or a series of connected meetings independent of any other meetings.
3. A convention is a showcase for an organization, providing members an opportunity to display their talents, achievements, growth and enterprises as an organization.

WHY DO WE HAVE CONVENTIONS?

Conventions are held:

1. To exchange opinions and reach compromises through cooperative group thinking on matters of concern to the organization.
2. To provide, periodically, a means for many to come to agreements, meet socially, exchange experiences, gain ideas, provide a clearinghouse, offer programs designed to enrich the minds of those in attendance.

3. Sometimes to form an association or federation of those interested in a common project.

WHO MAY ATTEND CONVENTIONS?

Every member has the right to attend, but only delegates and officers or other members, as specified in bylaws, may participate in debate and vote.

WHO AUTHORIZES A CONVENTION?

Conventions should be authorized in the bylaws, which should include:

1. When and how often they are to be convened.
2. Definition of powers and duties.
3. Fixing the quorum, usually a majority of delegates who have registered officially, whether or not they are present in the assembly room.
4. Provisions for qualifications for delegates and alternates based on the method for determining their number and the method for electing them.
5. Any particular rules applicable to the society.

CALL TO CONVENTION

The call is issued to every member according to the bylaws, usually at least 30 to 40 days prior to the date set for the event. It includes the theme for the convention, time, place, proposed rules, proposed program and proposed bylaw amendments (if any).

Timing and location are of paramount importance to fulfill the requirement of previous notice.

Many organizations include copies of proposed resolutions, particularly if they are to be presented as seeking congressional or legislative action. The report of the nominating committee, if any, is included, as well as information pertaining to travel and transportation, hotel reservations, room and board expenses and other pertinent information.

1. Because the volume of business usually needs to be transacted within a specific time limit, conventions must be carefully planned well in advance in accordance with the bylaw requirements, if any.

2. Since conventions are expensive in money, time and energy, they must:

    - Provide for the business, including reports from officers and committee chairmen, action on resolutions, nominations and elections.

    - Provide supplemental activities such as workshops, programs, tours, social activities.

    - Provide information and present programs to stimulate delegates and to leave them eager to report the results of the convention to the local unit.

    - Keep in mind the possible influence on legislative, judicial or bureaucratic institutions.

1. The president of the organization appoints the chairman of the arrangements committee, preferably one who lives in the chosen area of the convention site. This chairman selects the arrangements committee from nearby members.
2. The committee locates a convention hall, determines costs of accommodations and meals, travel routes and local attractions, may sign contracts with the approval of the board of directors, and makes reservations.
3. Arrangements are then made for accommodations and meals (but not for hotel reservations), for mechanical necessities such as audiovisual equipment, lecterns, chalk boards, etc., for meeting rooms and seating for voters and nonvoters, for banquets, protocol and whatever physical arrangements may be needed for the comfort and convenience of the registrants.
4. Kits containing information and other items are prepared for each delegate to receive upon registration.

PRE-CONVENTION BOARD PLANNING MEETING

This meeting provides for:

1. A detailed check of plans and a rehearsal of them.
2. Advice from the parliamentarian as to understanding of procedural rules and rules of debate.
3. Time to anticipate problems and consider strategy to remedy them.

STARTING TIME

1. The convention can be called to order at the designated starting time for opening ceremonies, but
2. No convention can begin **business** until legally ready to do so by adoption of the reports from three committees: credentials, rules and program, in that order.

CREDENTIALS COMMITTEE

1. This committee, appointed by the president: Supervises registration.
2. Distributes information to each unit about requirements for eligibility for delegates and alternates and the number and manner of their appointment, together with credential blanks as to their authenticity signed by the unit president.
3. Compiles an official list from the information received from the constituent units and the number of delegates allotted to each.
4. Determines who is qualified to vote and issues badges upon verification as delegates register on arrival.
5. Checks on irregularities and makes replacements as required.
6. In the event of a contested verification, solves it in committee or refers it to the assembly.
7. Registers alternates and guests to determine total attendance.
8. Prepares duplicate report of number of voters for use by the elections committee, including proxy votes, if any.

9. At call of the president, reads the credentials report and moves its adoption as the official voting record of the convention, which must be altered throughout the convention whenever there is a change in the voter registration.
10. Arranges for a time and place for registration and remains on duty until the final meeting.

RULES COMMITTEE

This committee:

1. Is appointed by the president to prepare a set of rules under which the convention can operate during the meeting.
2. May deviate from the adopted parliamentary authority but may not deviate from the bylaws.
3. Usually takes a single vote on adoption of the entire set, but any member, on demand, can require a separate vote on an individual rule or move an amendment to it.
4. Provides copy of the rules for every registrant, often in advance as in the call to convention.
5. Sees that the convention rules are adopted by a two-thirds vote.

PROGRAM COMMITTEE

This committee:

1. Is appointed by the president to prepare a proposed schedule of meetings, workshops, special events, exhibits and tours within the timetable of the convention. No such schedule may conflict with the business meeting plans.
2. Often engages clergy, pianist, speaker or other entertainment.
3. Designs program to appeal to all sections of those registered in attendance.
4. Phrases the motion to adopt with the words "with such changes as may become necessary" and avoids delay in moving to rescind any unexpected change in schedule.
5. Moves the adoption of the program (majority vote).
6. Stays on duty throughout the convention.

RESOLUTIONS COMMITTEE OR *REFERENCE* OR *PLATFORM COMMITTEE*

This committee:

1. Is the most important to convention business.
2. In accordance with bylaws, prepares, edits or eliminates all resolutions in violation with laws or the purposes of the organization.
3. Puts all duplicate resolutions submitted to it into one substance, after conferring with sponsors.
4. Sees that resolutions are prepared in proper form and correct grammar.
5. Presents them to the assembly in logical sequence.
6. Has no authority to adopt or reject resolutions but may present them with or without recommendation and give reasons.
7. Oversees that nonrecommended resolutions are separated from others to be brought to the floor for consideration by the assembly. Most rules permit any member to propose a resolution from the floor, with a second and a two-thirds vote to consider it, but only a majority vote to adopt it.
8. Presents resolutions of its own.
9. Is active throughout the convention.

The resolutions committee may prepare a **courtesy** resolution, as ordered by the president, to thank and acknowledge all those who served to make the convention a success. This is read and adopted just before adjournment. Only an affirmative vote is taken, if there is no objection. Copies are sent to the appropriate persons.

PUBLIC RELATIONS COMMITTEE

This important committee:

1. Provides news releases and press interviews, checking in advance on local media requirements.
2. Publicizes important speakers, guests and programs.
3. Publicizes important action taken, particularly if it involves legislative, judicial or administrative bodies or gives support to religious or charitable organizations.

There is need for such committees as hospitality, decorations, entertainment, finance, protocol and policy, all of which can be separate committees or subcommittees of the appropriate committees.

DELEGATES

1. Serve as elected voting members of the convention body, chosen according to bylaws of the parent organization, in ratio to the size of the chapter membership.
2. Should be qualified as to intelligence and responsibility.
3. Report to the credentials committee on arrival to receive delegate badges, to attend and participate in all business meetings, attend workshops, visit exhibits, listen to speakers, exchange ideas.
4. Take notes so as properly to report to their own constituency.
5. Enjoy fellowship with other delegates.
6. May be **instructed** by their unit as to how to vote on a particular issue or for a certain officer. However, such instruction is not always wise, as debate and amendments may alter the situation and make adherence to orders difficult.
7. Should have the confidence of their local unit as to their integrity and good judgment.
8. Should attend pre-conference orientations (warmups) for advance information, particularly that involving new delegates.
9. Should attend any called caucus.

ALTERNATES

1. Should have the same qualifications as delegates.
2. Must register with the credentials committee upon arrival and attend orientations and meetings as a possible replacement but without a vote.
3. Replace delegates who have officially departed, returning their alternate badge to credentials committee. The alternate then receives from the committee official recognition to replace the delegate.
4. Until becoming a replacement, have no vote.
5. After replacing delegates, have the same rights as the duly elected delegate.

ORDER OF BUSINESS

Order of business is adopted usually in rules committee as standing rules for the session, but each day's agenda is prepared by the president. Because of volume of business and the limit of time, strict adherence to procedural rules becomes necessary.

CAUCUS

A caucus is an informal meeting, run as if in committee, informally called by the chairman of resolutions or by the concerned sponsor of a particular proposition. Only delegates may attend, but experts may be invited to present information. There is no debate on the resolution, no voting, but delegates may ask questions, get clarifications, discuss freely any problem in order to iron out the difficulty. The delegates in caucus then deliberate in executive session to prepare the final recommendations and report to the assembly. In large conventions, this is a successful timesaver as the problems are often solved before debate is opened on the floor of the assembly.

PARLIAMENTARIAN

The parliamentarian sits close to the president for quick and easy conference, having first ascertained what method of communication is most comfortable for the president. Before the convention begins, the parliamentarian should be informed of the method of voting that will be used, attend the pre-convention board meeting, meet and confer with the president.

ATTORNEY

If an attorney has been engaged, her job is to monitor, clarify or explain statutory laws that are under discussion or business of the convention affected by them. The parliamentarian does the same for procedural rules.

ELECTIONS

1. A nominating committee is appointed or elected according to bylaws in advance or at least at the first meeting of the convention.

2. Ballots should be prepared, preferably printed in advance to include the nominated slate, space for nominations from the floor and a space for write-in candidates. List nominees in alphabetical order or in reverse.

3. Elections are conducted early in the session to provide time for re-balloting, if necessary.

4. Voting on propositions is the same as ordinary voting (by "Ayes" or "Noes").

5. Polling places and ballot boxes should be prepared in advance.

6. Delegates show badges to tellers who match them with the voting list supplied by the credentials committee.

7. Tellers issue ballots to voters who mark their ballots and hand them to tellers for deposit in the ballot box. Watch closely. Once in the ballot box, a fraudulent vote cannot be identified.

8. Tellers check voters' names off voting list.

9. Tellers, appointed by the president, should choose one teller as chairman of tellers, who reports the count to the presiding officer.

10. Tallying votes should be carefully and accurately conducted, as the report is prepared for announcement by the chairman of tellers.

USE OF MICROPHONE, COLOR CARDS

1. A sufficient number of accessible and strategically placed microphones for delegates wishing to speak should be provided.

2. Delegates, desiring a turn, stand before a nearby microphone.

3. Use of microphones should be included in convention standing rules so each delegate knows a microphone must be used to be recognized.

4. Each microphone will have an identifying number. These numbers will be used in numerical order by the president in assigning the floor to speakers.

5. If there is no debate, resolutions may be adopted by lightly striking the gavel once and announcing the adoption by the president, as stated in adopted standing rules.

6. Some conventions rule that debate is automatically stopped after a 15-minute discussion, and the resolution is put to vote.

7. When assigning specific microphones, the president may use color cards to expedite business as: green for those who wish to speak in favor; red for those who speak in opposition; yellow for amending; white for information, etc.

8. These cards are distributed by microphone monitors, who should be instructed as to their use.

CONVENTION MINUTES

The organization can save time and insure more accurate minutes when the president appoints a minutes approval committee in advance. These members may take notes during deliberations and meet to compare them with the secretary's minutes. After review and approval or correction, minutes are signed or otherwise officially noted. The secretary should not be a member of the committee.

ADJOURNMENT

If business is completed before the scheduled time for adjournment, any member may move to adjourn *sine die*, by suspension of the rules. Or, the Chair may declare adjournment with no objection.

┌─ **Review Quiz #1** ─────────────────────────────────┐
└──┘

LESSON 32: CONVENTIONS

1. What three essential procedures are required to validate convention business?

_____

_____

_____

_____

2. How are voting delegates determined?

_____

_____

_____

3. What is the essential function of a caucus?

_____

_____

_____

_____

4. Are delegates free to determine their vote? Explain.

_____

_____

_____

_____

5. What is the responsibility of the credentials committee?

_____

_____

_____

_____

6.   What is the main function of the rules committee?

_____

_____

_____

_____

7.   What are the program committee's responsibilities?

_____

_____

_____

_____

8.   What is the quorum of a convention?

_____

_____

_____

_____

9.   What are the duties of the resolutions committee?

_____

_____

_____

_____

10.   How are resolutions reported to the assembly?

_____

_____

_____

_____

11.   How is time between meetings best treated in a parliamentary sense?

_____

_____

_____

_____

12. What is the most efficient way to approve minutes?

_____

_____

_____

_____

13. How does an alternate replace a delegate?

_____

_____

_____

_____

14. What are the duties of a delegate?

_____

_____

_____

_____

15. What becomes of unfinished business at conventions?

_____

_____

_____

_____

16. When do newly elected officers assume office?

_____

_____

_____

_____

17. What is contained in the credentials report?

_____

_____

_____

_____

18. May the board hold meetings during convention? Explain.

_____

_____

_____

19. What are the parliamentarian's responsibilities during the convention?

_____

_____

_____

20. What is the purpose of the installation of officers?

_____

_____

_____

21. How does an organization officially provide for holding conventions?

_____

_____

_____

22. Do any federal laws affect elections or rights of members?

_____

_____

_____

23. If a special committee has not completed its assignment before convention adjournment, what becomes of the assignment?

_____

_____

_____

_____

┌─ **Review Quiz #2** ──────────────────┐

LESSON 32: CONVENTIONS

Mark "T" for True or "F" for False for each statement and explain why statements labeled "F" are incorrect.

_____ 1. A convention is an assembly composed of the membership.

_____ 2. Each unit may send as many delegates as desired.

_____ 3. Pairing of alternates and delegates is not recommended.

_____ 4. Temporary absence of a delegate entitles the alternate to substitute for the delegate.

_____ 5. A caucus operates as a committee to plan strategy.

_____ 6. The parliamentarian calls attention to every procedural infraction.

_____ 7. A convention quorum is a majority of voting delegates.

_____ 8. A parliamentarian's most important work is done before the convention.

_____ 9. Federal and state laws can affect voting rights of delegates.

_____ 10. Recess is used to terminate meetings during a session.

_____ 11. The convention must form itself into a single voting body.

_____ 12. The agenda is the business set for each meeting.

_____ 13. Resolutions committee must report all resolutions submitted to it.

_____ 14.   Each of the three essential committee reports is adopted by a majority vote.

_____ 15.   The credentials report may vary with each meeting.

_____ 16.   A convention standing rule, with notice, may be suspended by majority vote.

_____ 17.   Resolutions committee may recommend appropriate action to be taken by the assembly.

_____ 18.   Adherence to a prearranged schedule is imperative.

_____ 19.   Minutes need not be read before each meeting.

_____ 20.   Changing the program requires a two-thirds vote.

_____ 21.   Conventions are adjourned *sine die*.

_____ 22.   Resolutions committee may screen all resolutions brought to it.

_____ 23.   Policy statements are prepared by the executive board.

_____ 24.   It is not necessary to move adoption of resolutions reported out of committee.

_____ 25.   Elected officers should take up their duties immediately upon election.

APPENDIX A
MNEMONICS

Tips on Remembering Some of the Basic Rules in Parliamentary Law and Procedure

A number of basic rules in parliamentary law can best be remembered by resorting to mnemonics—a system used in the improvement of memory. The most effective mnemonics are those that one has developed for oneself. But the memory tips that appear below have been found helpful by some parliamentarians. Try them out. See if they work for you. If they do not, perhaps you can come up with something better.

Classes of Motions   **MY SISTER PLAYS IN RENO**

Main
Subsidiary
Privileged
Incidental
Restoratory

Standard Descriptive   **SAD MR IPA**
Characteristics of Motions

Secondable
Amendable
Debatable
Majority
Reconsiderable
Interrupt
Precedence
Applicability

Getting a Convention   CARS REALLY POLLUTE
Started

Credentials
Rules
Program

When "Adjourn" is   QED (*quod erat demonstrandum*)
Not a Privileged Motion

Qualified (adjourn to a future time)
Established (time preestablished for adjournment)
Dissolution (when adoption would dissolve the assembly with no
provision for a future meeting)

Basic Order of Business   R R R S U N

Reading and approval of minutes
Reports of officers, board, standing committees
Reports of special (ad hoc) committees
Special orders
Unfinished business and general orders
New business

Basic Content of Bylaws   NO MOME   C D P A

Name
Object
Members
Officers
Meetings
Executive board
Committees
Dissolution
Parliamentary authority
Amending process

Question of Privilege   S H I P

Safety
Health
Integrity
Protection

APPENDIX B
MOCK MEETINGS

This exercise provides practice in using the language of parliamentary procedure through three distinctly different types of mock meetings. The **fully scripted** mock meeting helps students develop a working vocabulary and provides specific parliamentary situations for group discussion and analysis. The **partially scripted** mock meeting demands a higher level of verbal skill and fluency than the fully scripted meeting. It provides a complete description of a parliamentary situation in which all motions are known in advance and the results of votes are controlled, but the students themselves must provide all of the language. Finally, the **unscripted** mock meeting demands the highest level of alertness, fluency and poise as the chairmanship is randomly rotated among members of the class.

*GENERAL
PROCEDURES
FOR ALL MOCK
MEETINGS*

1. Decide on the subject matter of the mock meeting (certain types of motions, rules for recognizing speakers, bylaw amendments, etc.).

2. Review the lessons in this book and recommended parliamentary authorities that relate to the subject matter of the mock meeting.

3. Decide on the type of mock meeting. Fully scripted meetings are best for beginners; partially scripted meetings are useful for all students as they progress from lesson to lesson; unscripted meetings are appropriate for advanced students who have mastered the basics and have the vocabulary required for fluency during business meetings.

4. Review the procedures for the type of mock meeting selected. All "ground rules" must be thoroughly understood and strictly observed.

5.   Assign roles to all participants.

6.   Allow participants time to prepare for the mock meeting. The type of preparation will vary according to the type of mock meeting selected.

7.   One person writes motions on the boards as they are moved, and erases them from the board as they are disposed of. Main motions should be written at the bottom of the board with other motions written above in their order of precedence.

Example:

Secondary Amendment: **"$3,000"**

Primary Amendment: **"at a cost not to exceed ($5,000)"**

Main Motion: **"That we purchase a new computer"**

8.   Except for unscripted meetings, a quiz should immediately follow each mock meeting to help ensure retention of the material.

PROCEDURES FOR FULLY SCRIPTED MOCK MEETINGS

1.   The instructor should play the role of presiding officer. Randomly assign all other roles to student participants.

2.   Students may not speak, except from the script, during scripted portions of the meeting.

3.   At points marked with an asterisk (*), the meeting is interrupted for discussion purposes and questions are permitted.

4.   All votes are controlled; students must vote as directed.

5.   Practice first from the scripts provided; then develop your own scripts according to the following guidelines.

1. Scripts will be more manageable if limited to one segment of the meeting, such as "New Business."

2. Scripts may be prepared by the instructor, by individual students or by groups of students who then role play their own scripts.

3. Scripts will be more instructive if focused on specific subject matter. One script, for example, may focus on the privileged motions while another may focus on selected incidental motions.

4. Scripts must provide for the recognition of each speaker by the Chair except for certain motions that do not require recognition.

5. Scripted discussion of motions should be held to a minimum.

6. Scripts should contain occasional planned errors in procedure. The functions of these errors are to facilitate discussion and to demonstrate how the errors may be corrected during the meeting.

7. Scripts must indicate the points at which the mock meeting is to be interrupted for discussion purposes.

8. Scripts must indicate how participants shall vote, and the result of each vote must be announced by the Chair.

PROCEDURES FOR SEMISCRIPTED OR PARTIALLY SCRIPTED MOCK MEETINGS

1.   Each member of the class plays the role of presiding officer for one or more mock meetings.

2.   The instructor plays the role of parliamentarian.

3.   All speaker roles are assigned in advance either by the instructor or by the student playing the role of presiding officer. One student is assigned to second all motions that require a second.

4.   Each performing group should be allowed time to rehearse prior to the classroom presentation of the mock meeting.

5.   No debate is permitted; however, the presiding officer must always call for discussion on debatable motions.

6.   Prior to taking any vote, the Chair must state the vote required to adopt the motion.

7.   Participation is strictly limited to what is stated in the script. The wording of each motion and the result of each vote are known in advance.

8.   Each mock meeting should be timed; speed and precision in handling motions are the primary objectives.

9.   Go through the meeting more than once, if necessary, to develop the desired fluency.

10. Practice first from the scripts provided in this appendix, then develop your own scripts according to the guidelines stated on the following page.

1. Identify speakers by letter: A, B, C.

2. State the motion assigned to each speaker but provide the language only when necessary to construct a specific parliamentary situation. In most cases the choice of language should be left to the speaker.

3. State whether each motion is to be adopted or defeated, but do not state the vote required for any motion.

4. Stating that "all motions put to a vote are adopted" places the burden on the Chair to determine which of the pending motions will be put to a vote.

1. **A** makes a main motion. **B** moves to **lay** the main motion **on the table** until 3 p.m. **C** raises a point of order that the motion to **lay on the table** as stated is out of order. The Chair rules that the motion to lay the main motion on the table until 3 p.m. is out of order. The main motion is adopted.

2. **A** makes a main motion. **B** moves to **lay** the main motion **on the table**. The Chair rules that the motion to lay **on the table** is out of order. **B** explains that an urgent matter has arisen and renews the motion. **C** raises a **point of order** that the motion to lay on the table cannot be renewed during the same session. The Chair rules that the motion to **lay on the table** is in order. The motion to **lay on the table** is adopted.

3. **A** makes a main motion. **B** moves to **refer** the main motion to the social life committee. **C** moves to **amend** by striking out "social life" and inserting "special committee of three to be appointed by the Chair." **D**, explaining that an urgent matter has arisen, moves to **lay** the main motion **on the table**. The motion to **lay on the table** is **adopted**.... (Other business intervenes during which the urgent matter is disposed of.) **D** moves to **take** the main motion **from the table**. All motions that are put to a vote are adopted.

4.   **A** makes a main motion. **B** moves to **postpone** the main motion indefinitely. **C** moves to **close debate**. **D** raises a **point of order** that the motion to **close debate** is out of order. The Chair rules that the motion to **close debate** is in order. All motions that are put to a vote are adopted.

5.   **A** makes a main motion. **B** moves to **postpone** the main motion **indefinitely**. **C** moves to **amend** the main motion by adding words. All motions that are put to a vote are adopted.

6.   **A** makes a main motion, and this is adopted. **B** moves to **recess**, and this is adopted. Following the recess, **C** moves to **reconsider** the vote on the main motion. **Reconsider** is adopted; the main motion is defeated.

7.   **A** makes a main motion that can be divided into two parts. **B** moves to **divide the question**, and this is adopted. The first part is adopted; the second part is defeated. **C** moves to **reconsider** the vote on the first part. **Reconsider** is adopted; the main motion is defeated.

PROCEDURES FOR UNSCRIPTED MOCK MEETINGS

Many variations of unscripted mock meetings are possible, the simplest being to assign one student the role of presiding officer and allow the class to make random motions while the instructor comments from the sidelines. The variations described below, one for an entire class and one for smaller groups, are especially challenging for advanced students because they provide for random rotation of students in and out of the Chair as the meeting progresses.

UNSCRIPTED MOCK MEETINGS FOR A CLASS

1.   The instructor initially assigns one student to chair the meeting.

2.   At specified time intervals, the instructor randomly rotates the chairmanship to other members of the class.

3.   Students should be alert to the fact that they may be called on at any time (even while several motions are pending) to chair the meeting.

4.   The instructor writes motions on the board as they are moved, and erases them from the board as they are disposed of.

5.   Students may move, second and debate any motions, and make points of order when errors in procedure are observed. Long speeches are discouraged.

6.   Students may vote as they please; however, the instructor may occasionally reverse the result of a vote to set up a learning situation.

7.   The instructor may interrupt the meeting from time to time to explain a relevant point of procedure.

UNSCRIPTED MOCK MEETINGS FOR GROUPS

1.   The class is divided into groups of six to eight students. Groups are given several days to prepare for the mock meeting.

2.   Each group prepares an outline of the motions and events that will occur in the meeting. The outline is approved in advance by the instructor.

3.   The total length of the meeting should be 30 to 40 minutes, with each member of the group in the Chair for about five minutes.

4.   Members of the group do not know who will be in the Chair at any given moment. The instructor randomly rotates the members in and out of the Chair at specified time intervals.

5.   Members of the performing group as well as all members of the class should have copies of the group's outline. No other notes, references or scripts are permitted.

6.   Participation in the meeting is strictly limited to group members.

7.   One member of the class who is not a member of the performing group is assigned to write motions on the board as they are moved, and erase them from the board as they are disposed of.

8.   Other members of the class as well as the instructor should take notes during the meeting. Errors in procedure as well as errors in proper parliamentary language should be noted.

9.   Following the meeting, the instructor and members of the class should critique the group's performance.

SCRIPTED MOCK MEETINGS

Sample Mock Meeting #1 - Focus: Amendments

Chair: Is there any new business?

#1:   Mr./Madam Chairman.

Chair: The Chair recognizes Speaker #1.

#1:   I move that the program committee be instructed to provide a program on volunteerism this year.

#2:   I second the motion.

Chair: It is moved and seconded that the program committee be instructed to provide a program on volunteerism this year. Speaker #1, you have the floor.

#1:   Our program committee has ignored repeated requests for programs to inform us about new opportunities for volunteerism in this community. This motion is necessary to ensure that the program committee doesn't continue to ignore our interests.

#3:   Mr./Madam Chairman.

Chair: Speaker #3 is recognized.

#3:   It seems to me that one program on volunteerism isn't going to do much good. I move to **amend** the motion by striking out the word "program" and substituting the words "series of programs."

#2:   Second.

Chair: It is moved and seconded to strike out the word "program" and substitute the words "series of programs." Is there discussion on the amendment?

#4:   Mr./Madam Chairman.

Chair: Speaker #4 is recognized.

#4:   I move to **amend** the motion by striking out the word "instructed" and substituting the word "requested."

#2:   Second.

(*):   **DISCUSSION.** Is this amendment in order? Why, or why not?

Chair: The amendment is not in order at this time. The primary amendment to strike out "program" and substitute the words "series of programs" is pending. After we have voted on this amendment, then the proposed amendment to substitute the word "requested" would be in order. Is there further discussion on the pending amendment?

#5:   Mr./Madam Chairman.

Chair: Speaker #5 is recognized.

#5:   I move to **amend the amendment** by inserting the words "audience participation" between "of" and "programs."

#2   Second.

(*)   **DISCUSSION.** Is this amendment in order? Why?

Chair: It is moved and seconded to amend the amendment by inserting the words "audience participation" between "of" and "programs."

#4   **Point of order**, Mr./Madam Chairman.

Chair: Please state your point.

#4:   You ruled my amendment out of order, but now you're allowing this amendment. I think we need some consistency here.

(*):   **DISCUSSION**. Is the point of order well taken? Why or why not?

Chair: Your amendment to strike out the word "instructed" was a second primary amendment. I ruled it out of order because only one primary amendment at a time can be pending. The amendment to insert the words "audience participation" is a secondary amendment. It directly amends the primary amendment to strike out "program" and insert "series of programs." It is in order. Is there discussion on the secondary amendment to insert the words "audience participation?" (Pause) Are you ready for the question? (Pause) We shall now vote on the secondary amendment to insert the words "audience participation" between "of" and "programs." All in favor, say "Aye." (Voices respond) All opposed, say "No." The amendment is adopted. The amended primary amendment now reads "series of audience participation programs." Is there further discussion on whether to strike the word "program" from the main motion and insert the words "series of audience participation programs"?

#4:   **Point of information**, Mr./Madam Chairman.

Chair: Please state your point.

#4:   Is it in order now for me to move a primary amendment to the main motion?

(*):   **DISCUSSION**. Is a new primary amendment in order?

Chair: This is not a point of information; it is a **parliamentary inquiry**. The answer to your question is no. We have a primary amendment pending, so another primary amendment is not in order at this time. Is there further discussion on whether to insert the words "series of audience participation programs" into the main motion? (Pause) Are you ready for the question? (Pause) The proposed amendment is to strike out the word "program" and substitute the words "series of audience participation programs." All in favor, say "Aye." (Voices respond) All opposed, say "No." (Pause) The amendment is adopted. The amended main motion now reads "that the program committee be instructed to provide a series of audience participation programs on volunteerism next year." Is there discussion on the motion?

#4:   I rise to a **parliamentary inquiry**.

Chair: Please state your question.

#4:   Is it now in order for me to move an amendment to the main motion?

(*):   **DISCUSSION**. How many times has the main motion been amended? How many more times can it be amended? Can speaker #4 now move an amendment?

Chair: Yes, an amendment is now in order. The main motion is now before us and no amendments are pending. However, you have not yet been recognized for the purpose of debating or making motions. Your parliamentary inquiry has been answered, and you must now wait your turn to be recognized in debate.

#6:   **Point of information.**

Chair: Please state your question.

#6:   Are funds available to the program committee to implement this motion, if adopted?

Chair: I am informed that the program committee has $5,000 of unencumbered funds.

#6:   Thank you, Mr./Madam Chairman.

#4:   Mr./Madam Chairman.

Chair: The Chair recognizes speaker #4.

#4:   I move to **amend** the main motion by striking out the word "instructed" and substituting the word "requested."

#2:   Second.

(*):   **DISCUSSION**. This amendment was moved once before by the same speaker, and it was ruled out of order. Is it now in order?

Chair: It is moved and seconded to amend the main motion by striking out the word "instructed" and substituting the word "requested." Is there discussion? (Pause) All in favor of the amendment, say "Aye." (Pause) All opposed, say "No." (Voices respond) The amendment is defeated. The pending main motion is "that the program committee be instructed to provide a series of audience participation programs on volunteerism this year." Are you ready for the question? (Pause) All in favor of the main motion, say "Aye." (Voices respond) All opposed, say "No." (Pause) The motion is adopted, and the program committee is instructed to provide a series of audience participation programs on volunteerism this year.

Sample Mock Meeting #2 - Focus: Filling Blanks

Chair: Is there any new business?

#1:   Mr./Madam Chairman.

Chair: The Chair recognizes speaker #1.

#1:   I move that we purchase new furniture for our headquarters office at a cost not to exceed $4,000.

#2:   I second the motion.

Chair: It is moved and seconded that we purchase new furniture for our headquarters office at a cost not to exceed $4,000. Is there discussion?

#3:   Mr./Madam Chairman.

Chair: Speaker #3 is recognized.

#3:   I move to **amend** the motion by **striking** out $4,000 and **inserting** $3,000.

#2:   Second.

Chair: It is moved and seconded to amend the motion by striking out $4,000 and inserting $3,000. Is there discussion on the amendment?

#4:   Mr./Madam Chairman.

Chair: Speaker #4 is recognized.

#4:   I move to strike out $4,000 and **create a blank**.

#5:   **Point of order**, Mr./Madam Chairman.

Chair: Please state your point.

#5:   The motion to **create a blank** must apply to the pending amendment.

(*):   **DISCUSSION.** Is the point of order well taken? Should the motion to create a blank apply to the main motion or the amendment?

Chair: Your point of order is not well taken. Even though a first degree amendment is pending, the motion to create a blank is applied directly to the main motion. Is there a second for the motion to create a blank?

#2:   I second the motion.

Chair: It is moved and seconded to strike out $4,000 in the main motion and **create a blank**. Is there discussion on the motion?

#5:   **Point of order!**

(*):   **DISCUSSION.** Why is a point of order being raised? Is the point of order well taken?

Chair: Please state your point.

#5:   The motion to **create a blank** is undebatable.

Chair: Your point is well taken, and the Chair stands corrected. We shall now vote on the motion to strike out $4,000 from the main motion and create a blank. All in favor, raise your hand. (Hands up) All opposed, raise your hand. The motion to create a blank is adopted. The Chair will now entertain suggestions for filling the blank in the main motion.

#5:   **Point of order**, Mr./Madam Chairman.

(*):   **DISCUSSION.** Why is the point of order being raised?

Chair: Please state your point of order.

#5: $4,000 was stated in the main motion, and $3,000 was stated in the amendment. These should be considered the first two suggestions for filling the blank.

Chair: Your point is well taken, and the first two suggestions for filling the blank are $4,000 and $3,000. Are there additional suggestions for filling the blank?

#6:   I suggest $7,500.

#7:   I suggest $2,500.

Chair: Are there any other suggestions for filling the blank? (Pause) The amounts to be considered are $7,500; $4,000; $3,000; and $2,500. Is there discussion on the suggestion to fill the blank with $7,500?

#5:   **Point of order!**

(*):   **DISCUSSION.** Why is the point of order being raised? Is the point well taken?

Chair: Please state your point of order?

#5: $4,000 was the first suggestion for filling the blank, so we should discuss this suggestion first.

Chair: Your point is not well taken. The correct order for considering amounts of money is to begin with the largest amount suggested. Is there discussion on filling the blank with $7,500?

#6:   Mr./Madam Chairman.

Chair: The Chair recognizes speaker #6.

#6:   I made the suggestion to fill the blank with $7,500. Our headquarters office is in shambles, and we really need some nice-looking furniture. In today's market $7,500 is not a lot to pay for furniture.

Chair: Is there further discussion on filling the blank with $7,500? (Pause) If there is no more discussion, we shall vote. All in favor, raise your hand. (Pause) All opposed, raise your hand. (Hands up) The suggestion to fill the blank with $7,500 is defeated. (Pause) The next suggestion to be considered is $4,000. Is there any discussion?

#1:   I made the motion to spend $4,000 on office furniture, and I think this is a very reasonable amount. If we go much lower than $4,000, we'll end up getting furniture that doesn't last very long.

Chair: Is there further discussion on filling the blank with $4,000? (Pause) We shall now vote. All in favor of filling the blank with $4,000, please raise your hand. (Hands up) All opposed, raise your hand. (Pause) The motion is adopted, and we will spend up to $4,000 on new furniture for the headquarters office.

#5:   **Point of order**, Mr./Madam Chairman.

(*):   **DISCUSSION.** Why is this point of order being raised? Is the point well taken?

Chair: Please state your point.

#5:   We voted to fill in the blank with $4,000, but we have had no opportunity to vote on the main motion.

Chair: Your point is well taken, and the Chair stands corrected. Is there discussion on the motion that we purchase new furniture for our headquarters office at a cost not to exceed $4,000?

#7:   Mr./Madam Chairman.

Chair: Speaker #7 is recognized.

#7:   I made the suggestion to fill the blank with $2,500 and I feel this is a very reasonable suggestion. Our present furniture only cost $1,500 when it was new.

#5:   **Point of order!**

Chair: State your point of order.

#5:   Our discussion should be limited to the main motion.

Chair: Your point is well taken. Speaker #7, your discussion is out of order. We are now discussing the main motion to purchase new furniture for our headquarters office at a cost not to exceed $4,000.

#7:   I speak in opposition to the motion. Our furniture isn't in that bad of shape, and $4,000 is exorbitant.

Chair: Is there further discussion on the motion? (Pause) We shall now vote on the main motion. All in favor, please raise your hand. (Hands up) All opposed, please raise your hand. (Pause) The motion is adopted, and we will purchase new furniture for our headquarters office at a cost not to exceed $4,000. Is there any other business?

APPENDIX C
CREATING ORDER OUT OF CHAOS

"Fairness, trust, good faith, and practicality are characteristics of the proper use of constructive parliamentary procedure."

Hermon Farwell, **The Majority Rules**

Use of this appendix is recommended as a learning experience in the need for order, rules and procedures to be used when groups work together for a common goal. The primary reference, *The Majority Rules*, is designed for those groups whose interest in parliamentary procedure lies in their desire to accomplish business both expeditiously and harmoniously in an atmosphere of courtesy, common sense and tact.

BACKGROUND

Today, the civilized world is a world of organizations. In the United States, the average adult belongs to a minimum of six organized groups and twice that many informal organizations. Such groups exist to accomplish some purpose, whether it be to decide a new policy for taxation or to provide an opportunity for interaction between members of a coffee klatch.

Depending upon the responsibilities of the group and its size, the sophistication of its members and the conflict among them, the detail and formality required for conducting business and attaining a goal may vary greatly. In general, a group of fewer than 10 or 12 can function well with informal and relaxed rules. Large deliberative groups, however, usually require rigid adherence to more formal rules.

Because of the informality of the small group, it may be sufficient that the members, especially the leader, be well acquainted with the fundamentals of parliamentary procedure and that they make for themselves the few rules necessary to operate. The larger group, partly because of the need for formality and partly to save time, can adopt for its guidance an already existing set of rules such as found in recognized parliamentary manuals.

Despite the number of rules and prescribed motions presented in *Robert's Rules of Order Newly Revised,* even that authority recommends that small groups such as committees and boards use no more parliamentary formality than is necessary to accomplish their work or is required by the bylaws of their organization. Other than that concession, **Robert** and many other authorities are strictly directive, in some cases not only prescribing the use of many rules but actually requiring specific words that must be used in proposing a motion.

Parliamentary procedure, as presented in this appendix, is based upon a sound understanding of the fundamental principles of successful decision-making in a democratic society and the belief that with that understanding, intelligent group members can formulate the few rules needed to accomplish their goals. It has long been known that self-made law is the most successful. More than five hundred years ago, Marsilius of Padua, at the request of Louis IV, ruler of the Holy Roman Empire, composed the Defensor Pacis, a document considered to be one of the most revolutionary of all medieval tracts. It held that all power is derived from those ruled and that there is no law except that of popular will.

Marsilius of Padua wrote:

> A law is useless if not obeyed . . . . Since that law is better observed by any one of the citizens which he seems to have imposed upon himself, the best law is made by the deliberation and command of the multitude of citizens . . . . This cannot be if a single man or a few make law by their own authority . . . In such case the remainder of the citizens, perhaps the majority, would endure such a law, however good, with impatience or not at all, and bearing contempt toward the law would contend that not having been invited to share in its creation, they would in no wise observe it. On the other hand, any citizen will endure and obey a law however irksome, that is made from the deliberation and consent of the whole multitude, because he himself seems to have imposed it upon himself and, therefore, cannot complain against it.[1]

---

[1] Alan Gewirth, *Marsilius of Padua and Medieval Political Philosophy,* 1951

In many societies and organizations, individualized rules exist. It is not uncommon, after a motion has been made and seconded, to hear the secretary ask for the name of the person who seconded the motion. Although no parliamentary authority requires that the official minutes identify that person, the organization has the freedom to require the information if a need exists. An organization could require three seconds before consideration of any substantive motion; although such a requirement may be restrictive, permitting worthy but unclear proposals to be eliminated without adequate explanation, the organization evidently might believe that there was a need for such a rule.

It should be clear that "informal parliamentary procedure" is a homemade code of decision-making procedures that can provide a fair and practical basis for the conduct of business in small, informal groups, especially when the climate of the meeting is tolerant and relaxed, even in areas of conflict. Probably the most significant of all rules that apply in the informal situation is that every existing rule must be applied consistently for all members, in all cases, under all circumstances.

┌─ PRACTICE EXERCISE ───────────────────────────┐

1. To the teacher: tell the students that the purpose of this section is to learn the need for parliamentary procedure.

2. Explain that, except for the laws of nature, the nation, the state and community, there will be no rules or regulations within the classroom for the duration of the exercise.

3. Inform the students of one of the following goals for the group, giving no instructions concerning the task.

   a. Placing greater emphasis on school sports, less on academic standards.

   b. Increasing the drinking age to 21.

   c. Abolishing student testing at the end of each semester.

4. Instruct the students to unite the class in an effort to implement this goal.

5. Do everything possible to interfere with any constructive effort made by the students. Create an atmosphere of chaos by remaining silent, or by interrupting speakers, or by talking about matters far removed from the classroom.

6. Let the class struggle as they try to decide what to do and how to do it.

CLASS ACTIVITIES

As the class tries to work toward their goal, the students will become more aware of the necessity for order. Emphasize how certain personal rights of each student are causing elements of conflict. Prominent among those rights will be the following:

The right to speak and be heard

The right to disagree

The right to speak freely about anything at any time

With guidance, a discussion will follow that should reveal some definite parliamentary principles:

1. Everyone should have equal opportunity to speak without interruption, necessitating some kind of control if others are to hear what is said.
2. Any matter related to the group may be proposed except when another matter is under discussion.
3. Speaking for or against a proposal is everyone's right, but order is essential.
4. Parliamentary procedure is not, nor was ever intended to be, a problem-solving process. (Problem-solving comprises a sequence of events: the analysis of a problem, the acquisition of relevant information, the development and evaluation of possible solutions, the selection of the best possible solution and the group decision to implement it; its use elsewhere is inappropriate and is usually inhibiting or confusing.)

In contrast, parliamentary procedure is designed to expedite making decisions concerning a particular course of action.

Make it clear to the students that when no rules exist, the conditions of chaos and anarchy prevail. However, if the group as a whole feels the need for a rule binding upon all members, then it may be made. Almost immediately after this announcement, some member of the class will make a suggestion or a proposal. Focus on the proposal, showing that it is indeed a main motion. By asking questions about the relevance of the proposal to the accomplishment of the group goal, you can lead the discussion into an explanation of the second for a motion. If you refrain from further interference, someone in the group will shortly suggest something about relevance. The students will also be aware that the best method of overcoming their confusion will be to sacrifice something of their right to uncontrolled speech and give someone—a leader—the power to control it. One member of the group should be given the authority to make certain that only one person speaks at a time, that the subject spoken of is related to the group and its goal, and that each person has an equal opportunity to speak.

To accomplish these procedural goals, the original proposal must be postponed for a time, and you should explain the process. Details concerning the motions to lay on the table, to postpone definitely and to postpone indefinitely are not necessary. You need only to explain that if the group consent, one matter may be put aside and another taken up. Further discussion will lead to the consensus that there is a need for several more rules.

With class participation, little time will be required to explore the fundamentals of parliamentary procedure and to see the need for specific rules and the methods to implement them. Chaos is nonproductive. The attainment of a group objective requires order, but order cannot exist without systematic procedures that are fair to all members. The guidelines are few and easy to understand and apply:

- Everyone is equal, with equal rights and responsibilities.

- Only one person should speak at a time.

- Only one subject should be spoken about at a time.

- Minority rights must be protected.

- Majority decisions should be accepted by all members of a group.

- Every proposal should be made in good faith for the good of the group and should be free of trickery and as simple as possible.

- No rule should exist unless it is needed, but if it exists, it must be applied consistently.

While the need for order, reached through parliamentary procedure, is being demonstrated by class activity, there will be frequent occasions for you to interject short explanations as the students realize the need for specified techniques. These techniques may be discussed in any order and are best explained and demonstrated when the group recognizes the need for a particular action. However, in view of the informality of this instruction and the desire to coordinate the learning experience with the realization of the need, you may wish to limit the discussion to the following specifics:

The need for a method of proposing action
(the **MAIN MOTION**)

The need for a signal to indicate group interest in a proposal
(the **SECOND**)

The need for a method for modifying a proposal
(the **AMENDMENT**)

The need for an opportunity to delay and investigate a proposal (the motion to **REFER TO A COMMITTEE**)

The need to postpone any action on a proposal
(the motion to **TABLE**)

The need for a means of correcting an act of the leader or asking for order (the **POINT OF ORDER**)

The need for a method of challenging the leader's decision
(the **APPEAL**)

The need for a method for terminating discussion and requiring a vote (the motion to **VOTE IMMEDIATELY**)

The need for a technique that will verify the vote
(**DIVISION OF THE ASSEMBLY**)

The need for a way to end the meeting temporarily
(**RECESS**) or permanently (**ADJOURN**)

APPENDIX D
WHAT COMES NEXT?

After participating in this book's learning process, you should be in agreement that the underlying concept of parliamentary law and procedure is to provide the basic fundamental principles that maintain the freedoms we enjoy today; also, that the desire for democratic freedom is burgeoning worldwide.

Your new talent in the parliamentary field is needed to help promote, protect and safeguard the democracy we enjoy.

A few suggestions on how to do this as an individual include:

1. Join civic, professional, educational, fraternal organizations of interest to you. Participate in their projects, attend their meetings. This will provide opportunity to learn and practice LEADERSHIP.

2. Take further study courses such as those offered by the American Institute of Parliamentarians (AIP) on procedural methods, use of motions, handling administrative problems. These studies instill CONFIDENCE.

3. Attend parliamentary workshops and seminars, such as scheduled at AIP Practicums, Educational Forums and Annual Sessions, which provide you the opportunity to practice your parliamentary skills, to share parliamentary opinions, to hear new ideas, to learn from others' parliamentary activities. This networking and participation provides EXPERIENCE.

4. Subscribe to and read professional parliamentary journals, such as the AIP *Parliamentary Journal*, and books by other parliamentary authorities available through AIP, leading bookstores and the library system. The development and broadening of the scope of your parliamentary knowledge provides STRENGTH.

Participation in any or all of these actions provides for your PARLIAMENTARY ENRICHMENT.

Again, after a time you may ask, WHAT COMES NEXT? If you are interested in becoming a professional parliamentarian, in addition to the continuance and expansion of the above suggestions, keep in mind:

Learning the rules is not enough. Through the leadership, confidence and experience you have achieved you need to further develop and build a thorough understanding of the parliamentary principles behind the rules. Also, you must be committed to a two-way street of giving and receiving parliamentary information for your continuing education in the professional parliamentary field.

Growth as a professional parliamentarian is obtained through many of the avenues mentioned earlier, but with a different approach— one of giving parliamentary information rather than always taking. Substantial growth is achieved through membership in parliamentary organizations, review and discussion of material in current parliamentary publications, participation in conventions, taking and participating in educational courses, doing research on new and difficult situations, writing parliamentary articles, seeking innovative ways to present a parliamentary topic.

A parliamentarian is a perpetual student expanding parliamentary horizons. You attend meetings to analyze the proceedings, to compare your parliamentary knowledge of what is right versus the parliamentary activities taking place in the meeting. You establish a mind-set where the use of the proper parliamentary processes and procedures is as important as the final decision.

You must be willing to grow—continuing to update your parliamentary knowledge, to learn by your mistakes, to gain by sharing information with others. The parliamentary field is not only the knowledge of many parliamentary authorities, but the ability to share this knowledge with others, a willingness to dig deep in researching materials, the know-how to provide meaningful, thought-provoking information to develop rapport with your audiences, to prepare effective handouts to make meeting participants more knowledgeable. To be successful in the parliamentary field, besides knowledge, you will need interpersonal skills, professional appearance and demeanor, confidence, voice control, knowledge of protocol—all important elements of a professional parliamentarian.

Other features that will add to your enjoyment and growth as a professional parliamentarian are an in-depth continuous interest in parliamentary law and procedure, a goodly amount of dedication, a sincere desire to be of assistance to others in what is often a "behind-the-scenes" role and, to a high degree, a flexible schedule.

If you want an up-front job, a leadership position, being a professional parliamentarian is not for you, unless you wish to specialize as a professional presiding officer. Foremost in the mind-set is that a parliamentarian is a consultant. You offer advice to the Chair as required—an opinion based on your knowledge of the parliamentary authority being utilized—an opinion to be accepted <u>or rejected</u> as the Chair decides. In essence one of your major obligations as a Parliamentarian is to "make the Chair look good." You accept as a compliment the remark by a participant that "the meeting went so smoothly we really didn't need a parliamentarian." You know then it was a job well done!

PROFESSIONAL PARLIAMENTARIAN? A goal for you? Try it! You'll like it!

APPENDIX E
AMERICAN INSTITUTE OF
PARLIAMENTARIANS

The American Institute of Parliamentarians is an Illinois not-for-profit, educational corporation. The following Action Program is its permanent platform, amendable by the same procedures as its bylaws.

ACTION
PROGRAM

The general purpose of the American Institute of Parliamentarians is to work for the improvement of parliamentary procedure to the end that decisions are made by parliamentary means rather than by violence or by dictatorial actions, and that mankind will learn to live in peace through the effective implementation of sound democratic principles. Objectives of AIP are:

A. PROMOTE USE OF EFFECTIVE, DEMOCRATIC, PARLIAMENTARY PRACTICES

1. Remove unneeded complications, confusing ambiguities and archaic terminology from parliamentary usage;
2. Emphasize parliamentary law, sound democratic principles and skillful, ethical tactics;
3. Provide a clearinghouse for parliamentary problems;
4. Research parliamentary practices in various times and places, and in all types of organizations; and experiment with numerous techniques;
5. Study assemblies and committees of ordinary associations and of legislatures, city councils, business corporations;
6. Develop techniques for obtaining better understanding of parliamentary procedure and for building leadership;
7. Help and encourage sponsors of student organizations in the study and practice of proper parliamentary procedure;
8. Cooperate with all groups interested in the improvement of parliamentary procedure, to maintain friendly relationships, to share its knowledge and results of its research to the end that democracy will function better through procedure;

B. PROMOTE PREPARATION AND USE OF PARLIAMENTARY LITERATURE

9. Publish a quarterly Parliamentary Journal, a scholarly, practical, interesting aid to AIP members;
10. Publish regular editions of a Parliamentary Directory as an aid to AIP members; and as a guide to organizations and individuals needing expert parliamentary service;
11. Maintain a parliamentary library of literature for reference, sale, circulation and free distribution;
12. Publish a Parliamentary Bibliography, parliamentary opinions and other parliamentary materials;
13. Encourage various organizations and individuals to prepare and have published literature;
14. Provide editorial assistance to prospective authors of parliamentary material;

C. PROMOTE TEACHING OF PARLIAMENTARY PROCEDURE

15. Encourage credit-bearing courses in parliamentary procedure in universities, colleges and law schools;
16. Encourage credit-bearing work in parliamentary procedure as part of other courses, at the elementary, secondary and college levels;
17. Encourage non-credit courses in parliamentary procedure in public and private schools as part of their adult education programs;
18. Organize high school pupils, college students and adults for the purpose of studying parliamentary procedure;
19. Encourage organizations to develop educational programs which include the study of parliamentary procedure;
20. Promote radio and television programs, articles and news items in newspapers and magazines as well as discussion groups, workshops, and symposia;
21. Train and supply competent teachers of parliamentary procedure;

D. PROMOTE THE TRAINING AND CERTIFICATION OF PARLIAMENTARIANS

22. Develop advanced courses in parliamentary procedure to include methods of teaching and of serving as parliamentarians;
23. Maintain facilities for accrediting qualified members as Certified Parliamentarians (CP's) and as Certified Professional Parliamentarians (CPP's);

E. PROMOTE WIDER USE OF PARLIAMENTARIANS

24. Distribute the parliamentary directory so that organizations and individuals may easily locate qualified parliamentarians;
25. Distribute information concerning the various services which parliamentarians are prepared to render, and the value of such expert services;

F. MAINTAIN A REPRESENTATIVE, DEMOCRATIC ORGANIZATION

26. Maintain a membership of parliamentarians, educators, lawyers, legislators and members of business, civic, labor, professional, trade, veteran, religious, service and fraternal organizations, and welcome to membership interested persons regardless of age, color, creed, financial status, nationality, race or sex;
27. Develop a sound system of representation in AIP's board, committees and conventions;
28. Stimulate general membership participation, thus involving more persons in policy formation and in activities that tend to develop leadership;
29. Promote effective techniques for the prevention of steamroller tactics, filibustering and other undemocratic practices;
30. Emphasize procedures which protect the rights of the individual without hampering the proper interests of the majority;
31. Emphasize reevaluation or practices to the end that there will be perennial development of our concepts and a continuous strengthening of our FAITH in true democracy.

ANSWERS

LESSON 1
PRINCIPLES AND RULES OF PARLIAMENTARY LAW

Review Quiz #1 - Answers

1. Parliamentary law is to facilitate the transaction of business and to promote cooperation and harmony among the members.

2. Principles of parliamentary law are:

    ·   Power and authority are vested in the members.

    ·   All members have equal rights, obligations and privileges according to their status as members as defined in the bylaws.

    ·   All business shall be conducted fairly, impartially.

    ·   Only one piece of business may be considered at a time.

    ·   Majority shall rule.

    ·   Minority rights shall be protected.

3. Parliamentary law was developed through usage and custom. Statutory law is enacted through the state legislative bodies.

4. An organization adopts a charter, bylaws, standing and special rules and a parliamentary authority. Rules are obeyed in that order.

5. *Jefferson's Manual* was written to systematize and regulate the decision-making process in the U.S. Senate, which currently uses the *Floyd M. Riddick's Senate Rules.*

6. Parliamentary rules are not an end in themselves. Principles, tact and fair play must be applied when interpreting parliamentary rules.

7. Procedures evolved by **Petyt** are:

   · One subject at a time.

   · Alternation between opposite points of view in assignment to the floor.

   · Requirement that the Chair always call for the negative vote.

   · Decorum in debate must be preserved, omitting references to personalities.

   · Debates must be confined to the merits of the pending question.

   · Division of a question that has more than one substantive part.

8. The adopted parliamentary authority goes into effect on any rules or regulations not covered in the organization's own bylaws or rules of order.

9. The ultimate authority of an organization is vested in its membership.

10. To be effective, rules must change to meet changing conditions.

11. The advantage of using parliamentary rules is they make it easier for members to work together more efficiently and effectively.

LESSON 1
PRINCIPLES AND RULES OF PARLIAMENTARY LAW

Review Quiz #2 - Answers

1. Failure to protect the minority and failure to announce the vote result accurately.

2. Failure to take a vote accurately and fairly.

3. Failure to protect rights of the minority and failure to take a vote.

4. Failure to consider one piece of business at a time. Amendment was not germane.

5. Failure to provide free and full discussion.

6. Failure to abide by majority decision.

7. Failure to abide by majority decision.

8. Failure to require decorum during debate.

9. Failure to state the motion to be voted on.

10. Failure to protect rights of all members, including absentees.

LESSON 2
DELIBERATIVE ASSEMBLIES
MEETINGS

Review Quiz #1 - Answers

1. The requirements for a meeting to be called are:

   · must be properly called, with a quorum present

   · must have the presence of a presiding officer to conduct the meeting and a secretary to record action

   · must adopt an agenda

   · must be adjourned properly.

2. A call to a mass meeting should include the purpose of the call, the time, place, date, who may attend and names of the sponsors.

3. A special meeting must be properly called as specified in the bylaws, including advance notice to all members and the purpose for the special meeting. A presiding officer, a secretary and a quorum must be present. Minutes are not read.

4. The business conducted at an adjourned meeting (continued meeting) is a continuation of the same meeting from the point of its adjournment. Minutes are read and approved. It must be convened before the next regular meeting.

5. A meeting may be called to order as soon as a quorum is present, after the specific time set for the meeting. In the absence of a quorum, the group may not conduct any business except to adjourn, recess to obtain a quorum or move for an adjourned meeting.

6. Notice Required—Business Conducted

Meeting	Notice	Business
Regular	Bylaws	Adopted agenda
Adjourned	By motion	Continuation of adopted agenda
Special	Bylaws	As stated in the call
Annual	Bylaws	Reports and election of officers
		Other business, as stated in the bylaws
Mass	To those invited	As stated in the call

LESSON 3
ORGANIZING A SOCIETY

Review Quiz - Answers - (T)rue or (F)alse

1.   T

2.   F - The newly elected Chair conducts the election of the
        secretary.

3.   F - Adoption of a resolution is only a formal consent to
        form a society.

4.   F - No dues may be collected until adopted bylaws
        state the amount. Donations would be in order.

5.   T

6.   T

7.   F - Only those societies that intend to sell stock to the
        public, that are organized for profit and will pay
        income tax on their revenues, and that wish to
        protect the assets of their principals from personal
        liability in doing business with the public need to
        incorporate as a legal entity.

8.   T

LESSON 4
ORDER OF BUSINESS
AGENDA

Review Quiz #1 - Answers

1. Special Meeting:

    Call to order, quorum present

    Reading of call—specifying purpose of call

    Transaction of business for which meeting was called

    Adjournment

2. The singing of the national anthem comes directly after any invocation or prayer.

3. Order of business is the reason for the organization's existence. With it, business is conducted systematically, in a predicted sequence, so that consistency and convenience are provided.

4. Agenda is the order of business adopted for the meeting, listing specific items in the adopted order.

5. Program can refer to the agenda and include the extra items planned for the meeting, or it can include the agenda, workshops, speaker, exhibits and tours planned for an entire convention.

6. Members seeking to adjust the adopted order of business may move to **Suspend the Rules**, which requires a two-thirds vote, in order to take up any business out of its proper order.

7. Unfinished business refers to business that was pending at the time of adjournment of the previous meeting, business scheduled but unmet, or that which was postponed to the next meeting which must be completed before new business can be introduced.

8. Consent agenda applies to those items listed on the agenda which can be adopted in a group by *general consent* with no objection, or by majority vote, because they do not require debate or amendment.

9. Special orders refer to what was ordered to be considered at a special time during a meeting. Because a special order may interrupt pending business, it requires a two-thirds vote. The Chair announces the special order at the proper time.

10. *Good of the order* is an agenda item in some organizations where the welfare of the organization may be discussed—usually informally in regard to the work, reputation, membership, certain announcements and so on. They do not require motions or action to be taken on them at the time.

LESSON 4
ORDER OF BUSINESS
AGENDA

Review Quiz #2 - Answers

1.   6

2.   4

3.   10

4.   7

5.   1

6.   3

7.   5

8.   9

9.   2

10. 8

LESSON 5
BRINGING BUSINESS BEFORE THE ASSEMBLY
MAIN MOTION

Review Quiz #1 - Answers

1. The steps required to make and complete a main motion are:

   a) The member rises, addresses the chair, waits to be recognized.

   b) On recognition says, "I move that ...." stating the proposal in the affirmative.

   c) Another member seconds the motion.

   d) The Chair states the motion as approved by the maker.

   e) The Chair opens the proposition to debate.

   f) When debate is completed, the Chair puts the motion to a vote.

   g) The Chair announces the result of the vote, which side won, states who is to implement actions to be taken, if any, and indicates the next item of business.

2. An original main motion introduces new business before the assembly requiring a decision. An incidental main motion is a main motion that is incidental to or relates to the business of the assembly, or its past or future action.

3. The chief characteristics of a main motion are that it must be seconded; is debatable; is amendable; requires a majority vote; can be reconsidered.

4. Main motions may be helped by the addition of germane amendments intended to correct or improve the original proposition.

5. Motions need to be accurate and well worded to avoid confusion as to their intent. Accurate main motions help save time as they require less amending.

6. Motions that may be ruled NOT in order are those that: are dilatory, conflict with any laws, propose actions beyond the purposes or authority of the organization, present the same question already disposed of, conflict with motions temporarily set aside, are not applicable to the business under discussion.

7. Its provisions should be implemented. The secretary should record the motion in the minutes.

LESSON 5
BRINGING BUSINESS BEFORE THE ASSEMBLY
IMPROPER MOTIONS

Review Quiz #2 - Answers

1. The motion is put in the negative and therefore is unnecessary.

2. The motion is probably dilatory.

3. The motion violates the provisions of the bylaws.

4. The motion cannot be implemented as the parent bylaws supersede local unit rules. The motion could be to send a protest.

5. It is too late to object, as the motion is already in committee.

6. The motion is worded incorrectly. It should be stated "I move to suspend . . ." or "to rescind . . ." the standing rule.

7. It is too late to appeal the Chair's ruling which must be done at the time the ruling was made.

8. The motion is put in the negative.

9. The motion is incomplete. Do what? By whom? It must be re-stated.

10. This motion, although long, is in good order.

LESSON 5
BRINGING BUSINESS BEFORE THE ASSEMBLY
ORDER OF PROCEDURE

Review Quiz #3 - Answers

1.   <u>4</u>

2.   <u>1</u>

3.   <u>6</u>

4.   <u>9</u>

5.   <u>2</u>

6.   <u>10</u>

7.   <u>7</u>

8.   <u>12</u>

9.   <u>5</u>

10.   <u>8</u>

11.   <u>11</u>

12.   <u>3</u>

13.   <u>13</u>

LESSON 5
BRINGING BUSINESS BEFORE THE ASSEMBLY
SUBSTANTIVE MAIN MOTION

Review Quiz #4 - Answers

1. Chair should ask member to rephrase, to make the motion a specific substantive motion—do what? Possibly a motion to refer the problem to the finance committee or ways and means committee or both, to make a study and report at the next meeting.

2. Chair should remind members that "expenses" is too loose an interpretation—suggesting that, if it is seconded, amendments would be in order, such as citing "necessary" expenses for travel, room and meals.

3. Chair should ask member to rephrase the motion, to be specific, naming the suggestions. Members are apprised of them before such a motion can be considered.

4. Chair would rule this motion not in order as illegal and in violation of city ordinances.

5. Chair should ask member to rephrase as motion is incomplete; (a committee of how many, how appointed or elected, to report when).

6. Chair should ask member to rephrase as the motion's intent is not clear. As stated, the dog owners would be muzzled.

7. Chair would rule this motion, as stated, out of order as a violation of city ordinances.

8. Chair would rule this motion, as stated, out of order as a violation of the bylaws.

9. Chair would accept this motion, possibly asking first whether the finance committee believes this is financially possible.

10. Chair's response would depend on the wording of the Rule 10; does the rule apply to members only, or does it include guest speakers as well? A guest speaker, invited by the assembly, is not subject to rules if he was not informed of them prior to the meeting.

LESSON 6
BRINGING BUSINESS BEFORE THE ASSEMBLY
RESOLUTIONS

Review Quiz - Answers

1. A resolution is presented in writing, written by a committee or a single member. It usually is written in a formal style, often prefaced by a Preamble (whereas) which explains the reason for the Resolve (enactment).

2. The Chair states the resolution as presented (seconded, if not out of committee), or has the secretary or chairman of the committee read it carefully aloud. The Chair then states that the resolution is open to debate.

3. A preamble has no legal significance, and should be brief because the debate should be on the real decisions asked for in the resolution.

4. The preamble is amended last, because changes in the resolves may require changes in the preamble.

5. A majority vote adopts a resolution.

6. If a resolution contains several clauses, they can be adopted en bloc, or by motions to divide the question. Each resolve can be considered separately, or any one of the clauses may be considered separately. The vote is then taken on the entire resolution as amended.

7. Because resolutions usually come from a committee which expresses a majority opinion, as an expression of a group statement, it has a strong psychological force that the resolution be adopted.

LESSON 7
THE AMENDING PROCESS

Review Quiz - Answers

1. Amendments have several forms and two degrees. This can complicate a situation, as well as show common lack of knowledge for using them properly.

2. Amendments may legitimately alter a motion by adding to it, striking words, inserting words, substituting paragraphs or sentences. By their use, one can either support, alter or defeat the original motion.

3. Amendments must relate to the motions to which they apply and may not negate a proposition.

4. The substitute motion is a complete alternative proposed to the main motion. It must be germane to it. It is voted on first. If adopted, it must be voted on again as the main motion. If defeated, the original main motion, as amended or not, is voted upon.

5. Friendly amendments are suggestions to the maker of the motion, probably of words he would have used had he thought of them. With his approval, they are usually adopted by *general consent* with no objection.

6. Primary amendments are germane to the main motion. Secondary amendments are germane to the primary amendment. There can be no third degree amendment, but any number of amendments can be offered, one at a time, after pending amendments are disposed of.

7. Amendments are sometimes used to help a motion's acceptability by offering some change to it, or they may defeat the motion by altering its intent.

LESSON 7
THE AMENDING PROCESS

Review Quiz #2 - Answers - (T)rue or (F)alse

1.   T

2.   T

3.   F - One votes first on the substitute, the motion to amend.

4.   F - The amended motion must still be adopted.

5.   T

6.   F - Any number may be applied to the main motion, but one at a time.

7.   T

8.   F - It may be germane, although hostile.

9.   F - The reason for the proposal may be debated.

10. F - The secondary amendment need only be germane to the primary amendment.

11. T

12. T

13. F - The amendment only rewords the main motion. It must still be adopted.

14. T

15. T

16. T

LESSON 8
PRECEDENCE OF MOTIONS
TABLE OF MOTIONS

Review Quiz #1 - Answers

1. Subsidiary motions provide ways to dispose of pending motions and always apply to another motion.

2. They arise as needed and are disposed of in order of rank from highest to lowest.

3. They have complete control over the pending motion and are designed to expedite the pending motion.

4. Subsidiary motions are disposed of in order of precedence, from highest to lowest.

5. Incidental motions relate to pending business arising out of the matter at hand.

6. Incidental motions occur as needed, but must be resolved before business can resume and are usually undebatable, resolved by the Chair.

7. Privileged motions occur as needed due to special circumstances.

8. They are sometimes disposed of by the Chair. They must be resolved before business can continue, and they may interrupt pending business.

9. Incidental main motions are main motions that are incidental to, or related to, the business of the assembly, or its past or future action.

10. Precedence means order of rank, not importance, that provides a priority of order for action to be taken.

11. Secondary motions are those that can be made and considered while a main motion is pending and which must be acted upon or disposed of before direct consideration of the main motion can be continued.

12. Secondary motions are the subsidiary, privileged, incidental motions.

LESSON 8
PRECEDENCE OF MOTIONS
TABLE OF MOTIONS

Review Quiz #2 - Answers

<u>C</u>   1.   Immediately after the reading of the minutes you wish the assembly to consider your motion to raise dues.

<u>E</u>   2.   The motion on the floor is to raise dues from six to 12 dollars a year payable monthly instead of yearly, as in the past. You want the dues raised, but you want them payable yearly.

<u>J</u>   3.   Another member insults you while having the floor.

<u>B</u>   4.   You think the motion too silly for discussion.

<u>G or K</u>   5.   The Chair calls for new business immediately after the reports of the committee chairmen.

<u>A</u>   6.   The Chair made a decision. You think his judgment is wrong.

<u>L</u>   7.   The motion you favor is under discussion. It is obvious that it will be defeated. You do not want this to happen.

<u>L</u>   8.   You are a member of a group supporting a Valentine dance. Someone outside your group moves to amend for an Easter dance. You wish to consult your fellow supporters of the original motion to decide what action to take.

<u>M or N</u>   9.   There is a motion to rescind a main motion. You wish to know the vote required to adopt the motion to rescind.

<u>H</u>   10.   There is a motion to adjourn pending. What is the only motion in order at this time?

<u>I</u>   11.   Your motion was adopted, but now you think an addition to it should be made.

<u>F</u>   12.   You agree with the proposition except for one sentence in it.

LESSON 9
SUBSIDIARY MOTIONS

Review Quiz #1 - Answers

What motion would you use?

1.   Main motion

2.   Amend

3.   Limit debate

4.   Previous question (vote now)

5.   Refer to committee

6.   Lay on the table, or postpone to a set time

LESSON 9
SUBSIDIARY MOTIONS

Review Quiz #2 - Answers - (T)rue or (F)alse

1.   F - Motions from a committee need not be seconded.

2.   F - Members may second motions in order to have them discussed, not because they favor the motion.

3.   T

4.   T

5.   F - Refer to committee is of higher precedence than postpone indefinitely.

6.   F - An amendment to the amendment cannot be amended. Tertiary (third degree) amendments are not permitted.

7.   F - Lay on the table cannot be discussed or amended. It never includes the time limit for the postponement.

8.   F - Refer to committee may be a main motion.

LESSON 9
SUBSIDIARY MOTIONS

Review Quiz #3 - Answers

1. The Chair should refuse to accept this motion. The Chair may explain to the members how its use would deprive members of their right to debate (which should require a two-thirds vote), and inform members that this motion is for emergency use only (**Robert**).

2. Members calling "Question" usually indicate impatience and can be ignored by the Chair. It is not a motion made after due recognition by the Chair. Explain the use of the motion to the assembly. If many members call "Question" and it appears to the Chair that most members seem ready to vote now (without the proper use of the motion **Previous Question**), the Chair may say, "It appears to the Chair that the assembly is ready to vote." If there is no objection, the Chair will assume the proper motion to close debate (**Previous Question**) has been made and will put the motion to a vote. If there is an objection, the Chair will accept the formal motion, **Previous Question** (close debate and vote now), when properly proposed.

3. The Chair would ask the member to complete the motion, stating which committee, if a standing committee is to be referred to, or, if not, to move to complete the motion by moving to *create a committee* of how many, how selected and to report.

4. The Chair should rule on whether the amendment is in order, because it does not contradict or negate the main motion. If the Chair is in doubt, the assembly may decide by majority vote.

5. The maker of the main motion has the right to speak against the amendment but not against the main motion.

6. The Chair could explain that business may not be postponed beyond the next regular meeting but may be postponed once again at the next meeting, if necessary.

LESSON 9
SUBSIDIARY MOTIONS

Review Quiz #4 - Answers

1. Lay on the table

2. Main motion

3. The main motion, sometimes other motions

4. Amendment

5. Not in order, lower in precedence

6. Lay on table, previous question, postpone indefinitely

7. Previous question, limit debate

8. Lay on the table

9. Reverse order of precedence, highest to lowest

10. As amended

11. Cannot

12. Meeting or session

13. Order of precedence, lowest to highest

14. Limit debate, postpone to set time, refer to committee

15. Lay on table, previous question, limit debate

LESSON 10
PRIVILEGED MOTIONS

Review Quiz #1 - Answers

1. Fix the time to which to adjourn

    Adjourn

    Recess

    Question of privilege

    Call for orders of the day (return to the regular order)

2. Privileged motions are not debatable because of their importance and urgency which permits them to be considered ahead of pending business.

3. A motion to **Recess** suspends the meeting temporarily and business is resumed at the point of interruption. A motion to **Adjourn** closes the meeting and the next meeting begins as an entirely new meeting with a new agenda.

4. "I rise to a *question of privilege*" or "I rise to a *point of order.*" The Chair will ask the member to state the question. The Chair will then rule on whether the question is in order or not in order.

5. The motion to **Adjourn** does not require a quorum since without a quorum a meeting must **Adjourn**, or take steps to obtain a quorum, or move for an adjourned meeting.

6. The motion to **Adjourn** may be moved at any time, even after the call to order. If no business is pending, it is a main motion.

7. If the business was scheduled, it is taken up under unfinished business at the next meeting. If not scheduled, it is introduced under new business.

8. The Chair may **Adjourn** the meeting when there is no further business or in an emergency or when no quorum is present.

9. The motion to **Fix the Time to Which to Adjourn** provides for continuance of the same meeting at the time stated.

10. In the absence of an emergency, the *question of privilege* may be stated as a main motion, and the members are granted the right to debate.

LESSON 10
PRIVILEGED MOTIONS

Review Quiz #2 - Answers - Motions

1. To limit debate

2. Call for orders of the day, or point of order

3. Amend

4. Refer to committee

5. Postpone indefinitely

6. Question of privilege, to suspend the rules, to lay on the table

7. Previous question

8. Move for an adjourned meeting

9. Adjourn

10. Recess

11. Question of privilege

12. Move for an adjourned meeting

13. To adjourn, or recess to obtain a quorum

14. Call for orders of the day

15. Previous question

16. Adjourn

17. Postpone to a set time, recess

18. Divide the question or amend

19. Recess, refer to committee, postpone definitely

20. Refer to committee

21. Postpone to a set time, lay on the table

22. Extend debate

23. Postpone to a set time

24. Substitute

25. Postpone to a set time

26. Question of privilege

LESSON 11
INCIDENTAL MOTIONS

Review Quiz - Answers

1. Division of assembly

2. Point of order

3. Appeal

4. Object to consideration

5. Division of a question

6. Request

7. Parliamentary inquiry, point of information

8. Point of order

9. Informal consideration

10. Withdraw

11. Point of information

12. Parliamentary inquiry

13. Division of a question

14. Object to consideration

15. Appeal

16. Suspend the rules

LESSON 12
RESTORATORY MOTIONS
CHANGING PREVIOUS DECISIONS

Review Quiz #1 - Answers - Comparison of Reconsider and Rescind

Comparison	Reconsider	Rescind
When Proposed:	At any time	No business pending
	Can interrupt a speaker	Not in order when reconsider has been moved
Precedence:	Over any main or restoratory motion. Double precedence for making and for consideration	None
How Proposed:	By one who voted on the winning side (Robert)	Any member
Action Taken:	Is debatable, not amendable	Is debatable and amendable
Vote Required:	Majority	Two-thirds without notice. Majority with notice
Effect:	Opens main motion to debate	Countermands main motion
Special Consideration:	Stops action on the adopted motion. Must be called up	Giving notice of this motion does not prevent action being taken on the previously adopted motion. Out of order when main motion has been implemented

LESSON 12
RESTORATORY MOTIONS
CHANGING PREVIOUS DECISIONS

Review Quiz #2 - Answers

1. The motion has the same rank as when **laid on the table**, including all pending amendments.

2. The motion can be taken from the table in the same session or the next session in an organization meeting quarterly or more often.

3. To **Amend Something Previously Adopted** is used when changing only part of a text.

4. Any member can move to **Rescind** at any time provided action on the motion has not been taken.

5. **Rescind** requires a majority vote with notice, a two-thirds vote without notice.

6. **Reconsider** stops any action on the adopted motion.

7. **Reconsider** takes two actions, one to make it and one to call it up for consideration.

8. If a committee is discharged, all action on what was referred to it stops. The assembly makes any further decisions as to the status of the referral.

9. **Amend Something Previously Adopted, Rescind** and **Discharge a Committee** may require previous notice.

10. The purpose of **Rescind and Expunge** is to condemn action and strike it from the minutes.

11. **Reconsider and Enter on the Minutes** permits any two members to halt action on a motion adopted by a majority.

12. If a member did not vote on the prevailing side, he can persuade another member to move to **Reconsider (Robert)**. Any member may vote to **Reconsider**.

13. Motions upon which action has been taken may not be **Reconsidered** or **Rescinded**.

14. **Reconsider** is debatable and includes debate on the main motion as well.

15. If members neglect to call up the motion to **Reconsider**, the Chair may remind the assembly of this.

16. In committee, **Reconsider** can be proposed at any time, no limit on it, by any member who did not vote on the losing side (**Robert**).

17. Adoption of the motion to **Reconsider** does not adopt the main motion which is put to vote again, after the reconsideration.

18. If the motion to **Reconsider** fails, the motion under consideration remains as adopted.

19. If **Rescind** is adopted, the main motion is cancelled as though it never existed.

20. Adopting the motion to **Reconsider** places the main motion before the assembly for another vote.

LESSON 12
RESTORATORY MOTIONS
CHANGING PREVIOUS DECISIONS

Review Quiz #3 - Answers

1. a

2. b

3. d

4. c

5. c

6. b

7. d

8. d or b

LESSON 13
THE PRESIDING OFFICER
PRESIDENT - CHAIRMAN

Review Quiz #1 - Answers

1. When serving as presiding officer, the Chair should be impartial. It is the members who decide.

2. "The meeting will come to order." Strike gavel firmly. "The Chair will not continue business until all are quiet and in their seats." Wait calmly, with dignity. Look at the assembly with intensity.

3. "The Chair will not recognize any member, nor entertain any motion, until this meeting comes to order." Tap gavel firmly. Pause. If some members persist, the Chair may say, "Shall these members be allowed to continue to disrupt the meeting? A motion will be in order to have them escorted from the room."

4. Ignore it.

5. As a member of the organization, the Chair has the same voting rights as any member, but disenfranchises those rights to preserve the appearance of impartiality, except if the vote is by ballot or roll call (in which the Chair votes last) or when the vote can affect the result.

6. "The Chair will recognize each member in turn. Please be seated and rise for a turn when the floor has been yielded. The Chair recognizes . . . . "

7. The gavel is used to call the meeting to order, when there has been a break in decorum and to adjourn the meeting. Some authorities like the tap of the gavel at the conclusion of the announcement of each vote to signal that that particular business has been acted on.

8. The Chair should announce which side (majority) has won as "The Ayes have it and the motion to . . . is adopted," or "The Noes have it and the motion to . . . is lost." He should then see that those who are to implement the motion receive the order.

9. The presiding officer should have a knowledge of procedural rules and how to use them, and the ability to deal fairly in human relations.

10. As an administrator, a president must set goals, be responsible for the welfare of the organization and preserve order.

LESSON 13
THE PRESIDING OFFICER
PRESIDENT - CHAIRMAN

Review Quiz #2 - Answers

President (Chair) May	President (Chair) May Not
Announce unfinished business	Close debate
Close nominations	Order a vote by ballot
Validate voting results	Declare a close vote unanimous
Assume motion to adopt auditor's report	Preside at committee of the whole
Rule a motion out of order	Conduct business in absence of a quorum
Preside at own election	Preside ex officio
Order the secretary to note offensive remarks	Be counted in committee quorum
Call an offender to order	Vote twice on a proposition
Appoint a temporary chairman	Order a bylaw revision
Assume office immediately	Move to adopt own recommendation
Order a counted vote	Be ex officio member of all committees
Appoint the parliamentarian	Refuse recognition to the floor
Take a vote on an assumed motion	Depart from the adopted agenda
Adjourn the meeting	
Take a vote on an unseconded motion	
Assume full authority to make rulings	

LESSON 14
DEBATE

Review Quiz #1 - Answers - Practice Exercise

The reasons to favor a raise in dues:

a.   Last year's budget showed a deficit.

b.   Dues are currently less than for a comparable membership.

c.   More revenue can provide better services.

The reasons to oppose a raise in dues:

a.   Revenue can better be raised by more effective ways to recruit new members.

b.   Last year's deficit was due to an unusual circumstance.

c.   Increased dues may cause some members to resign.

Dilatory comment (unacceptable)

"Now that I've reviewed the first two budget items, I'll review the other 17."

Comment lacking in decorum:

"We could solve our financial problems with a more competent treasurer."

LESSON 14
DEBATE

Review Quiz #2 - Answers

1. Most motions are debatable except when debate would defeat the purpose of the motion.

2. **Limit or Extend Debate, Recess, Adjourn, Previous Question, Object to Consideration, Lay on the Table.**

3. The presiding officer may debate if he leaves the Chair, and he must not return to it until final action has been taken on the motion. He may participate in debate during informal consideration or, without leaving the Chair, may explain the result of the vote if members vote "Aye" or "No" on the proposition. He may clarify obscure or complex points as long as this is done impartially.

4. Decorum is courtesy, propriety and fair play during discussion of an issue.

5. Dilatory tactics are efforts to delay or hinder progress in debate by using motions that would adversely affect the progress, such as moving to *postpone* when a prompt decision is required.

6. Debate provides for group thinking, for interchange of facts and ideas that "gives truth a chance to emerge."

7. The Chair may not impatiently hurry debate by taking the vote too soon.

8. Member may interrupt a speaker if the need is urgent by moving a *point of order* or *of personal privilege* addressed to the Chair.

9. Motions that help control debate are **Previous Question, Limit Debate, Lay on the Table, Refer to Committee, Postpone Indefinitely and Object to Consideration.**

10. Voting on a proposition without debate violates the fundamental principles of the decision-making process; e.g., before deciding "yes" or "no" by vote, know all the facts—listen to all the arguments pro and con. Debate clarifies the issue; debate is informative; it tests the merits of the proposal; it evaluates the need; it challenges the credibility of the proposed action; and it projects the expected results of the proposal.

LESSON 15
STRATEGY OF DEBATE

Review Quiz - Answers

1. When preparing to debate, be sure to **organize and simplify your arguments.**

2. To persuade others to your opinion, always **be agreeably courteous.**

3. When speaking as an adversary, **be specific, be accurate, be germane.**

4. When the opponent is speaking, **pay close attention to the remarks made.**

5. If debate gets heated, it is often wise to **call for a recess.**

6. To support your arguments, prepare with **facts and provable statements.**

7. A member about to propose a subject for debate should **get support in advance whenever possible.**

8. Base your arguments on the psychological **needs of human behavior.**

9. Confound your opponent by asking **for proof. Ask questions.**

10. To save your position if losing, **move to Recess, to Amend, to Refer to Committee or to Postpone.**

11. Remember that procedural motions are not **debatable.**

12. After rising to speak, be sure to identify yourself and **speak audibly and clearly.**

Note: Many correct answers are possible to these questions. The answers given above are suggestions only. The questions may be used as the basis for a class discussion.

LESSON 16
QUORUM

Review Quiz #1 - Answers

1. A quorum is the number of members in good standing required to be present to validate action taken at a meeting of an organized group.

2. A quorum should be small in number to assure the presence of a sufficient number of members, even under hardship conditions.

3. Mass meeting: Quorum is those present.

   Convention: Quorum is a majority of
                            registered delegates.

   Special Meeting: Quorum is the same as a
                            regular meeting.

   Committee or Board: Quorum is a majority of
                            membership, or as
                            specified in bylaw.

   Ordinary Society: Quorum is as specified
                            in the bylaws.

4. Move for an *adjourned* meeting, for a *recess*, or to *adjourn*.

5. Qualified voters who are present or as stated in the bylaws.

6. In four and five, quorum is three; six and seven, quorum is four.

7. Yes, action is valid if a quorum is present.

8. Once established, a quorum is assumed to be present throughout the meeting until adjournment or until challenged. If some members have departed from the meeting leaving less than the required number constituting a stated quorum, the quorum is said to have disappeared.

LESSON 16
QUORUM

Review Quiz #2 - Answers

1. Yes, a quorum of 10 is six.

2. One of three actions: set a time for an *adjourned* meeting, *recess* to obtain a quorum, or *adjourn*.

3. Yes, the meeting was scheduled. Anticipating the arrival of a quorum, the Chair kept the members present without conducting any business or making any announcements. Any member could have moved to **adjourn**.

4. As a *point of order*, ask for a quorum count. If there is no quorum, all business must discontinue. Or the members could refrain from calling attention to the fact, since a quorum is presumed to be present unless challenged. Once challenged, the absence of a quorum cannot be ignored.

5. Quorum of committee was eight. Majority of 11 was six. The motion was lost.

6. Quorum of committee is seven. Vote was invalid as no quorum was present.

7. Quorum was present plus one. Vote was adopted. Majority of five is three.

8. Yes, if those present are willing to take the responsibility to take action in good faith that it will be ratified later by the assembly. If not ratified at a later date, responsibility and/or damages to the organization (if any) because of the unauthorized action taken will be borne by those members taking the action.

LESSON 17
MINUTES

Review Quiz #1 - Answers

1.   To preserve accurate, official records of action taken by the organization as well as to keep a historical record.

2.   To verify the record.

3.   Yes, by use of the motion to **Amend Something Previously Adopted** (changing adopted motions), which requires a two-thirds vote.

4.   Exactly as stated by the Chair with the approval of the maker. No motion such as "I so move" (which requires the secretary to paraphrase the motion) is valid.

5.   Yes. It must be made available to them for reference purposes.

6.   The board.

LESSON 17
MINUTES

Review Quiz #2 - Answers

_4_   Who presided

_1_   Kind of meeting

_5_   Disposition of previous minutes

_2_   Name of society

_3_   Date, time, place

_8_   All points of order and appeals

_9_   Hour of adjournment

_6_   All main motions as stated by the Chair

_7_   All notices of motions to be made

_10_   Signature of who took the minutes

LESSON 17
MINUTES

Review Quiz #3 - Answers - (T)rue or (F)alse

1.   T

2.   F - Only those stated by the Chair.

3.   T

4.   F - Only motions as proposed by members.

5.   T

6.   F - No minutes are read at a special meeting—the call is
         read.

7.   F - All counted votes only.

LESSON 17
MINUTES

Review Quiz #4 - Items not included in minutes - Answers

1. Name of seconder
2. Any discussion or remark unless adopted by a motion to do so,
    which is included in the minutes.
3. Any slanderous comments.
4. Motion not stated by the Chair.
5. Withdrawn motion, unless necessary for the record.
6. Previous comments or opinions of the secretary.
7. Incidental motion resolved by the Chair.
8. Roll call attendance (unless group is very small).

LESSON 18
FINANCES

Review Quiz #1 - Answers

1. Allocation of an organization's expenditure of funds is determined **by preparation of a budget.**

2. Two main items included in preparing a budget are **source of revenue** and **anticipated expenses.**

3. Adoption of a budget is authorized by **the assembly by majority vote.**

4. A budget may be amended if the **amended amount does not exceed anticipated income.**

5. An audit is valuable because **it is used to verify the treasurer's books or to expose an error.**

6. The treasurer's report is not submitted to vote because **it has not been verified.**

7. Adoption of a budget does not permit the treasurer to **pay bills automatically.**

LESSON 18
FINANCES

Review Quiz #2 - Answers

Monthly Report of Treasurer

Amount on hand at previous meeting (date)   _____

     Receipts   _____

     Disbursements   _____

Amount on hand at current meeting (date)   _____

     Date   _____

     Signature   _____

LESSON 19
OFFICERS

Review Quiz #1 - Answers

1. Officers should be selected for **integrity and competency.**

2. Bylaws should contain the following information about officers: **title, qualifications, term of office, method of election, succession to office, how to fill a vacancy.**

3. A president has the duty and responsibility to **protect the rights of members and to preserve order.**

4. As administrator, the president is responsible to **set goals, maintain a well-run organization, supervise the execution of goals.**

5. As presiding officer, the president must know **procedural rules and how to use them, the organization's documents of authority, how to preside fairly.**

6. The vice president should be highly qualified because **the vice president serves as "standby" for the president.**

7. After a term of office expires, the president-elect **automatically becomes president without actually being elected to that office.**

8. The treasurer reports at each regular meeting on the financial condition of the society but no **action is taken on the report because it has not been verified.**

9. The most important role of the secretary is to **keep accurate, up-to-date minutes.**

10. Officers required to be present for a meeting to be valid are the **president and the secretary.**

LESSON 19
OFFICERS

Review Quiz #2 - Answers

1. Title of officers, how elected, term of office, how vacancies are filled, number of terms in office, qualification and duties for each office.

2. By numerical order, the first vice president moves up, then others move up. The vacancy is in the lowest office.

3. To keep financial records in order through a verified statement which is adopted by the society.

4. The president-elect is never elected president directly, assuming office at conclusion of the term of the current president.

5. Legal representatives are those authorized by the bylaws and/or by appointment of the board or assembly of the organization, to act for the organization in legal matters: usually a presiding officer (president) and a secretary.

6. To accurately record action taken by the assembly and read the minutes.

7. To submit an accurate statement of amount on hand at previous meeting, receipts, disbursements, amount on hand currently.

8. No, not without permission of the assembly.

9. No, only by approval of the assembly, unless authorized to do so.

10. Duties are like those of a caretaker of the meeting—keeping members from interfering, doing errands for the presiding officer, delivering messages, escorting dignitaries or guests, escorting unruly members from meetings.

LESSON 20
EXECUTIVE BOARD

Review Quiz #1 - Answers

1. The purpose of an executive board is to manage and to administer the business of the organization, to carry out its duties as defined in the bylaws or by order of the assembly.

2. The composition of a board is established in the bylaws usually including elected officers, and any others as the bylaws may authorize. Board members are considered officers of the organization.

3. A board may make its own rules if not in conflict with the parent organization or other laws.

   It must provide for regular meetings properly called, with a quorum present; must keep minutes; may conduct meetings as formally as size may require; must resolve all problems by majority vote or *general consent.*

4. A board's duties and powers are defined in the bylaws and come from authority outside itself. It correlates activities, recommends policies, carries out assignments, controls finances subject to membership approval and acts for the society when it is not in session.

5. Board minutes are confidential, read and approved by the board, unless permission is granted for regular members to hear them.

6. With the exception of the president, all board members hold equal rank and may not act or speak individually on behalf of the board unless empowered to do so. All decisions are by group majority action.

7. Boards must take directions from the assembly, which can amend or rescind any board action. Boards cannot create offices, fill vacancies, nor add to their membership except as bylaws provide. Boards may not assume powers not expressly prohibited in bylaws.

8. Motions adopted by preceding boards continue in effect until completed or rescinded.

9. Executive committee may only exist if established in the bylaws. It usually is composed of the president and a few other board members. It reports to and is subordinate to the board. Its report is included in board minutes. It usually functions for delicate personal matters or for financial transactions.

10. Specific exclusive powers may be cited in the bylaws. If the assembly meets less often than quarterly, the board may be empowered to act for the assembly.

LESSON 20
Executive Board

Review Quiz #2 - Answers - (T)rue or (F)alse

1. F - Only between meetings or as empowered.

2. F - May make own rules if they do not conflict with parent bylaws.

3. F - Only if permitted in bylaws.

4. T

5. T

6. T

7. F - Reports recommendations, action taken.

8. T

9. T

10. T

11. T

12. T

13.   T

14.   T

15.   F - Only by permission of the board.

16.   T

17.   F - Such a conference must be authorized and conducted legally.

18.   T

19.   T

20.   T

LESSON 21
MEMBERSHIP

Review Quiz - Answers

1. Yes, a member is eligible to vote until he has been suspended or dropped from membership or unless bylaws prohibit him from voting.

2. Yes, if not obligated to serve as a condition of membership.

3. Yes, she may vote for any position or office in which she is included among others.

4. Membership may be terminated for: nonpayment of dues, if so stated in the bylaws; by expulsion, after a trial; by resignation; and upon dissolution of the society.

5. An honorary member is a person who holds a complimentary title, which usually permits the holder to attend meetings and to speak— without payment of regular dues—but not to vote, unless bylaws allow it, or unless full payment of dues is made as an active member. The title is for life or until rescinded.

6. If obligations of office are compulsory and the member cannot fulfill them, a resignation from office is in order. If the obligations are not compulsory, no excuse for resignation is required. A member may request from the assembly, citing the reason, to be excused from certain obligations or to be excused temporarily.

7. Common law provides that such a member should be disqualified from voting on that issue or should abstain from voting, but the member is counted in the quorum for the vote at the time the action is taking place.

8. A member in good standing is one who has fulfilled the requirements for membership and who has not voluntarily withdrawn from membership or been expelled or suspended. Bylaws must include any statement that suspension may result from nonpayment of dues. The member is then deprived of his right to make motions, debate or vote.

9. List any five as listed in Lesson 21 material.

10. List any five as listed in Lesson 21 material.

11. Bylaws on membership should include requirements for eligibility, application and acceptance procedure, dues and any other required fees, provision for resignation, suspension and expulsion, members' rights according to classification, and classes of membership, if any.

12. Membership provides rights and obligations to participate in the activities of an organization according to the classification of membership.

13. An ex officio member has all the rights of a regular member but is not counted in the quorum.

14. No vote is taken on a resignation.

LESSON 22
COMMITTEES

Review Quiz #1 - Answers - Practice Exercise

1. Sample answers:

   a. To investigate:

      The committee is to request an interview with the town library board to request permission to meet in their Aegean Meeting Room each Wednesday evening from 7:00 p.m. to 10:30 p.m. and to report to the society at the next meeting.

   b. To recommend action:

      The committee shall obtain prices, delivery time, and payment methods from Sears, Montgomery Ward, and J. C. Penney for the purchase of a computer and, at the next meeting, recommend the best choice and give its rationale.

   c. To take action:

      The committee shall review the list of newly published books on parliamentary law and purchase 10 copies each of its first two selections, to be paid for from the miscellaneous fund. The books shall be placed in the school library.

2. a. The advantage of a committee is that it may take more time fully to deliberate the problem and come to a group discussion.

   b. Standing committees are created in the bylaws. Other committees are **appointed** by a motion from the floor which may or may not included specific members; or **appointed** by the Chair, if authorized in the bylaws, or by a motion to refer to a committee appointed by the Chair; or **elected** after being nominated by the Chair or nominated and elected by the assembly.

   c. Committee business is conducted informally with no time limit on debate and no limit on the number of turns to speak. No motion to close debate is in order. **Reconsider** may be moved as often as required. The committee chairman participates fully.

   d. The committee chairman must: select a time and place to meet convenient to all members; supervise an orderly meeting; start on time with a quorum present; have assignment and any instructions and copies of all necessary documents; ensure full and free discussion.

LESSON 22
COMMITTEES

Review Quiz #2 - Answers - (T)rue or (F)alse

1.   F - Already seconded in committee.

2.   T

3.   T

4.   T

5.   T

6.   F - Membership only from appointing power.

7.   T

8.   F - Not always competent.

9.   F - Established in bylaws, adopted authority.

10.   F - Not obliged to attend.

11.   T

12.   T

13.   F - Discharge is automatic.

14.   F - Only if empowered to do so.

15.   T

16.   F - By motion from the floor.

17.   T

18.   T

LESSON 22
COMMITTEES

Review Quiz #3 - Answers

1. A committee should keep some records of its meetings. One member may be designated as an official recorder. Charts could be prepared to define the problem; what ideas have been proposed to solve the problem; what has been considered; what needs further consideration; who is responsible for any specific assignment; what has been accomplished to date. Such records of progress help the committee prepare its final report. The notes are intended for the committee members only and are usually destroyed after the final report.

2. The first committee meeting is important. Members should be introduced to help them get to know one another and feel more comfortable about working together. Ground rules should be set, such as: Meetings will begin and end on time; members are expected to attend and participate. The assignment should be clearly defined. Members should be told what is expected of them; that they will, from now on, work as a team. Dates and times for future meetings should be established.

3. "Brainstorming" is a method where each member may contribute ideas for solving the problem freely, no matter how improbable they may seem at the time. No comments are made until a list of suggestions is ready. Each suggestion is open for discussion and the elimination of the least appropriate begins. When one or two really useful ideas emerge, these are given concentrated study until a good solution emerges after each alternative has been evaluated from the new information, reexamination and consideration of alternatives.

4. The "Delphi Technique" is a method often used in committees where meetings can present a hardship because of distance, expense or time. The chairman circulates the assignment or problem to each committee member by memo. Each member considers the message carefully and responds to the chairman with questions, suggestions. The chairman compiles these and recirculates the message with alterations. This continues as often as needed, usually not more than three times. This method permits each committee member time to study the problem before answering. The final result becomes a truer expression of group opinion as agreed to by a majority of the members.

5. Difference of opinion is a healthy sign that members are thinking about the assignment, but sometimes this causes friction among them. The chairman must maintain leadership: by getting more facts provided, by insisting they are understood, by citing areas of agreement, by keeping discussion germane. Good humor should be maintained, never permitting sarcasm. Emphasize the team work of the group. Insist on only constructive criticism.

6. Committee decisions are best made by consensus, a compromise of opinions that comes to a final agreement among the members—a win/win solution wherein members who have changed their opinions still keep their dignity. Decisions made by a majority vote, while correct, still leave some of the members dissatisfied with the resulting decisions.

LESSON 23
COMMITTEE REPORTS

Review Quiz - Answers - (T)rue or (F)alse

1.   T

2.   T

3.   T

4.   T

5.   F - It is placed on file for reference.

6.   F - Usually.

7.   F - Only with permission of the assembly.

8.   T

9.   T

10. F - The report has already been received. No action is taken
          except on recommendations contained in the report.

LESSON 24
BYLAWS
PART I

Review Quiz #1 - Answers

1. Executive boards may not assume powers not granted in the bylaws, can act for the society only between its meetings, can take no action that conflicts with action taken by the assembly, must carry out instructions of the assembly.

2. Executive boards may be granted full power to act independently, may act for the assembly between its meetings, may formulate policy for recommendation to the assembly.

3. Standing committee information should include the following: Enumeration of committees; how they are appointed or elected; whether a chairman serves as director on the board; the duties of the committee; authority to act, if necessary.

4. To amend bylaws requires: previous notice, two-thirds vote or as provided in the bylaws information about the amendment, such as endorsement by two members' signatures.

5. The adopted bylaw goes into effect immediately upon adoption, and thus can only be amended according to the bylaws. A negative vote may be reconsidered.

6. While the adoption of the bylaw is immediate, its implementation may be delayed if a provision is adopted which states an effective date.

7. A motion to rescind the bylaws, with previous notice and a two-thirds vote.

8. A bylaw may be suspended only by a provision for its suspension stated in the bylaws.

    Note: **Robert** says that if the bylaw is procedural in nature, it does not belong in the bylaw and may be suspended.

LESSON 24
BYLAWS
PART I

Review Quiz #2 - Answers - (T)rue or (F)alse

1.   T

2.   F - Special meetings are provided for in the bylaws.

3.   F - This is the right of any member.

4.   F - This method has a disadvantage. It requires changes
             in computation.

5.   F - At least the annual meeting date should be specified.

6.   T

7.   F - Only after all commitments, taxes, are paid—and not
             ever if incorporated.

8.   F - Boards act for the membership whenever authorized
             to do so.

LESSON 25
BYLAWS
PART II

Review Quiz #1 - Answers - Practice Exercise

1. A membership article should include: classes of membership; limitations; rights; dues and initiation fee (if any); joint or family membership.

2. A membership article could include the following rights: to enjoy all social privileges; to nominate and be nominated; to nominate oneself; to vote for oneself; to change one's vote before announcement of the result; to make motions; to debate; to vote or abstain; to receive a trial if accused; to resign; to serve on committees; to hold office if eligible.

3. Officers in order of rank: president, first, second, third vice-presidents, president-elect, recording secretary, corresponding secretary, treasurer, financial secretary, sergeant-at-arms, directors—or as stated in the bylaws. If the organization is incorporated, the chairman of the board supersedes the president. The president may hold both offices.

4. The recording secretary takes and keeps minutes, is custodian of all records, has custody of the seal of the corporation, signs documents, keeps current list of all committees and their chairmen, and files copies of all adopted rules and policies ready for quick reference.

  The corresponding secretary of an unincorporated society sends out all notices, notifies members of appointment to committees, writes all correspondence for the organization or the board.

5. The financial secretary prepares the budget, sends all bills, receives payment, maintains a ledger for the treasurer, sends out notices of dues, turns all monies received over to the treasurer.

  The treasurer is custodian of all monies, deposits and withdraws funds as directed, keeps books of accurate accounts for audit, reports to assembly as provided, disburses monies as authorized, assists in preparing budget.

LESSON 25
BYLAWS
PART II

Review Quiz #2 - Answers

1. In practice today, constitution and bylaws are a single document.

2. Bylaws define the primary characteristics of an organization.

3. A member should be familiar with bylaws if she looks forward to full participation.

4. Bylaws on members' rights bear on those present and absent.

5. Bylaws may sometimes be subject to rules of a parent body.

6. Bylaws should be made no more restrictive than necessary.

7. Writing bylaws places a demand on clarity and precision.

8. Each sentence should be impossible to quote out of context.

9. Specifications in bylaws should not be unnecessarily detailed.

10. Articles are designated by Roman numerals, sections by Arabic numerals.

11. Provisions of a temporary nature should not be included in the bylaws.

12. The use of a parliamentarian is recommended when drafting bylaws.

13. Subordinate units should not adopt provisions that have no local application.

14. Conditions may be prefaced with **"except that."**

15. No proposed amendment to an existing bylaw provision is in order which proposes a change greater or less than the range covered by the existing bylaw and the proposed amendment to it.

16. An amendment becomes part of the bylaws **immediately** upon adoption.

17. An amendment to the bylaws may have a **proviso** as to when it shall take effect.

LESSON 25
BYLAWS
PART II

Review Quiz #3 - Answers - (T)rue or (F)alse

1.   F - Constitution's rules are usually permanent.

2.   T

3.   T

4.   T

5.   F - There must be no opportunity to misread bylaw rules.

6.   F - Unless a private group. This would violate federal law.

7.   T

8.   F - If a change is required, amend the bylaw.

9.   F - Not unless the bylaws provide for it. A procedural rule does not belong in bylaws.

10.   T

11.   F - This is contrary to democratic procedure.

12.   T

13.   F - Never on the nominating committee.

14.   F - Not if there is a recording secretary.

15.   T

LESSON 26
STANDING RULES

Review Quiz - Answers

1. A bylaw may not be suspended; a standing rule may be suspended.

2. Standing rules remain in force until amended or rescinded.

3. Standing rules may supersede any rules in the adopted parliamentary authority, but not bylaws.

4. They may be proposed at any time during the life of the organization when no business is pending.

5. They are adopted by a majority vote.

6. No. Most organizations adopt standing rules as needed, rules that will apply to each meeting and are kept separate from bylaws.

7. So that any part of the agenda could be suspended for the duration of the meeting.

8. As in Question 1, so that any rule can be suspended or amended at once. Bylaws generally require previous notice and two-thirds vote and cannot be suspended without a bylaw provision to do so.

9. Custom is a standing rule and is binding on the organization until rescinded.

10. Organizations may have special problems relating to their objects, programs or standards, and need to state their views in regard to them as a guide for future action.

11. Policies are the organization's philosophy. Once adopted, the policies set a pattern or precedent for all like situations. Policies are as binding as bylaws.

LESSON 27
VOTING METHODS

Review Quiz #1 - Answers

1. Majority is over half of the votes cast by eligible voters present and voting, a quorum being present.

2. A plurality vote is used when there are three or more options. It is the most votes cast for any member or issue.

3. **Division of the Assembly** is a demand by any member to retake the vote by a show of hands or standing vote. It may also be ordered by the Chair.

4. The minority of one-third plus one can control the assembly's decision.

5. No, all 15 members would have had to vote yes or no.

6. Since the bylaws do not require a ballot vote, if there is no objection, the Chair declares_____ elected to the office of_____ by acclamation.

7. No. Abstentions are counted to determine the presence of a quorum. However, abstentions affect the result of the vote by reducing the size of the majority required to win.

8. Yes, up until the announcement of the result, except in a ballot vote when the member's vote cannot be identified.

9. A counted vote is obtained by ballot vote, by roll call or by a motion to take a counted vote adopted by a majority. It is done by taking a standing vote and counting off.

10. No, not even by unanimous vote, since bylaws may not be suspended. Nor may the secretary cast one ballot for the assembly, which then discloses the vote in violation of the secrecy of a ballot. Only if bylaws allow for this may it be done.

11. Yes, the candidate receiving the highest majority.

12. No, another ballot must be taken, unless the organization has provided for a plurality election, which is not recommended. It would be difficult to serve as president without majority support.

LESSON 27
VOTING METHODS

Review Quiz #2 - Answers

SOLUTION:

A. **Without** the Chair voting:

1.   Total votes cast—31

2.   20—2/3 or 21

3.   Defeated

B. **With** the Chair voting:

1.   Total votes cast—32

2.   21—1/3 or 22

3.   Defeated

4.   Defeated

RESULT:

Will an affirmative vote by the Chair change the final result? <u>No change</u>

Will a negative vote by the Chair change the final result? <u>No change</u>

ADVICE:

If you were the **parliamentarian advising the Chair**, what would be your advice?

<u>Since his vote would not affect the result, the Chair should refrain from voting to preserve impartiality.</u>

LESSON 28
NOMINATIONS

Review Quiz - Answers

1. Any member in good standing who meets the qualification for office may be nominated. Any member may nominate. Members may nominate themselves for any office.

2. A single slate presents the best selection of a nominating committee. By presenting a second slate, they would appear to be offering second best choices.

3. Nominations are debatable as to the qualifications of the nominee but not to criticize the candidate.

4. Seconding nominations is not required but is frequently done to signify endorsement.

5. Existence of formal nominating procedures tends to assure that serious thought will be given to the qualifications of those members who are being proposed to serve in a society's leadership positions.

6. The five methods of nomination are: by the chair, by a committee, from the floor, by ballot, by petition.

7. Yes, the report must be officially announced at a proper meeting.

8. The Chair may nominate in unorganized groups or at a mass meeting.

9. Yes, and if elected may choose which office to accept.

10. No, it provides the opportunity to perpetuate the old group leadership.

11.

Advantages:	Disadvantages:
a) from floor: freedom of choice	hasty selection
b) by ballot: reveals sentiments of nominated group	too many may be nominated
c) by committee: saves time, also provides research of qualifications to serve	limits nominations for each office

12. Bylaws should determine the method of nomination and eligibility for office.

13. A nominating ballot permits every member to nominate, so there is no need for nominations from the floor.

14. Yes, if the bylaws do not require a vote by ballot.

15. A minority member on the nominating committee may always nominate from the floor.

16. The report is "legal"—a majority report. Majority of five is three.

17. Yes, no member should be penalized for service to the organization.

18. Yes, nominations from the floor are always in order, unless prohibited in the bylaws.

19. A member may make only one nomination at a time for each office.

20. To vote on a nominating report is to elect without an opportunity for further nominations from the floor.

21. Each nominee should have agreed to serve if elected.

22. a) Completing all nominations for office decides nominees for each office.

    b) To nominate for each office one at a time permits more flexibility. A member who was not nominated for one position may be nominated for another.

LESSON 29
ELECTIONS

Review Quiz - Answers

1. To elect is to choose by due process someone to serve in a particular office.

2. The group should look in its bylaws or in its adopted parliamentary authority for the election procedure.

3. Generally, elections are conducted by ballot, but the method must be specified in the bylaws.

4. No. A write-in candidate may be elected, if eligible, without nomination.

5. Ballot vote provides the right to secrecy and freedom from intimidation.

6. Every member present may vote, unless under suspension, even if in arrears for dues, unless bylaws provide otherwise.

7. Acclamation may be used by *general consent*, with no objection, if only one person is named.

8. Polls are opened by prior announcement, by the Chair, or by a motion adopted by a majority vote.

   Polls are closed by prior announcement, by the Chair with *general consent*, or by a motion requiring a two-thirds vote.

9. The president may vote at any time, but usually exercises this right when voting is by ballot, or when it could affect the result.

10. No. A formal installation ceremony has no effect on the time when office holding begins unless bylaws provide otherwise.

11. Usually members under suspension, or who have some personal or monetary gain not in common with others, may not vote. Usually honorary members have no vote.

12. When more than the required number of nominees receive a majority vote, those with the largest number of votes are elected up to the required number on the board.

13. When no nominees receive a majority vote, balloting is repeated until a majority is achieved. All nominees remain on the ballot unless the nominee withdraws.

14. In any election where two leading candidates represent factions within the society, members of both sides may prefer, in a tight election, to cast their votes for a compromise (or "dark horse") candidate.

15. The presiding officer directs the voting process and declares the results. Leaving the room or adjourning the meeting may not be done. No motion is in order that would force disclosure of a member's vote or views.

16. Absentee ballots are those wherein a member may vote by mail or may hold proxy (right of attorney) to cast a vote for another. This may only be done if provided for in the bylaws or by state statutory law, where pertinent.

17. Yes, if no bylaw says otherwise. However, if the bylaws impose a limit of one term, a member who has served more than half a term is considered to have served a full term.

18. A ballot vote refers to a situation in which voters indicate on slips of paper, or by machine, their choice among nominees or alternatives to a question, in such a way that the voters cannot be identified.

LESSON 30
THE "PROFESSIONAL" PARLIAMENTARIAN

Review Quiz #1- Answers

1. A professional parliamentarian is one who has demonstrated experience and knowledge of principles and procedural rules, who is familiar with several parliamentary authorities, who is qualified as an expert witness before courts of law, who has ability to preside well and whose qualifications are attested to by recognized authorities.

2. A parliamentarian should be impartial, flexible and patient.

3. A parliamentarian serves during meetings at the direction of the presiding officer and advises the board and the membership.

4. A parliamentarian serves as consultant, gives oral or written opinions, attends board and regular meetings, as requested, and teaches orientation classes.

5. Fees should be commensurate with skills and time spent for research, opinion writing, classes taught and duration of session, plus expenses.

6. When it could affect the outcome of a decision or when a problem harmful to the organization may develop.

7. Through the Chair or as directed by the Chair.

8. Before meetings—in consultation with the president and board members.

CHAPTER 30
THE "PROFESSIONAL" PARLIAMENTARIAN

Review Quiz #2 - Answers

1. a. If the meeting was a regular meeting, notice for such meetings is in the bylaws and no further notice is required. Therefore, business undertaken will be legal with a quorum present. It is a member's responsibility to attend meetings.

    b. If the meeting was not a regular meeting, previous notice is required to protect the absentees, and without previous notice the meeting cannot be valid even if a quorum is present. Previous notice, unless otherwise specified in the bylaws, may be given at a previous meeting, by mail or in the call to the meeting. Every member should be notified and should be sent the notice in adequate time to attend. To be valid, the action requires a majority vote at a properly called meeting at which a quorum is present.

2. No parliamentarian can correctly advise without pertinent facts and the name of the adopted parliamentary authority. Many such problems are people problems, not procedural problems, and the questioner may merely desire confirmation of only what he wishes to reveal. Insist on obtaining the proper data, getting the whole picture. Put the advice in writing and retain a copy. You may need to turn down the request for an opinion, even if it means the loss of a fee. Explain that, like a lawyer, physician or other professional, you cannot give sound advice without sufficient knowledge of the problem.

3. This problem cannot be advised without your obtaining a copy of the bylaws. Is the executive secretary employed? What powers are permitted? Sometimes it is necessary to see what is contained in the employment contract. Is the executive secretary given the right to vote? To speak but not vote? To do both?

    The executive secretary is valuable in providing continuity to the organization. Officers are temporary, and therefore the concern of the secretary is understandable. However, the presiding officer directs the meeting and should allow the executive secretary no more turns to speak on a motion or issue than any other member, without such permission being granted by the assembly. Usually, the executive secretary may speak but not vote, unless he is also an elected member of the board or of the assembly.

LESSON 31
DISCIPLINE

Review Quiz - Answers

1. Yes. It is a main motion, precisely, an incidental main motion.

2. A vote to censure is a warning to the member. It indicates disapproval of his conduct.

3. No. The offender is disqualified as it affects him personally, not in common with other voters.

4. Continuation of offenses may result in suspension, removal from office or expulsion.

5. Results are kept private to protect the organization from a possible libel suit.

6. A trial must be conducted in a closed meeting.

7. Yes. Misconduct outside a meeting may reflect on the good name of the organization.

8. A two-thirds ballot vote is required for expulsion.

9. Yes, hearsay is permitted, since legal proof of facts is often difficult to obtain and witnesses are not sworn in.

10. Officers may be removed from office, but generally with valid cause. The power to appoint or elect carries with it the power to remove.

11. Conduct tending to injure the good name of the organization, disturb its well-being or hamper its work is subject to disciplinary action.

12. Members who disagree with the Chair's rulings may appeal the ruling, seconded by any other member.

    Other possibilities are to use parliamentary inquiry or point of order, appeals, move for a vote of no confidence, to censure or with cause to expel from office or membership.

13. The Chair's power to control a meeting is established by common law.

14. The Chair may withhold recognition, point out the inappropriate behavior, call a member to order, ask the assembly to order the member to leave, or entertain a motion to censure. The Chair may order removal of a non-member from the room.

15. Freedom of speech is the right to express publicly, within the boundaries of the laws as established by society, what one believes, and to exercise that right with civility and acceptable behavior without abuse or in a manner designed to incite the performance of unlawful acts and violence.

LESSON 32
CONVENTIONS

Review Quiz #1 - Answers

1. The three essential procedures required to validate convention business are the adoption of the credentials committee report, the standing rules committee report and the program committee report, in that order.

2. Voting delegates are members appointed or elected by their local units to represent their respective membership as determined by the parent body.

3. The essential function of a caucus is to become informed and to clarify in order to determine support for or against a nominee or a proposition before it comes to a vote.

4. Delegates are free to vote according to their best judgment unless they have been instructed how to cast their votes by the unit they represent, regardless of any amendments and debate on the convention floor that could affect the situation.

5. The credentials committee registers attendance, verifies and issues voting credentials to delegates, replaces alternates with delegate badges, as needed, and verifies proxy votes, if any. The committee reports to the assembly, moves adoptions of its report to determine the voting body, remains on duty in the event of a change in delegate attendance.

6. The rules committee prepares convention procedures as standing rules under which the convention will operate. The rules are adopted by a two-thirds vote.

7. The program committee provides the schedule of all convention events. The program is adopted by a majority vote.

8. A convention quorum is a majority of the registered voting delegates regardless of their presence or absence from the floor, unless otherwise defined in the bylaws.

9. The convention resolutions committee, in accordance with the bylaws, prepares and edits resolutions, eliminating all resolutions in violation of laws or purposes of the organization.

10. Resolutions are reported by the resolutions committee or are offered from the floor for consideration by the assembly, with or without recommendation. Those out of committee need no second.

11. Time between meetings is best treated as a recess so that, after reconvening, business may continue at the point of interruption.

12. Minutes are best approved by the early appointment of a minutes committee or by authorizing the board of directors to approve the convention minutes.

13. Alternates must register with the credentials committee. They replace delegates who have officially departed or failed to attend. After replacement, they have the same rights as duly elected delegates.

14. A delegate reports to the credentials committee to be registered as officially holding rights to participate and vote; a delegate attends all business meetings, attends programs that have been provided, takes notes and prepares a report on return to the local unit. A delegate must vote as instructed by the unit on specific matters.

15. Unfinished business at a convention ceases to exist but may be introduced as new business at the next convention.

16. Newly elected officers assume office according to the bylaws, usually at the end of the convention.

17. The credentials report contains the total number present, the number of registered delegates and the number of other voting members, if any. Supplementary reports are given when the voting attendance changes.

18. Board members should not hold meetings during a convention business meeting. Assumed to be the best informed, they take their places on the floor of the convention to participate in the debate.

19. The parliamentarian at convention is to serve as principal advisor to the president, both at the pre-convention board meeting and during the convention business. The parliamentarian gives advice and opinions but never makes a ruling.

20. Installations are merely ceremonial and have no legal significance in regard to elections.

21. Conventions are provided for in the bylaws, specifying when and how often such meetings convene, the powers and duties of the governing body, qualifications of delegates and alternates and the method for selecting them.

22. Federal and state laws affect the rights of members, such as prohibiting discrimination in respect to race, sex, religion.

23. The special committee continues until it gives its final report at the next convention or is discharged.

LESSON 32
CONVENTIONS

Review Quiz #2 - Answers - (T)rue or (F)alse

1. F - Elected delegates.

2. F - As entitled to.

3. T

4. F - Only if credentials were surrendered to alternate.

5. T

6. F - Usually only if it may affect decisions.

7. T

8. T

9. T

10. T

11. T

12. T

13. F - Not if in conflict with bylaws or purpose of organization as stated in articles of incorporation, if the organization is incorporated.

14.   F - Convention standing rules require two-thirds vote.

15.   T

16.   T

17.   T

18.   T

19.   T

20.   T

21.   T

22.   T

23.   T

24.   T

25.   F - As designated in adopted rules.